D0504185

SPECIAL MESSAGE TO READERS

This book is published under the auspices of

THE ULVERSCROFT FOUNDATION
(registered charity No. 264873 UK)

Established in 1972 to provide funds for research, diagnosis and treatment of eye diseases. Examples of contributions made are: —

A new Children's Assessment Unit at Moorfield's Hospital, London.

•

Twin operating theatres at the Western Ophthalmic Hospital, London.

•

A Chair of Ophthalmology at the University of Leicester.

•

The establishment of a Royal Australian College of Ophthalmologists "Fellowship".

You can help further the work of the Foundation by making a donation or leaving a legacy. Every contribution, no matter how small, is received with gratitude. Please write for details to:

THE ULVERSCROFT FOUNDATION,
The Green, Bradgate Road, Anstey,
Leicester LE7 7FU, England.
Telephone: (0116) 236 4325

In Australia write to:
THE ULVERSCROFT FOUNDATION,
c/o The Royal Australian College of Ophthalmologists,
27, Commonwealth Street, Sydney,
N.S.W. 2010.

I've travelled the world twice over,
Met the famous: saints and sinners,
Poets and artists, kings and queens,
Old stars and hopeful beginners,
I've been where no-one's been before,
Learned secrets from writers and cooks
All with one library ticket
To the wonderful world of books.

TWIGGY IN BLACK AND WHITE

Twiggy was the world's first supermodel: a skinny kid with the face of an angel who became an icon. Here, she recounts her extraordinary journey from working-class schoolgirl in North London to model, recording artist and award-winning actress. She reveals the truth behind her suffocating relationship with Justin de Villeneuve, her boyfriend and manager. She describes her traumatic marriage to Michael Whitney, an alcoholic whose inability to cope with her success nearly destroyed both their lives. Now happily married to actor Leigh Lawson, Twiggy's road to contentment has been long and hard, won through her unfeigned charm and ability always to see the funny side.

TWIGGY LAWSON
WITH PENELOPE DENING

TWIGGY
IN BLACK AND WHITE

Complete and Unabridged

CHARNWOOD
Leicester

First published in Great Britain in 1997 by
Simon & Schuster Limited
London

First Charnwood Edition
published 1998
by arrangement with
Simon & Schuster Limited
London

Cover photograph Brian Aris

British Library CIP Data

Twiggy
Twiggy in black and white.—Large print ed.—
Charnwood library series
1. Twiggy
2. Models (Persons)—Great Britain—Biography
3. Large type books
I. Title II. Dening, Penelope
746.9′2′092

ISBN 0–7089–9029–0

Published by
F. A. Thorpe (Publishing) Ltd.
Anstey, Leicestershire

Set by Words & Graphics Ltd.
Anstey, Leicestershire
Printed and bound in Great Britain by
T. J. International Ltd., Padstow, Cornwall

This book is printed on acid-free paper

For my darling Leigh, Carly and Ace,
and all my wonderful family

Acknowledgements

My thanks go to Penelope Dening; Helen Gummer, Ingrid Connell and Marian McCarthy at Simon & Schuster; Abner Stein; Marian Rosenberg; Shirley Russell; Philip Jenkinson; Barry Hanson; Shirley Bowler; Vivien Smith; and of course my wonderful husband Leigh Lawson

'Experiment'

Experiment
Make it your motto day and night
Experiment
And it will lead you to the light
The apple on the top of the tree
Is never too high to achieve
So take an example from Eve
Experiment

Be curious, though interfering friends
May frown
Get furious, at each attempt to
Hold you down
If this advice you only employ
The future can offer you infinite joy
And merriment
Experiment — an you'll see.

Cole Porter

1

'Roll camera. Mark it. Action.' That Easter Sunday in 1967 the vocabulary of film making was still new to me. We were in downtown Manhattan, where even the sky has to fight for space, cut into remnant-sized pieces of bright blue by skyscrapers so tall you can't even see where they end. Not that you get even a glimpse of sky in what was shot on Fifth Avenue that morning. It was like a canyon just filled with people heading up from Broadway to Central Park, on the mass stroll known as the Easter Parade. But what you do see, right in the middle of all the Jackie Onassis lookalikes (or Jackie Kennedy as she still was) dressed in their new spring outfits, neat suits with high collars and pencil skirts and pillbox hats, is this funny-looking thing that looks like it's escaped from a Disney cartoon, all knees and legs and big eyes. And everyone staring like it was from outer space. So, what do you think of this girl from England? asks the man with the mike. 'She's cute,' says a balding man in his best Bronx. 'She'll last a couple of weeks.'

Somehow that couple of weeks has stretched into thirty years and people still turn their heads, in cars, in the street, and stare. And although I don't look like I did then — at least I hope not — they still recognise me and I catch a mouth shaping my name. Twiggy.

The documentary of that first insane trip to New York was directed by Bert Stern, who made the legendary *Jazz On A Summer's Day*, about the 1959 Newport Jazz Festival. He was also a top stills photographer who I'd worked with a few months before in Paris doing the collections for American *Vogue*, where my untutored gaffes had raised not only laughs but a good many hackles among the Paris couture houses. No doubt it was then he recognised the mileage to be had in throwing this innocent seventeen-year-old Londoner into the snake pit of Manhattan. But watching the film now all these years later is an extraordinary experience. Perhaps everyone feels distanced like this when they see early footage of themselves, though few people in the sixties had cine cameras and even fewer had documentaries made about them so it's hard to know. But for me it's literally like looking at someone else.

Although I didn't think there was anything very odd about the way I dressed at the time, now I can't help seeing it from the point of view of those bemused onlookers. With that boyish haircut and eyelashes like woolly bear caterpillars, there's no getting away from it. I look like an alien. Bambi meets ET. Those butter-wouldn't-melt-in-their handbags American girls lining the sidewalk can't have been much older than me, but with their gloves and matching court shoes we were from different planets. Bert Stern may not have known it then but he was recording the end of an era. And I was just the most visible part of what was to come.

Watching it on film does trigger real memories of course but it's hard now to piece together what happened when, and in what order. It comes back to me in disconnected flashes. From beginning to end everything about that trip was surreal, from the huge apartment that Bert Stern lent us on the Upper East Side, empty except for two beds and a massive blow-up of me as a baby on the wall — to photographer Melvin Sokolski's idea to have masks made of my face and get everyone in shot to wear them. Originally they got twenty-four made up. But the passers-by, who were supposed to wear them and then hand them back, kept them as souvenirs — so as the days went by more and more had to be made. Imagine what it felt like being surrounded by a mob wearing black and white masks of your own face. Unnerving isn't the word. And when we come to a later sequence in the film where the crowd just goes berserk, even now I can feel my heart beginning to race as I remember the terror, the sheer panic, the just wanting to be back at home with Mum and Dad, or in fact anywhere but about to be crushed to death outside B. Altman's on Fifth Avenue at 33rd. After all I was only seventeen. I wasn't the first to enjoy New York's over-the-top hospitality — it had happened to the Beatles two years before, but at least there were four of them. It's amazing they let me go, but then nobody ever dreamt what lay in store.

But at the same time I can barely believe that this young girl on the screen, who casually admits to earning more an hour than my Dad earned in a month, is the same person that these days picks over the carrots in the market so as not to get a duff one. And when I think that my adored daughter Carly is the same age now as I was then, my blood runs cold. If I'm honest I don't really like her going on the bus on her own; as for flying to New York with only a half-boyfriend, half-manager, total Jack-the-lad (which is how Justin de Villeneuve, my so-called Svengali, was recently described in the *Daily Telegraph*) to look after her — forget it.

Above all I can't help thinking, how did it happen? And, even more extraordinary, how did I survive when so many others didn't?

A shelf-life of only two weeks might have been a slight exaggeration but in essence that old New Yorker was right. And he wasn't alone. One newspaper called me The Paper Girl. (These were the days of throw away paper knickers.) 'She's like fashion,' it continued. 'The big thing of the moment, but you'll be able to crumple her up and throw her away like a piece of paper.'

Endurance was not a hallmark of the sixties. Although it was only in April 1966 that *Time* magazine coined the phrase 'Swinging London' that put the US seal of approval on what had been going on since 1963, by the time of that first trip to New York the sixties were already half-way through. Everyone accepted it was a time of shooting stars: a brief arc of brilliance then nothing. The sixties were full of 'whatever happened to' names. Some disappeared quietly, happy to have survived with their sanity intact and, hopefully, a bit of money in the bank, but others paid a terrible price for their fifteen minutes of Warholian fame and worse still, bequeathed a terrible legacy to their children.

I had been launched into the media stratosphere, courtesy of the *Daily Express*, as 'the Face of '66'. The implication being that twelve months on there would be a Face of '67. But it (she?) never materialised. At least not in the same way. What happened was that for some extraordinary reason I came to represent not just that one year, but the whole decade, the whole free-wheeling, free-loving, free-thinking sixties revolution.

A lot of what happened to me was time and place. After all Jean Shrimpton — who I idolised and whose pictures I had plastered all over my walls — had already begun the change of direction in the early sixties. She was the first of the natural models. Before her models were very elegant, sophisticated and mostly over twenty-five. Then came the beautiful and much younger Jane Birkin with the beginning of the waif look.

Fashion was undergoing a complete renaissance. Suddenly, and probably for the first time ever, young people were the focus. The boom years of the early sixties had put money in their pockets and so young designers like Mary Quant and Barbara Hulanicki of Biba were emerging to fill the new hunger for clothes that were different, not cut down versions of their parents', but which reinforced their wearers' new-found status. These clothes needed to be photographed on very young girls, as conventional, sophisticated models would have looked ridiculous in the mini skirt; as was demonstrated over and over again by misguided women on Britain's high streets, not only in the sixties, but more recently when the mini made a comeback. To wear those skimpy fashions you had (and have) to be young and thin. The change from models just being anonymous coat hangers to actually having a personality was part of this sea change and both designers and the media recognised it as central to the spirit of the times. My famous Twiggy painted eyes were just one of the things that set me apart, although my eye make-up was downright plain compared to a model called Peggy Moffat who was one of the first people I worked with and who taught me so much about how to move in front of the camera. Her eyes were a veritable art work of colour and pattern.

And I was obsessed with clothes: a Dedicated Follower of Fashion as the Kinks put it. I always had been long before I became Twiggy, when I was still the schoolgirl called Lesley Hornby, when me and my friends would spend the whole week planning what we were going to wear on Saturday night. Because for the first time ever it was possible for anyone to be up there at the sharp end. It was no longer a question of waiting to see what filtered down to C&A from the Paris collections. Fashion was what was being worn by Cathy McGowan on *Ready Steady Go* on Friday evenings or the local trend-setters on the dance floor on Saturday nights. In those heady days fashion changed not by the season but by the month, and by the time Biba got into full swing, sometimes even by the week.

Yet in a more important sense I suppose I was, and still am, a child of the sixties; a time when ordinary people could do extraordinary things. For most people, at least for girls who came from my kind of background, the whole sex, drugs and rock 'n' roll thing was just window dressing. The sixties gave young women the freedom to earn good money and spend it on what they wanted. Records and clothes. Feminism had nothing to do with it.

What happened to me certainly couldn't have happened before, and that amazing mix of ego and confidence that had allowed anyone who could play three chords on a guitar to get up on a stage and sing of love and revolution without anyone saying 'boo' only lasted a few years before the men with calculators took over. Not altogether a bad thing. Being talented doesn't automatically make you able to handle the money side. It amazes me to think anyone ever imagined it did. When I think what should have been done with the money I earned over the four years I was modelling, I can only sigh.

Better minds than mine have tried to fathom why the sixties happened. But it was all about not accepting limitations that till then had always been accepted as inevitable, recognising that the barriers were only psychological. Like space travel, which is now so commonplace it only gets a mention when things go wrong. Then it was the most amazing thing to happen. Like everyone else I'd got used to the idea that space travel was just science fiction, something that happened in the cinema (*Flash Gordon* on Saturday mornings at the Neasden Odeon) or on the radio. Once a week I was allowed to come downstairs in my pyjamas and we'd all sit around the wireless set which was as big as a sewing machine, and listen to *Journey Into Space*. It was so exciting. And not just the being allowed up. But like *Quatermass* when it came on the television, I was absolutely terrified, although I knew it was only pretend. It was never really going to happen. So when it did, the feeling was incredible. When John Glenn circled the earth it was my first moment of knowing that history was being made. After that, anything was possible. Breaking through the earth's atmosphere was like a symbol.

But for all the speculation, in the end what it boils down to is money. There was just more of it about. Suddenly ordinary young people, people with jobs, had money to spend exactly as they wanted. And there were more of them; these were the baby boomers. All the old rules went out the window. All those old barriers to success — family background, education, age, class — were forgotten. It didn't matter where you came from, nothing could stop you if you were ambitious enough.

Not that I actually was. Although I loved drawing and designing and making clothes I certainly had no ambitions to be a model myself. About the age of ten I had rather fancied being a champion ice-skater — largely I suspect because of those great outfits — but in spite of tagging along with my long-suffering middle sister Vivien who took me every week to Wembley ice rink, when I later discovered boys I gave it up. I never even learnt to skate backwards. Jean Shrimpton might have been my hero but only in the sense that I thought she was incredibly beautiful and I wished I looked like her. Like a fawn. But I never thought 'Oh, I could do that'. It just wasn't a thing that happened to working-class girls. Even Jean came from a well spoken family which was what gave the whole thing with David Bailey — always known as being a bit rough and ready — its edge. In those days models were always middle or upper class. It was something for the pretty ones to do before they got married. Models were sophisticated and glamorous. Not words anyone could have associated with Lesley Hornby, least of all Lesley Hornby herself. I knew I looked really funny. Far too skinny in spite of the weekly spoonful of cod liver oil and malt my Mum gave me every Sunday night to 'build me up', which I absolutely loved. It looked like Marmite but tasted like toffee.

But already in 1966, times were changing and even if I didn't know what I wanted to be, I knew what I didn't want to be. I knew I wasn't prepared to take any old job. My older sister Shirley was a secretary, and Viv was a hairdresser. But I was already talking with my teachers about trying to get into art school and doing a fashion design course. But it was no more focused than that.

Then I met Justin. People have this idea of Justin as the Svengali who 'made' me. But my view is very different. If anyone can be given the credit for recognising my potential, it's his brother Tony. But Justin knew how to sell. And he was very keen on making money — and spending it — and once he knew he had a golden goose, he wasn't about to hand it over to anyone else. And if this meant protecting his investment, both physically by not letting anyone else near me and by exaggerating his own role in the phenomenon known as Twiggy, then that's what he would do.

There is no doubt the combination worked. For real sixties cred you had to have been born and bred on the wrong side of the tracks in Liverpool, or failing that on an East End council estate. Justin fitted the bill perfectly and although I was born a good fifteen miles away from the sound of Bow Bells, I had this terrible voice that to those who didn't know any different sounded pure Stepney. And it wasn't just the accent. Because my Dad was deaf, I'd got used to speaking much louder than most people. When technicians do sound checks even now, they still can't believe the decibels I put out — though having a voice that can fell a tree at twenty paces has proved very useful over the years. The accent has calmed down a bit now, but so it should, having lived for the last twelve years with the man who has the most gorgeous voice in the whole of the British acting profession and speaks Shakespeare as if it had been written for him. My wonderful husband Leigh Lawson. Not that I'm biased.

Back then, I was in every sense of the word,

'loud'. Justin used to say I sounded like a demented parrot. Before the sixties I'd only have been allowed to open my mouth in an Ealing comedy, or a Carry On. That was the only time you ever heard working class accents in the cinema, which I suppose is why when I did get to speak, everyone thought it was so hysterical, with this Peggy Mount voice coming out of my teacher's-pet face. If by some amazing chance I had been 'discovered' by one of the British film industry's roving talent scouts I would have been 'groomed' and given a posh voice at the Rank Charm School and probably sunk without trace. Nobody had laughed at me before I was famous — at least not at my voice. At school they'd laughed about what I looked like. I was known as Olive Oyl, because of my stick legs and Mod uniform of Hush Puppies and plastic mac flapping around my ankles. It was so hurtful. But perhaps thinking about it in retrospect it was things like that which helped me cope with all the adulation that followed. Because I never really believed a word of it, and thought they were all mad.

If I had been conventionally beautiful, I might have somehow accepted what happened to me as my due. But I didn't. I took what I looked like seriously in terms of my job, but that was it. To get the best out of you photographers have this running monologue, along the lines of — 'Oh yeah, you're gorgeous, yeah baby' as they click, click, click. I felt like saying, it's only me, this funny skinny little thing. In Hollywood it's even worse. If you believe the 'Oh God, darling, you were so wonderful' aural wallpaper, it can destroy you. You have to be so grounded not to believe the crap they give everybody. Over the years I've noticed that people who don't take their 'stardom' seriously handle it better, both the ups and the downs. I've been incredibly lucky. Not that I haven't had difficult times. But I've learnt over the years that although the down times are hard, the wonderful thing about show business, which any performer can confirm, is that the phone can ring and suddenly you're off on a new adventure.

By choice my modelling career only lasted four years. And although it's what everyone still seems to remember about Twiggy, in terms of my life, it's only a small part. Amazingly, when I was only twenty, even before I did *The Boyfriend*, Thames Television did a *This Is Your Life* on me. For some reason Marje Proops, the *Daily Mirror's* famous agony aunt, was brought on to explain my appeal. She said I had 'brought the look of the sixties to every ordinary girl's doorstep. She could be anyone's daughter.'

But I wasn't just anyone's daughter. I may owe my success to my ordinary background and to the spirit of the time — but I owe my survival, both professionally and personally, to the very early days, to my own individual family and the values I learnt subconsciously through them. Values that seem as rare now as a four-leaf clover but which because they were so deep within me, I also recognised in Leigh. I can imagine how trite and saccharine this must sound. But the Hornby family circumstances were far from idyllic. For years my mother suffered from recurrent nervous breakdowns which resulted in absences from home of several months, the first one soon after I was born. It could have led to terrible insecurity. That this never happened I owe not only to my father's extraordinary sense of family, responsibility and duty, but also to both my sisters who at different times in my life took over entirely the role of mother when Mum was no longer able to. Everyone accepts that the breakdown of the family and the fragmentation of society over the last two decades have led to an unhappier world. And the family is the first thing they analyse when things go wrong. But nobody much bothers to analyse why things go right. I only have happy memories of my childhood, but it could have been very different. It is only recently that I have been able to piece together what actually happened.

2

No matter how much fashion has moved on over the last thirty years, one thing that stays the same is the media's preoccupation with 'skeletal' models. You would think that anorexia hadn't existed before I arrived on the scene; yet I get blamed as regularly (and with as much regard to logic) as the weather gets blamed for trains not running on time. I can understand why: I appear to be the epitome of the first skinny teenager. But that is exactly what I was. A naturally skinny teenager.

'What do you eat?' was one of the standard questions thrown at me on that first trip to New York. 'Food,' I told them. Looking at the documentary footage now you can see the disbelief at this inanity in my face. What did they think I ate? Pound notes? When they found out I had porridge for breakfast, they went mad and even wanted pictures of me eating it. What I should have told them was that I really liked it with condensed milk, which at home I used to dribble on to my steaming Quaker Oats straight out of the tin.

My memories of childhood are a bit like memories of old films. A scene here, bits of dialogue there. Some things I can almost smell and taste. I can see our kitchen in Neasden and the table laid with a plate of salad, which was always a slice of ham or cold chicken, a lettuce leaf, half a tomato and a spring onion. And of course, Heinz salad cream. It's the vinegar in it. I love anything pickled. Pickled onions, pickled eggs. Home-made pickled eggs are sensational, and yes, I make them myself. I have always been able to cook, although it was only through Leigh's passion for cooking and food that I got into experimenting and cooking for sheer pleasure.

At home life revolved around food; buying it, preparing it, cooking it, eating it. I was never faddy. I was a good little girl and ate whatever was put in front of me. Mum's speciality was puddings: syrup sponge with custard, spotted dick. Just the thought of them makes me drool even now. Though nothing seemed to put on any weight. By the time I was about six, Mum, her friend Doris and Auntie Joyce (not a real aunt, but my friend Geraldine's mother who lived over the road) had a little catering business going: children's birthday parties and bar mitzvahs, mostly for Jewish families in Hendon, Hampstead and Golders Green. How it began I don't know, though it's possible my mother being half Jewish might have had something to do with it.

Mum's maiden name was Reeman, and, though no one's ever checked it out, the story goes that her grandparents had emigrated to England from Germany some time in the nineteenth century when we think they changed their name from Reemansburg. By the time Mum was born in Greenwich in 1909, they were to all intents and purposes cockney-speaking

English: two of her uncles ran a stall on Petticoat Lane and one of her aunts was married to a park keeper in Kensington Gardens, who Mum remembered visiting in what was obviously their tied house, tucked away in the park itself.

Although Mum's job meant she would sometimes be away on Saturday or Sunday afternoon, there was a huge bonus for me. The people she cooked for were usually wealthy, and she would come home loaded down with bags of left over goodies: iced cakes, sandwiches. If it was a bar mitzvah there would be canapés, which to us were so posh, and piles of smoked salmon, which always got given to Binkie the cat, as none of us could stand it. Our cat must have been in seventh heaven: I could live on it now. For Mum it was more a hobby than anything else, something that 'got her out' and that she enjoyed. It wasn't every weekend by any means. But one of the great excitements, if she didn't finish till late, was going out at night to collect her. Dad would get me out of bed, put me in the car, and I'd be all cosy in my pyjamas and my dressing gown as we drove through the dark and I'd be chattering away non-stop, like I always do. When we got there Mum would come out, still in her black skirt and top with a little white frilly apron, and hold up a bag, as tantalising as if it were looted treasure, and say 'Guess what I've got for you, Lesley.'

I have never had to diet in my life. It's a question of metabolism. Until I had Carly I ate anything and everything. These days I admit I watch what I eat but only for health reasons.

I simply believe that if you're fit, life is better. And as far as cream cakes are concerned, you've only got to look at the people who are eating them — rarely the Miss Skinnies. Most women now in their forties and fifties look a good ten years younger than their mothers did at the same age because we've learnt to look after ourselves better. The upper classes might have played tennis, but the only exercise people like my mother got was walking to the bus stop. Eating sweets was even encouraged by the government, who gave everyone a sweet ration throughout the war (six ounces a week). And they all smoked like chimneys. Mum says that, in the forties, she was prescribed cigarettes 'to calm her down'.

I'm glad I'm thinner rather than fatter. But it's not a question of choice. It's genetic. You only have to look at my sisters. We're like three peas in a pod. Thankfully I'm now about twenty-five pounds heavier than I was in 1965 when my bust (if you can call it that) was thirty and a half inches and my hips thirty-two. Time, or rather dancing, has improved my stick-like legs. (Twiggy was one of the nicer nicknames my legs landed me with. Shirley's second husband Colin used to call me Razor Blades.) I first began to put on a bit of muscle during *The Boyfriend* but only really developed calves and thighs you could call the name during my time on Broadway, although the punishing eight performances a week schedule took me down to a trim seven and a half stone. (Best way to lose weight: do a musical.) The bumps on my chest only became breasts after I'd had Carly.

I've been very lucky with my sisters. They are the kindest, most wonderful people and we've always got on really well. Although we were so physically similar there has never been any jealousy; I know it's been difficult for them at times having such a famous sister. Perhaps it's simply that the age gap was so big (there are seven years between each of us) that we were never in competition. By February 1966 when the whole Twiggy thing blew up, Viv was a happy young newly-wed of twenty-three, and so sweet and timid she's the first to admit she could never have hacked all the publicity. Not like Shirley who was the rebel of the family and did all the naughty things, like staying out all night — something I would never have dreamt of doing.

I was born on 19 September 1949, when Mum was forty-one. The story goes that when Mum found out she was expecting me, she was so cross she didn't speak to Dad for a week. But as we used to say, 'Mum, it takes two.' Not that I knew about that side of things until I was grown up. In those days you didn't talk about things below the navel. But as usually happens with afterthought babies, I was eventually seen as someone very special. I was adored and spoilt. Not indulged with toys or sweets or anything. Just loved. Mum used to say, 'Shirley was the naughty one, Vivien was the sweet one, but you were the best.' Dad used to say, 'When Shirley left home I thought we were going to have a bit of peace. Then you came along.'

Along with the spoiling came the worrying.

There is no getting away from the fact that as a child I was very thin and they were worried enough to take me to the doctor, who told them very firmly that there was nothing wrong. 'You can't expect to make an elephant out of a mouse,' he said. Nowadays they'd have been told to look at photographs of themselves at the same age. But if there ever were any (unlikely, as both Mum and Dad grew up in the First World War) they're long gone now. Like many of their generation, my parents had no interest in old things. To be modern was what mattered. I suspect it had a lot to do with escaping the poverty of their backgrounds where everything was make do and hand-me-down. Modern meant you had money.

My father had bought our house in Neasden in 1937 when it was brand new. St Raphael's Way was part of the great sweep of suburban infilling that followed the building of the new London orbital road, known as the North Circular. Number 93 was one of those thirties houses, like the classic doll's house, where the central bay swings open to reveal the standard three up, three down (including kitchen) semi-detached pre-war house with a little garden front and back. In our case complete with coal bunker and garage. We were the first family in our street to have a car and also the first family in our street to have a television set. Dad made the cabinet himself and put together the insides from components which I imagine he got from MGM film studios in Borehamwood, Elstree, where he was by then working as a carpenter.

The film industry has always paid comparatively well, which is why I never remember wanting for anything. We certainly weren't poor.

Dad was forever making 'improvements'. When he and Mum first moved in he converted the upstairs into a separate flat for Mum's parents, complete with kitchen. It wasn't that he wanted them there, neither of them did. From what I can make out Nanny Reeman was a martyr to her nerves. But they had fallen on hard times and Dad was not one to shirk family responsibility. Even if it wasn't his family. They lived with us till they died.

What really surprises me now that I look back on it is that although the fireplaces were all blocked up (they were old fashioned), Dad never put in central heating. You knew it was cold, but you couldn't do anything about it. The one-bar electric fire didn't do much good. I can still remember freezing winter mornings when the insides of the windows were patterned with wonderful frosty ferns, and when I finally plucked up courage to jump out of bed and grab my clothes from the chair I'd nearly fall over myself running downstairs to the kitchen, which was the only really cosy room. Mum would already have lit the oven which stood with its door open just waiting for me to get dressed in front of it.

Dad's not appreciating anything old led to him having a massive clear out when they finally left Neasden in 1968. With the proceeds from my trip to Japan I had bought a house in Twickenham. If Mum had been around it might have been different. But she was ill again. And as this was the height of my modelling career I was no help. So Dad was in charge of the move and, although there must have been a lot of accumulated rubbish in the loft — after all, they'd been there thirty years — from old family photographs, to granddad Reeman's war medals (Boer War), to Mum and Dad's ballroom dancing trophies, very little was ever seen again.

One photograph however did survive. For me Mum has never been anything other than her wonderful homely self, soft and rounded, but the twenty-year-old Nell Reeman was a beauty. I can see her now, looking coquettishly over a bare shoulder at the camera, all dark lidded eyes (soot, she told us) and rosebud mouth. It was taken for a publicity shot to hang in the window of the photographers on Neasden Parade. Box Brownies were the only cameras that ordinary people had then and if you wanted anything better than a snap the size of a passport photo, you had to go to a professional. It was a studio shot, taken about 1930. A perfect period portrait. So perfect that I thought I'd show it to Ken Russell when we were making *The Boyfriend*, particularly for the hair which is blonde and in tight finger waves (sugar water, Mum said, 'sets like concrete'). It was given to the production department. What a mistake. That was the last I ever saw of it.

The only other pictures I have of my parents date from about fifteen years later, towards the end of the war. By then they were in their late thirties but if I look beyond the face of the father I love and miss so much, I see Carly. Other people can spot family resemblances much more easily and I have to agree that although I've inherited Mum's lovely complexion, her tiny feet — and her quirky sense of humour — the rest is pure Dad. Eyes. Nose. High forehead. Thick hair. He looks just like a Battle of Britain pilot, though in fact because he was deaf in one ear he wasn't able to go to war and worked on Spitfires and Mosquitoes being made at the aerodromes at Heston, Slough and Harmondsworth.

It might have been the Hornby looks that got me into modelling, but what you can't see in the photograph are the other qualities of Dad's which I must have inherited that gave me the wherewithal to go further, to sing and to dance, and above all not to lose my head while all around me were losing theirs.

Norman Hornby was born in Bolton, Lancashire in 1910 (Hornby is an old Lancastrian name) and he was the kindest, gentlest man you can imagine, but not at all tactile. When I came back from America that first time, I was so happy to see him I threw my arms around him and gave him a kiss and I remember him being quite shocked, and saying in his broadest Lancashire ('Lan-ki-sheeere') — he never lost his wonderful accent — 'Ee now, Lesley. There's no call to be soppy.' He hadn't been brought up to show emotions.

Family responsibility was something he learnt early in life. Dad's own mother died when she was only thirty-four and he was only fourteen, leaving five children and a husband who never recovered from the double blow of losing his wife not long after losing the family business, a corner shop. He had been too kind-hearted for his own good and had allowed just about everyone to buy on tick during the First World War. (After the Second World War Dad went into business for himself repairing war damaged houses and exactly the same thing happened.) As the eldest child and the only son, young Norman, my Dad, had to take over as breadwinner to keep the family ticking over until his sisters were old enough to start work at the local cotton mill. For him it was a double tragedy as he had just been awarded a scholarship to an art school, quite a thing for a boy from the backstreets. Instead he was apprenticed to a local cabinet maker. As an apprentice's pay was only nominal, to earn money he worked in the local mortuary, laying out dead bodies.

Dad never let his lack of education stop him learning. He was always reading. Architecture and politics were his two favourite subjects. Two of his sisters had emigrated with their husbands to Rhodesia to try their luck with mining, and there was nothing Dad didn't know about southern Africa. And he was always drawing, although I don't think any of his early pictures survived the move to Twickenham. But I'm lucky enough to have one of Dad's oil paintings hanging in the flat and people who know say it shows real talent. It's of a cat but he has somehow given this imperious old tabby real personality. Not an ounce of sentimentality.

He was also very musical, something which I think came from his mother's side of the family who were originally from Ireland. He'd had piano lessons when he was little, so as well as being able to play anything by ear — and I mean anything, from classical to Cole Porter to Bill Haley — he could also read sheet music. While he was still living in Bolton, Dad had played piano in a dance band. Going dancing on a Friday or Saturday night was about the only entertainment ordinary working people had in those days. And that's how Mum and Dad met, at Cricklewood Palais, shortly after he'd moved down to London and was working for Bovis, fitting out Marks & Spencer shops. (He was offered shares at five shillings each and turned them down. Even at that price he couldn't afford it.) Mum was engaged to somebody else at the time, but fortunately for us, her fiancé didn't like dancing. So she got shot of him, handed back the ring and that was that. I used to love hearing that story. But it always ended with Viv and me wagging our fingers and chanting, 'You should have kept the ring, Mum.'

They may have been perfect dancing partners — Dad five foot seven and Mum five foot and half an inch — but in many ways I realise now they were a bit of a mismatch. Dad was always so interesting and interested in everything around him. He was hungry for knowledge. He had this hunger to travel, to see buildings and paintings. Mum just didn't share his horizons. She even hated him playing the piano ('that horrible noise', she called it) and when Shirley's first marriage broke down and she moved back home into the front room which Dad fitted up for her as a bed-sit, he took the piano out into the garden and hacked it to pieces with an axe. That was when I was six. He said it was because Shirley needed the space. After that, the only music we had in the house was the radio.

Much as I love her — her warmth, her quirky humour — I don't think Mum can ever have been an easy person to live with. But my coming along made things worse. Her first reaction was probably right. Forty-one was too old to have a baby. Soon after I was born she had to have a hysterectomy. After the operation she had the first of her nervous breakdowns, probably what we would now call postnatal depression, but serious enough to land her up in a mental hospital for several months. At that time all most people were told was to pull themselves together. One thing that she never got over was the death of her sister Alice of rheumatic fever at the age of thirty. She clearly idolised Alice, although because of the ten-year age difference they can't have been that close as children, and Mum went to live with her when she was about seventeen, having fallen out with her parents. When Alice died Mum was twenty. She always talked about it as the source of all her unhappiness. It must have been so traumatic for her.

Housewives in the fifties didn't go out to work — at least not around us — so there was no shortage of neighbours to look after me while Mum was away. Foremost among these was Mrs Garahan from two doors up, her daughter

Teresa who later went on to become a nurse, and Auntie Joyce and the Ports who lived at the end of the street. Looking back I realise that there must have been complicated rosters to make sure I was all right. But I suspect it was Shirley who really took the brunt of it. I remember her as always being a grown up. She used to wear big fifties dresses and high stiletto heels and a feather haircut. She and her friends were so glamorous. Shirley was more like a second mum to me — she had her first baby, my nephew Paul, when she was eighteen, when I was only four. When she married again and had two more children I would always be included in their holidays. It was like having another level of family.

Partly I suspect because I was her last baby and partly through the trauma of having to leave me when she went into hospital Mum was incredibly protective. Over-protective probably. It's understandable: her other two daughters were growing up, so I was doubly precious. I was a very clingy, shy little girl. Always hiding behind the curtains when somebody came to the house; going to parties, handing the present in at the door, then running back to Mum who was already half-way down the road. Perhaps subconsciously I was frightened that she might not be there when I got back or perhaps I was just responding to her signals. But however easy it is to speculate now, the truth is that at the time I was never aware of anything wrong. When you're little you assume that what happens to you happens to everyone. I can't remember how old I was when it finally dawned on me that everyone's mum didn't go away for 'rests'.

There was no pattern to Mum's absences. Her natural tendency to depression, probably inherited from Nanny Reeman, was made worse by the shock to her system after the hysterectomy. There was no such thing as HRT (Hormone Replacement Therapy) then. Instead they gave her ECT (Electroconvulsive Therapy). It makes me so angry that this kind of radical treatment was meted out in such a cavalier fashion. Who knows what long-term damage it did — destroying millions of brain cells. In the sixties, they put her on Mogadon. I remember once reading on the side of the bottle 'not to be taken for more than three weeks'. That was thirty years ago. And it's only very recently that she's been weaned off it. None of it worked. Her bouts of depression, her 'nervous condition' continue to this day.

The plus side was that I had a very close relationship with my father, closer I suspect than I would have done otherwise. Sundays are the days I remember most clearly, because they were the most different. Dad was always at home so it was often just him and me playing house on our own. There was a blackboard hanging up in the kitchen and we'd play noughts and crosses and hangman. Then there were board games and jigsaws. For me it was the beginning of a lifelong passion for both. Most people think I'm mad: they'd do anything rather than get roped in for a game of Monopoly. But I love them. And I'm incredibly competitive. I can't even let Carly win Chinese Chequers, but there's nothing competitive about jigsaws. They're just extraordinarily relaxing. My dream is to have a whole room just for jigsaws and of course a sewing room — my other great passion. My dreams are very simple: I don't want yachts, I don't want private aeroplanes, I want a jigsaw room and a sewing room.

* * *

My father never complained and never stopped adoring my mother, however difficult she was. I know she couldn't help it, but he was like a saint. Her illness has manifested itself in many ways and one was a fear of travel. Dad loved his car but Mum would only go in it if she sat in the back and only if he went no faster than 30 m.p.h. Even then out would come the regular refrain 'Don't forget, Norman. Thirty miles an hour.'

One of the greatest sadnesses of my life is that my father never saw me on Broadway. Mum wouldn't fly and he wouldn't leave her. Shirley, who'd already been out to see the show and knew how much it would mean to both Dad and me, offered to go and stay with her while he was away. We even suggested going on the QE2. But it was no good.

In many ways it was an idyllic childhood. I was a very happy child and I only have happy memories. For all the difficulties I can't ever remember any arguments. All that was kept away from me. I was the peach. Cosseted. Protected. Whenever I wanted someone to play with all I had to do was cross the street, knock on Auntie Joyce's door and ask if Geraldine could come out and play. If it was cold we'd play inside. If it was warm we'd play in the street. Although there were garden gates, the pavements were as much our playground as anywhere else. We'd play mothers and babies with our prams when we were younger, or later on we'd skip or play hopscotch or jacks. I can still play jacks now. Once a week, I got my comics, *Bunty* and *Judy*. How I used to long for Thursdays, the day they came out. Then at Christmas came the annuals. Simple pleasures.

There was something very innocent about those days. An innocence that, however much we try to retain it in our own children, has largely disappeared. We had Bill and Ben and Muffin the Mule. Sparky and his Magic Piano and Tubby The Tuba. Now kids have Beavis and Butt-head and MTV. When I did *Desert Island Discs* a few years ago, I chose my all-time favourite 'The Laughing Policeman' because it reminded me of those Sundays and always hoping I'd hear it on *Two-Way Family Favourites* on the wireless, and the house filled with the smell of the roast. The record had exactly the same effect in the studio as it had in our kitchen long ago. Everyone was in hysterics. It's so infectious, you just can't help laughing. But that's all gone and it's so sad. That was the last of it. That was the end of England how it used to be. England where childhood meant just that. Being a child. I still have a longing for it. But with the sixties everything changed.

3

One of the things that has really irritated me over the years is the way that just about everybody has swallowed the line that Justin was the Svengali and I was the dumb blonde. It might have made a good story for the newspapers, but it wasn't, isn't, true. When it comes to the media, particularly newspapers, they just make you what they want to make you. In reality I was one of those much maligned creatures who always loved school. Not a swot perhaps, but a real goody two shoes, always doing my homework, keeping my exercise books neat. I was always among the top ten, even at Kilburn and Brondesbury High School For Girls, the best grammar school in the area and which needed a high pass mark at the Eleven Plus to get into. I was never top of anything except once when I got first prize for my weather map on our school journey to the Isle of Wight. Years later Mr Singer, my favourite teacher, told me he was still using it as an example of how it should be done. Just think, I could have been a weather girl.

If you have a special teacher it can change your life. I had two. First there was Mr Singer who was my form master for four years at Bridge Lane Junior School. He was one of those wonderful old-fashioned teachers who did it because he loved it. In our family with its overabundance of overprotective 'aunties', this comfy and round-looking man in his tweeds and woolly jumpers gave me enormous confidence and was hugely important in my life. At home I might have been clingy but with Mr Singer I was myself.

Then there was Miss Downer, who taught me to play the recorder. She was inspirational, passionate about music. Her mentor was Carl Dolmetch, the man who single-handedly brought the recorder back into the concert hall and who she may well have studied under. Most children learn the descant recorder and that's it, but with Miss Downer the descant was only the beginning. First step up the rung was the treble and I eventually ended up playing the tenor. Our recorder group would regularly play in competitions and concerts, playing Purcell and Handel. While other teachers dressed in modern fifties clothes, Miss Downer was different, I now realise. I remember her vividly because of the hair. She had a centre parting and flat finger waves — like a real thirties hairstyle. She wore big flared cotton skirts and flat sandals and tight little jumpers with embroidered flowers, that Edina Ronay brought out later in the seventies, but were then very old fashioned. She never wore make-up and used to stride through the school as if oblivious to everything except music and you, if you needed to talk to her. Through her I learned to read music. If I hadn't, God knows if I'd have had the courage to attempt even *The Boyfriend*, let alone Broadway. It still causes eyebrows to be lifted in something very like disbelief when musical arrangers or conductors first find out I'm not musically illiterate.

Although I enjoyed playing the recorder, whenever anyone asked me what my best subject was, the answer was always the same. Art. There was one girl I remember at Kilburn and Brondesbury High who was seriously good. I wasn't like that. But when I was seven, Mr Singer (who taught everything from art, to sums, to reading and writing) entered a painting I'd done in the *Sunday Pictorial* Children's Art competition. I ended up being one of twenty-four children all of whom 'had done something they could be proud of' at a party in a swanky Park Lane hotel. It was my first appearance in the press and I was described as 'Pretty Lesley Hornby, of Willesden'. I can't imagine why they chose me. Most of the others seemed to have done good deeds. There was one who saved her brother and sister from death and another who saved her mongrel dog from being put down after it had bitten her, by arguing the toss with a magistrate. Perhaps it was because my painting was patriotic: this was after all 1956 and the picture was entitled 'The Queen Going For A Walk'. The *Daily Mirror* had actually reproduced it, saying that it would amuse Her Majesty and surprise the royal dressmaker. It appears my ideas about clothes were unconventional even then.

Each child had a celebrity to look after them. I had Rolf Harris but the real thrill of the party was meeting Alma Cogan, a wonderfully glamorous singing star famous for her frocks with a catch in her voice who died incredibly young. When I told her how much I loved her dress (yards and yards and yards of skirt) she asked me if I would like to know what she would be wearing on her Christmas TV Show. It was to be our secret, she said, and I wasn't to tell anyone. I imagine I nodded in quivering anticipation as she told me that her dress would be gold.

Although the paper described it as 'an unforgettable day', the only other thing I can remember is the dress I wore, which was pink chiffon with little white flowers, puffed sleeves, and a net undersksirt which Mum had bought for me from C&A. I'd first worn it for my best friend Jennifer Read's seventh birthday party. I remember because she had the same dress, but in a different colour; turquoise with yellow flowers.

I've always been aware of clothes. I can still remember outfits I had when I was really quite little. Mum made nearly all of them in those days. She loved American-style dresses which you couldn't get in fifties' England, except perhaps in a posh shop like Daniel Neal's in Oxford Street. But the American pattern companies, like McCalls and Butterick had plenty. Sometimes she would even manage to dress Viv and me the same — quite a feat given the seven-year gap. From early on I had a big say in what I was wearing and I loved the whole business of going with her to choose patterns and material. It meant a real journey, to the drapers in Harlesden High Street (where we'd also buy my liberty bodices, a kind of vest, with their strange rubber buttons) or sometimes all the way to Barkers in Kensington High Street when we'd 'make a day of it'.

When I was about eleven or twelve, we began to buy things from Kay's catalogue. Shirley was a rep so she'd get the commission. She'd come back with this huge book, as big as a telephone directory, filled with more children's clothes than I had imagined existed, and we'd sit down at the kitchen table to look through it together and pick things. I remember one dress I got from there. A cotton print, royal blue with great big red-orange roses, tied at the back with a bow. In the front it had a scoop neck filled with three rows of white lace. I'd have one new dress every summer. And one new pair of white sandals. Every autumn everything would get put in a suitcase, washed and ironed and ready for next year. You really knew when summer was round the corner, because out would come the suitcase smelling of mothballs and then there would be all that trying on and letting down of hems.

But by the time I was thirteen I was making my own clothes. The sort of things I wanted you couldn't get even from Kays, because by then I was a Mod. At least I was on Saturday nights. At school we had to wear uniform which was navy pleated skirts, white shirts and ties. The skirt I used to turn up at the waist over and over. Not only because skirts were starting to get shorter, but because uniforms were expensive and Mum had bought mine 'to last'. The other thing was stockings. They were brown and made of cotton and bagged like mad, epecially on my skinny legs, so I wore socks, mostly knee socks. Also stockings couldn't be trusted. My friend Angela was what you'd call a big girl. She was very funny and always had us in hysterics. Across the road was the boys' grammar school and the whole focus of the day was to attract the boys on the bus on the way home. One afternoon we had just arrived at the bus stop which was as usual seething with hair-tossing boys and giggling girls when without any warning, the fastening on Angela's suspender belt popped and down came her stockings and her suspender belt, landing in a heap around her feet. There was this split second of silence and then everyone collapsed on the pavement. Boys included. I don't think I have ever laughed so much in my life.

Breaktimes would be spent discussing what we were going to wear at the weekend. Some of us pooled our money in order to buy Vogue patterns which, although expensive, could easily be adapted if you knew how. And I knew how. Learning to sew was just part of growing up. Viv turned into a proper seamstress and I remember her making a beautiful bouclé tweed suit. She even made her own wedding dress. I began with dolls' clothes, using bits and pieces left over from Mum's sewing box. I still love sewing though I have never learnt to cut my own patterns and am always promising myself to go on a course to learn how. In those days I could buy a yard of cotton for 2/11d (14p) and wool gabardine for 12/11d (64p). (Whereas the new invention, tights, were incredibly expensive and a real luxury costing 19/11d (99p) each.)

Even now half the pleasure comes from making something for a fraction the price it would cost in the shops. The other pleasure is choosing the fabric. Forget Bond Street or Fifth Avenue. For a real taste of paradise there is nothing like a wholesale fabric shop. They're not limited to the rag trade, anyone can go there. My favourite is in Berwick Street in Soho. It's like finding yourself in a treasure house. Moving through the aisles of colour is like being on the inside of a kaleidoscope and I go into imagination overdrive, seeing a dress, trousers, or jacket in every roll. It's not just clothes. It's sewing itself that I find so creative and satisfying. I made all the curtains and cushions and bedspreads in our cottage in Oxfordshire and for our flat in London.

Being a Mod was a serious business. It was perhaps the first time the working class had set the pace in fashion. And Mods were all working class. The great thing was to follow the pack. The boys had the best of it. They were like peacocks, strutting around like never before. They wore suits and desert boots, ankle swingers they were called, and Ben Sherman button-downs or giraffe-necked gingham shirts and black leather jackets. Buttons, flaps and vents were all very important, but used to create their own look. Most of the boys were older than we were, earning but still living at home. The boom after the austerity of the fifties meant they could walk into a job and be earning £10 a week when the average weekly wage was only £13. So they had all this money which they would spend on clothes, on made-to-measure suits (costing £9 from Burton's or John Steven's) like rich people did, but they were able to create their own look.

And where it all happened was dance halls on Saturday nights. The routine was always the same. First we would watch *Dr Who* on television then it was upstairs to get bathed, dressed and made up. The first time I went, with Jennifer Read and Ellen Chad, was to the Kingsbury Ritz, just the other side of Wembley, and I remember I wore a grey pin-stripe pinafore dress, down to mid-calf, at a time when normal skirts stopped at the knee. It was A-line with a big V to the waist and crossover straps over a white silky blouse with a big pointed collar. I can't remember what the others were wearing but it was something similar. The whole point was we had to look the same. Make-up was white lipstick from Woolworth's and black mascared eyes. Although we'd planned it for weeks, we were terrified. Even more when we got there and saw all these people who looked like grown-ups standing about. And girls chatting to boys leaning on scooters. We immediately backtracked toward the station in a fit of giggles. After calming down by putting on more layers of mascara we went back again. The doors were just about to close but the doorman saw us coming and shouted out, 'Come on girls, I'll let you in if you're quick.' So in we went.

Those dance halls were huge. They were the same places that Mum and Dad had danced in all those years ago — *palais de danse* — designed for big bands. And every town and suburb had one. The only one you hear of now is the Hammersmith Palais. But this wasn't dancing as they had known it, with a partner. We only danced with girls (except for the slow songs). You'd put your handbags in the middle and dance around them. On the stage there would be three or four fresh-faced boys with guitars and drums who were known as the group. All the groups started off that way, playing at dance halls. Like The Dave Clark Five and the Kinks. Even the Beatles. These were the days when you just screamed and screamed and screamed. Jennifer and I got tickets to see the Beatles at the Finsbury Park Astoria, which was miles away.

But the place we usually went to was the Starlight Ballroom in Sudbury which was over towards Harrow. We'd go there and back on our own by bus and train. To get there took over an hour, with three changes. By then I was used to travelling on public transport: the journey to school took an hour and a half and I'd been doing that since I was eleven. People weren't frightened like they are now.

At Sudbury the acknowledged leader of the fashion pack was a boy called Mick O'Connor. He had a Lambretta, and Lambrettas were much more stylish than Vespas. Part of the thing was to see what Mick O'Connor was wearing. And that would set the fashion agenda for the next few weeks. Once he actually spoke to us. He had jet black hair, about an inch long all over, which stood up as if he'd had an electric shock, presumably done with Brylcreem. Only the week before he'd had hair parted in the middle.

As for the girls, their hair was mostly cropped. Except for me. I wanted to look like Jean Shrimpton and had been growing it for years. I wore it parted in the middle. At the weekends I would curl it under and I remember going to bed in great big rollers that prickled. I'd had this thing about long hair ever since Shirley had cut mine off with Dad's wallpaper scissors when I was about five. It was when I'd had the first of my dizzy spells and the doctor had told Mum that perhaps my long hair was using up my energy. I'd had these dizzy spells from when I was about five and grew out of them when I was twelve. They were probably due to low blood pressure, certainly not long hair.

Our Mod uniform was a long plastic mac, a brand known as Pakamac, worn over whatever was the thing to wear at the time. We used to freeze in them. But that wasn't important. You had to be 'with it'. You had to look the same. One Saturday night the group of seventeen-and eighteen-year-old girls who were the trend-setters (I don't think the sixties word 'trendies' came in till later) were all wearing ankle length skirts and granny blouses in chiffon with cameo brooches. If that was the look, we had to have it, and we did. The following week, armed with our pocket money, Jennifer and I went up to C&A on our quest and bought two chiffon blouses, one in royal blue (mine) and one in brown. The sleeves and the Peter Pan collars were see-through, but the rest was lined in satin. As for the skirts, they had to be made. So I bought two yards of tweed each, black and grey for me with a blue slub, and one with a brown slub for Jennifer. She couldn't sew so I had to do both: there was no way I'd have worn one on my own. The trouble was that Jennifer's mother wasn't as understanding as mine. (Shirley's gallivanting fourteen years earlier had proved very useful, and I was given much more leeway than many of my friends.) She was not going to have Jennifer going out looking like that, she said. 'In case of what the neighbours might say.' The fact that you couldn't imagine anything more modest was beside the point. We looked like the suffragettes. So both skirts were kept at my house until D-Day and the next Saturday night we set off, me in mine, Jennifer in an ordinary skirt, and she changed under her mac on the top of the bus. We were hysterical.

There was never any alcohol. Not drinking was part of being a Mod. These were the days of Coca Cola and purple hearts. Purple hearts were barbiturates. My friends, the brave ones, used to take them. The boys took them by the handful, drank Coke and chewed gum; girls generally were a little more careful. I had nothing to do with them. Not because I'd been told not to, because my parents didn't even know about pep pills then. They hadn't really hit the press. Friends had told me what the effects were and they sounded to me just like the dizzy spells that I used to get sometimes and which frightened the living daylights out of me. So I stayed well clear. Then and later. Though I started to smoke, which was stupid, because once you've started it's so difficult to stop.

Of course the point of all this was boys. My problem was that I knew I was totally the wrong shape. At school I was teased mercilessly. All the boys laughed at me. Their name for me was Oxfam. The only girls they were interested in were ones with boobs, preferably big ones. One of the things I did to get over this was to stuff a bra I bought for the purpose (by no stretch of the imagination did I need one) with paper tissues. There had always been boys I thought were gorgeous, ever since I was five when I was in love with Carl Webb who went to nursery school with me. What you might call my first real boyfriend was Christopher. I met him at the Kingsbury Ritz. He gave me a lift to the station on the back of his scooter, so he must have been over seventeen. Going out with someone in those days meant going to the pictures. The film we were going to see was on in Wembley. He lived in Watford, so we arranged to meet at the station. I waited and waited and waited. It was dreadful. I remember I was wearing a black and grey double-breasted coat. Eventually I went home to find he'd phoned to say there had been something wrong with the line. The train had never even left Watford. I suppose I hadn't thought to ask anyone at the station if anything had happened. After our second date he telephoned and told me that as he was saving up to buy a new Lambretta, he couldn't afford a girlfriend as well. So I lost out to a scooter. I remember being devastated and crying my eyes out and Viv being so kind to me. She said all the right things. But whatever anyone says to you, it's ever so hard. You're so vulnerable. For days afterwards all anyone heard in our house was Peter and Gordon singing 'World Without Love' which Christopher had given to me.

In about 1961 Viv had given in to her passion for Paul Anka and bought his hit single 'Diana'. It was her pride and joy and she guarded it with her life but we had nothing to play it on so we would sit around the table and she would hand it round and let us look at it. This went on for weeks until one day Dad took pity on her and appeared with a turquoise and cream portable gramophone, a second-hand Dansette that he'd got from someone at work.

Viv was a hairdresser. She had started as a Saturday girl at the salon in Edgware where Shirley used to have her hair cut. They'd taken her on as a favour but she turned out to be really good and left school when she was fifteen, a term before she took her O-levels, to work there permanently. What was the point, she said, of having O-levels when you didn't need them to be a hairdresser. Dad was furious. Viv, like me, went to Kilburn and Brondesbury High where everyone was expected to stay on in the sixth form to do A-levels, not leave before they'd even taken their Os. By the time I was fourteen she'd moved on from Edgware and was now working in Queensway. Queensway was then a very cosmopolitan street, filled with Chinese restaurants with windows hung with rows of ducks that looked as if they'd been sprayed with red hair lacquer. It's just off the

Bayswater Road that runs along Hyde Park. In other words, West End. Or so we mistakenly thought. My usual idea of going Up West was to take a bus to Trafalgar Square and just wander around. When I was little it meant the twice-yearly trip to Oxford Street for the sales and, most importantly, a visit to Lyons Corner House at Marble Arch, where we'd have ham, egg and chips and I would feel so posh. So when Viv told me that Mr Vincent, where she worked, had a vacancy for a Saturday girl, I jumped.

Life was beginning to open up. For a start I had more money. My wages were about £1 10/- (£1.50) and with tips, sixpence here, sometimes even half-a-crown, it gave me about £2 10/- (£2.50) a week. A fortune. At Mr Vincent's I did the usual things a Saturday girl does: wash hair, sweep the floor, keep the basins and surfaces clean. The clients were mostly middle-aged ladies who had perms and sets. The junior stylist was called Kay. We used to talk clothes together because she, too, was a Mod. Don't imagine that everybody in London at the beginning of the sixties was a Mod. Far from it. Viv wasn't, for example, although she and Kay were about the same age. Students weren't either. They had their own uniform of polo necks and jeans (usually imported from France) which no one had seen except on American films until then. And of course there were the Rockers who drove motorbikes and were the Mods' natural enemies. I had always longed to go down to Brighton or Margate on one of the famous weekends but Dad had never allowed it. To me it seemed so unfair. Of course now that I know the truth of those pitched battles between the Mods and the Rockers he was absolutely right.

Although she was tiny, only four foot eleven, Kay always looked amazing, with heavy black eye-makeup and short spiky hair. It was Kay who first took me to Biba. From then on every Saturday lunchtime when I got my lunch break I would run to Bayswater tube, take the Circle line two stops to Kensington High Street, and run for another four minutes until I reached Biba. There should be a plaque on 87 Abingdon Road. It transformed the way the ordinary girl in the street dressed. Mary Quant might have invented the mini skirt, but her shop, Bazaar in the King's Road was for rich girls. Biba was for anyone. Biba was Barbara Hulanicki. Not literally, in fact Biba is the name of her sister — but it was chosen when they needed a name for their 'postal boutique' because it was short and easy to remember. Barbara had been an art student and had a job drawing corsets for an old-fashioned lingerie catalogue. Her husband Fitz suggested she design something herself and try to sell it mail order. Although they hadn't even made anything, the fashion editor of the *Daily Mirror* agreed to feature a very cheap gingham shift, with matching head scarf. The whole thing sold for £2 2/-(£2.10), or two guineas as it was called then. The rest is, as they say, history. The mail order was soon dropped, as they couldn't cope with the volume. Instead they opened a shop. It was a tiny corner shop, an old chemists in a quiet residential street. But before long, Biba was Mecca to everyone from shopgirls to debs. (A couple of years later they closed the shop to customers to let Princess Anne roam around. It must have been very odd being on her own. The whole thing about Biba was that it was always seething with bodies.) Not only did the clothes look amazing, you could afford to buy something every week. I remember I bought a dress in brushed cotton jersey, lemon with shocking pink zig zags which I later wore to Viv's wedding. Already the hemlines were creeping up. It was two inches above the knee. The first dress I bought was a linen shift with a keyhole neck. Another one I remember was A-line with tight, tight sleeves that ended in a puff at the shoulder, with little pearl buttons at the neck. All classics. If only I had kept them.

It wasn't like any other shop I had ever seen. There were no rails, just clothes hanging off wooden hat stands and wicker baskets filled with T-shirts like vests with shoe-lace necks. There wasn't even a proper changing room and not even that much choice. The clothes changed all the time. If you didn't buy what you wanted there and then, it wasn't worth coming back next week and hoping it would still be there. Sometimes it would look half empty, if they were waiting for a delivery. There were no women saying 'can I help you, madam?' just young girls with long blonde hair wandering about tidying up the clothes that littered the floor and hanging them back on the hat stands again and putting clothes in the famous black and gold bags and taking the money in a big old-fashioned cash register.

It wasn't long before Cathy McGowan was wearing something from Biba every week on *Ready Steady Go*, ITV's answer to the BBC's *Top Of The Pops*. No one ever went out on Friday. *Ready Steady Go* was the Mod Bible and Cathy McGowan with her amazing dark hair, so long and heavy it just seemed to hang there, and a fringe she could barely see out of, was the queen. Our dream was to get on the show. They used to go round the country doing auditions, looking for good dancers, so one week, when they were in London, Jennifer and I went along. A man would tap you on the shoulder and if you got tapped you got given your ticket. And we were tapped. Oh the excitement! The great hope was that the Beatles would be on, but they weren't. I wore a white pleated knee-length skirt and mustard and grey two-ply jumper and a string of pearls. There were no videos in those days to record magic moments like that. But Mum said that she thinks she caught sight of my skirt.

A year or so later, when Biba had moved from Abingdon Road to Kensington Church Street, after all the madness had happened to me, I was at the shop for some shoot or other and Barbara came out and just said 'Hello'. I am so glad she did. Not only is she one of the greatest design talents England has ever produced (though she is in fact of Polish and Russian descent) but she's an extraordinary, wonderful woman and I feel very lucky to count her among my friends. Sadly Fitz died far too young early in 1997.

They lived in what had been an artists' studio off Melbury Road, to the north of Kensington High Street. It was all open plan and huge. It even had the bath in it (though the loo was separate). I was completely captivated and from the first time I stepped into this magic room I knew that someday I would live in somewhere decorated just like it, and now I do. It was all velvets and tassels and tapestries and it was like going into Aladdin's Cave, with ostrich feathers in blues and purples. I'd never seen anything like it. They didn't decorate like that in Neasden.

Now that I was buying things from Biba and I had my money from Mr Vincent's, I began branching out, away from Pakamacs and Hush Puppies. Because we were much the same size, I had always borrowed Viv's clothes. She must have been earning about £15 a week and always bought fabulous things, though I drew the line at a pair of black and red high boots she had bought at the dance shoemakers, Annello and Davide. I thought they were hideous. (Little did I realise that boots would become a passion with me. At one point I had thirty pairs.) And when I bought a pair of dark green leather shoes from Galleries Lafayette in Regents Street, it was Viv's green polo jumper and green leather gloves that I borrowed to go with them. Those shoes cost seven guineas. Incredibly expensive. I didn't dare confess to Dad and told him they'd cost £3. But they were worth every penny. They were my pride and joy and they made me feel beautiful.

I suppose I was beginning to feel a bit happier

about the way I looked. After all, the girls in Biba's looked much the same as me. And one Saturday night when a boy at a dance asked me, as his opening gambit, 'Are you a model?', I really felt I'd arrived. By then things had moved on and my friends and I were going further afield. I met him in Harrow where I saw the Yardbirds (Eric Clapton in the band, and Jeff Beck), and the Who, whose mad drummer Keith Moon I had known when he worked as a delivery boy for Viv's boyfriend's dad who ran a greengrocers in Wembley. This boy's name was Roger. He was a photographer's assistant, and suggested doing a few head shots. I was only fifteen and still at school so this was a real come-on, though until that moment the idea of being a model had never crossed my head. Also I thought he was gorgeous: blonde and about eighteen and so grown up. So we arranged to go out. This time the meeting place would be at Neasden Station. Neasden Station is one of the most dispiriting places in the world. It's where all the train lines into London from the north cross and that's about it. There's no parade of shops. Nothing. Just a narrow pavement next to a narrow bridge. I waited there for far too long. All I remember is not wanting to go home. Not wanting anyone to know that I'd been stood up. This time there was no phone call when I got back.

But the story has a coda. A year or so later, after the whole thing happened to me, I was booked to do a job for a women's weekly magazine. The photographer's studio was in

Kilburn. And as I walked in with my model's bag and paraphernalia there he was, Roger. The photographer's assistant. He went beetroot red. But as nobody else there knew what had happened, we just said hello and chatted and it wasn't embarrassing, at least not for me. I still thought he was really nice but although he phoned up a week or so later, and in fact came to the house — I remember us sitting in the rarely used front room — it was too late. By then I was with Justin.

4

There's nothing journalists love more than pigeonholing. So when I first hit the headlines ('cockney kid') Justin became immortalised as 'former hairdresser', which is why people assume I met him through my Saturday job. In a way I did, but only indirectly. Justin's brother Tony worked downstairs at Mr Vincent's and Justin would sometimes pick him up from work and come upstairs for a laugh and a joke with the girls. In those days men and women had their hair done separately so we were up on the first floor and the barbers was downstairs. And that's how we met.

I was only fifteen. But Justin was twenty-five and during the ten years since leaving school and meeting me, he had been a hairdresser, so it's not surprising that when it all happened, that's what he told the press — it sounded better than some of the other jobs he had had: nightclub bouncer, debt collector for the bookmakers William Hill and front man for 'auctioneers' selling fake watches. Not that I knew any of this at the time. When we met in the spring of 1965, he was running a stall in the Chelsea Antique Market with an architect friend of his called Ben Maurice-Jones.

It was Tony who had first called me Twigs. (His first name for me was Sticks but, like most nicknames, it changed without anyone really noticing.) He was younger than Justin, rather plump and very funny and it was Tony who first suggested I could be a model — a customer had said to him that I ought to get photographs done. Justin got involved only because he had a car, a wonderful little red sports car, a Triumph Spitfire, which I remember us all cramming into one Sunday morning to shoot some pictures on Wimbledon Common. The photographer was a friend of Tony's and for all I know the pictures were shot on an Instamatic. Anyway, they were a disaster and nothing was ever done with them.

Justin (whose real name was Nigel Davies) was very different from the boys I was used to. For a start he was ten years older than me and married with a little girl, Melanie, though by the time I met him he had been separated for three years. He didn't bother to hide any of this because for quite a long time he was nothing more than Tony's big brother. He was very flamboyant. A twentieth-century dandy. He wore outrageous clothes, velvet jackets with handkerchiefs flopping out of them, or denim jeans so tight that Viv was convinced that he was gay. Although he was certainly camp, he was by no means gay, though it wasn't till several years later that I found out just how great a womaniser he was. He wasn't tall, about five foot nine, but with the coiled-spring body of a boxer, another of the things he had done in the past (he'd been an amateur welterweight known as 'Tiger' Davies, but had given it up because of his asthma) and there was always this edge about him that let people know he could get himself out of trouble — and them into it.

Tony's girlfriend was called Louise. She was older than me, about eighteen I suppose, and very pretty with long blonde hair parted in the middle. She and I got on really well and so the four of us would often spend Sundays together, just having fun and a lark. When the weather was fine we might go for a day trip to the seaside. Or spend the afternoon at Tony's flat in Albany Street near Regent's Park. Louise and I used to spend hours playing with make-up. False eyelashes were her thing. I bought my first pair at the chemists next to Mr Vincent's in Queensway and Louise and I used to make up our eyes so we looked like dolls. You couldn't stick false eyelashes on the bottom lid, so we would draw them in, like a rag doll I'd had when I was little.

It was all above board between Justin and me for months and months because I was still at school. During that summer term he would turn up with the hood down on the Spitfire and wait for me outside. The other girls were amazed. So much for Olive Oyl. Sometimes a whole lot of us would pile in. Looking at it now, all those girls in uniform, short skirts and stockings — it was all a bit suspect. But it wasn't like it was a date and he would ask me out. He would just come and pick me up and say did I want to go for a ride. As the summer wore on, it got a bit more romantic but I'd always have to be home by ten. At first Mum and Dad didn't approve — after all, he was ten years older then me — so I'd say I was seeing a girlfriend and we'd arrange to meet round the corner. Eventually they had to accept the inevitable. Justin had the gift of the gab and could talk his way into and out of anything, so it wasn't long before he had Mum eating out of his hand, though Dad never entirely trusted him. It was Mum who convinced him that I'd be safer with Justin in a car than on my own at the mercy of anyone. By October, when Viv got married, Justin was accepted enough to come along to the wedding.

Since Justin had separated from his wife, he'd been camping out with various friends. When I met him he was living in a house belonging to an American writer, Philip Oxman. It was an amazing studio house in Dukes Lane, a small cobbled mews just off Kensington Church Street. In fact Justin lived in a little stone summer house in the garden which had once been a chapel, and which to me seemed like it had jumped straight off the pages of a fairy story, covered in vines. He had met Philip through another friend of his, Louis de Wett, who was very grand and forbidding and who lived in an equally grand and forbidding house in Holland Park. Inside the walls were painted black and covered with huge canvasses. There was even a gym in the basement where Louis used to hone his already amazingly honed body. Both Louis and his enormous paintings terrified me. I soon learned not to look at them too closely, otherwise I'd see things young girls shouldn't. He was an intellectual, very tall and seemed to me to be terribly old though he was probably only about forty. When you're fifteen, anyone over thirty is ancient. But another of this group, Gabrielle Drake, I adored. She was the complete opposite of me, dark-haired and voluptuous just like I'd always imagined an actress would be. She looked like Ava Gardner and was so beautiful she took my breath away. But however friendly Gabrielle was toward me, I never really felt comfortable with Louis. Another artist friend of Justin's, Brian Robbins, was quite different. He was a kinetic sculptor and lived in a basement flat in Primrose Hill. He was very Welsh and very homely and made fried egg sandwiches, something I'd never had before but which I adored, homely yet somehow naughty, with the yolk dribbling down your chin.

Part of Justin's world was a world of mad artists. They did mad things, even something like eating in the garden seemed mad to me then. It was a wonderful world to look into. And for quite a long time that was all I did, hardly daring to open my mouth. My world had been very happy but it had been very suburban.

For all his intellectualising, Louis de Wett had his practical side. Justin was trying to sell art at this time. To be successful Louis had told him he needed a name that was more exotic than Nigel Davies. It was then he changed it to Justin de Villeneuve. It wasn't his first *nom de guerre*. Justin the hairdresser had been known as Mr Christian.

It was only after about six months that our relationship became serious. It wasn't that I fell madly in love with Justin. When you're in love with someone you know it and you certainly don't feel your knees go weak when you see other people, which from time to time I must admit did happen — though I would never have dreamt of doing anything about it. It was just that he introduced me to this other world. Looking back he should never have taken me out, I was far too young and he was far too old. In my opinion a ten year age gap is all very well when you're in your twenties or thirties, but not at fifteen and twenty-five.

I must always have known it wasn't right because although we were together for nearly seven years and he was always asking me to marry him, I never did and I never even moved in with him. Home was always with Mum and Dad: in Neasden until 1968, then Twickenham. In 1969 Justin and I bought a mews house just off Tottenham Court Road. Upstairs was used as an office, and downstairs was Justin's studio, a place to entertain and where Justin lived. Often the only reason I'd stay the night was because we'd be going out or I'd be working the next day in town and it was easier than schlepping in all the way from Neasden, but I never lived there full time. I would always spend two or three nights a week at home. That was when he would have his little liaisons. The reason he had the red sports car was that it had been given to him by a much older woman who he would 'see' twice a week. Of course I had no idea. But when she found out about me, just before Viv got married, that was the end of the little red Spitfire and it was back to buses. Justin fobbed me off with some story. It never occurred to me not to believe him. I'd led a very suburban existence where people told the truth and I was vulnerable and very gullible.

Ever since the Wimbledon Common fiasco, I had really given up on any idea of modelling. My ambition was now to make my living designing and making clothes. After all it's what I'd always dreamed of and I had already made a small start by making hipster trousers which Justin was selling to other stallholders at the Chelsea Antique market for £5 a pair — a profit of £4 each. I only had to sell two pairs a week to make enough to live on.

One of the pluses of working in Mr Vincent's, the hairdresser, was the glossy magazines which I could never have afforded to buy. And I would spend hours flicking through them, getting ideas. Not everything was successful. I remember one particular outfit of Jean Shrimpton's. It was a summer dress, a paisley cotton print in purples and reds, just above the knee. It had short sleeves and a round neck. But what made it amazing was a bare midriff, covered with mesh. I managed to find some fabric that was quite close but couldn't find a pattern, so I used one I had and just cut out the middle. The mesh was a bit of a problem. In the end I cut up and dyed a string vest. It didn't quite work out as it should have done. But I wore it anyway.

By now school had come to seem an irrelevance. I might still be spending my weekdays at school but I was living in another world, spending my time with people whose interests and horizons were very different — and much more interesting — from those of my contemporaries. I'd stopped going out with my friends to Mod dances and I'd fallen out with Jennifer Read.

Although we'd been friends since junior school, after the Eleven Plus we went to different schools. At Brondesbury and Kilburn High School my new best friend was Janet Davis. Janet had a hard life; her mother had died and she was very shy and was always having to go back to get her dad's dinner. To get her out a bit, I introduced Janet to Jennifer and the three of us went to dances together. The summer before I met Justin, Mum had another one of her difficult patches and I spent a few weeks of the school holidays with Shirley who was by then living in Hayes, Middlesex, on the outskirts of London. When I came back to Neasden one of the first things I did was to go round to see Jennifer who lived only a few minutes away on the North Circular itself. They didn't have a phone so I walked over to her house, feeling all happy, looking forward to seeing my best friend. I remember it all so clearly, knocking on the door and her mum coming out and saying she wasn't in. But in the background I could hear Jennifer and Janet giggling. I'll never forget that awful feeling. It was horrible and it broke my heart. I don't think I ever spoke to Janet again. There was nothing I could do but to walk away.

When I told Dad that I wanted to leave school, he was apoplectic. And you can understand why. He'd been forced to leave school at fourteen and here was I, at fifteen having gained a place at grammar school, and everything to play for, saying I wanted to give it up. It's hard now to even imagine what I thought I was doing, but to be fair setting up in business on your own wasn't as ridiculous then as it might seem now. Biba's was just the tip of a very big fashion iceberg. Boutiques were opening up by the day. Clothes were everything and there was money to be made. My O-level GCE's were just a few months away. I knew I couldn't hope to do well in those and make clothes at the same time. And who knew when the youth bubble would burst? If I was to go into business it had to be now. After all these years I don't remember exactly what we said to Dad but I suppose it must have been something like that. Heavy of heart, he agreed and wrote to the headmistress. But when her reply came back Dad was incensed. Rather than use sensible arguments to persuade me to stay at least till the summer, her letter was aggressive and rude. She even called Dad stupid. I left with his blessing.

Justin's arty friends never stopped saying that I should seriously think about going into modelling and one of them, Annie Harris, mentioned me to a friend of hers who worked on *Woman's Mirror*, a new young magazine which was trying to do for the cheaper end of the magazine market what *Nova* was doing at the glossy end. It had already caused a rumpus by having a cover of a foetus. It wasn't into knitting patterns. They were looking for new faces. The friend, Susan Robbins, phoned Justin and asked if I could go in and see them.

In the meantime another friend of Justin's, a fashion photographer called Michel Molyneux who'd been big in the fifties had said we should contact *Queen*, which was very glossy and in those days vied with *Vogue* as top fashion magazine. I remember I decided to wear a trouser suit in a Liberty cotton print which I'd made. Rather advanced and also rather cold, as it was November. The editor was Prudence Glynn. She was blunt. They never worked with models who were not with bona fide modelling agencies. So that was that. I was five foot six and minute. No model agency would even look at you under five foot eight. Not to mention my unconventional vital statistics of 30:22:32. A year or so later I remember walking into San Lorenzo in Beauchamp Place, my favourite restaurant — it was rather amazing, it had a tree in the middle of it — and noticing Prudence Glynn sitting at another table. I saw her and had this urge to sashay over to her and say 'You goofed'. But being a nicely brought up little girl, I couldn't bring myself to do it. I'm glad I didn't. As she left the restaurant it was she who came over to me. And she said, 'I goofed, didn't I?' Which I thought was really brave and very sweet. In 1968 I finally got to work with her at the *Sunday Times*.

Back at *Women's Mirror* Susan Robbins was equally realistic but a little less blunt. 'You've got a sweet little face but you'll never make a model because you're too small.' Hearing this harsh truth for the second time in under a week didn't make it any easier. But before I'd had time to feel sorry for myself, she added, 'But you might be able to do beauty and head shots.' And there and then she offered me a year's contract at £9 a week, for one day's work. This was amazing. Nine pounds was what most people earned for five days' work. It meant the other four days I could be getting on with my clothes business. I said I'd have to think it over but in the meantime she said I should get some head shots done. And I would be paid. Oh the excitement. My first booking. The first thing I had to do was to see the photographer, and the first thing he said was that I had to do something about my hair. Working at Mr Vincent's I'd been able to tint and bleach my naturally mouse hair as much as I'd wanted. And it was in a terrible state. So the magazine booked me in to Leonard's.

Leonard's was then the top, most exclusive hairdressers in London, perhaps even the world. I'd obviously heard of him, but people like me didn't go to places like that; so when we found ourselves outside the salon in Upper Grosvenor Street in Mayfair it was a bit of a shock. Not another shop in sight. No flashing sign, just a discreet plaque by the solid front door. Just one of a terrace of eighteenth-century town houses. High class wasn't the word. I was booked in with Mr Clifford, for a trim and general conditioning, but then fate took a hand. It turned out that Justin and Leonard, the great man himself, knew each other. Justin hadn't connected his old friend Len (Leonard was actually his real name) with this amazingly famous hairdresser.

They hadn't seen each other since they'd worked together at Vidal Sassoon's several years before. So while my hair was being done Leonard came over to say hello. After I was finished, he asked us if we would mind going over to see another photographer. It was just round the corner, a few minutes by bus.

Barry Lategan had recently come over to England from South Africa and he specialised in hair and beauty and did all Leonard's salon photographs. I later learned that after Leonard had seen me he'd called Barry up and told him that he had a girl in the salon who he thought was interesting, who he thought was photogenic and who, if Barry thought she had something, he'd like to do his new haircut on.

Barry's studio in Baker Street was enormous. Not that I had anything to go by, as this was the first one I had ever been in. While Justin was doing his usual chat-up line, I just wandered around looking at the blow-ups on the walls. It was so exciting but Barry had a nice soft voice and was so friendly and gentle that I felt completely comfortable. At some point while he was talking to Barry and I was just wandering around, Justin noticed that my hands were in my mouth again and he shouted at me. 'How many times have I told you, Twiggs, don't bite your nails.' Then Barry said, 'What was that he called you?' I'd been introduced to him as Lesley Hornby.

'Twiggy,' repeated Barry. 'That's the name you should use.'

I was a terrible nail-biter and a thumb-sucker

and by the time I was eleven I had very protruding teeth as a result of sleeping with my thumb in my mouth. It was the beginning of orthodontics and our dentist in Neasden, Mr Pal (he was from India) said I should have a brace. In fact I had two. One on the bottom and one on the top. The one on the top was on a bridge and I could take it out. But without my thumb I couldn't get to sleep so for the first few weeks I took it out when I went to bed. I didn't think anyone would find out. But when I went back he knew, and I went bright red. He knew because although my bottom teeth were moving back, nothing was happening to the ones on the top. He made me so ashamed that I never did it again. And he straightened my teeth. Because of the PAL dog food adverts, we used to call him Prolongs Active Life. It should have been Prolongs Active Teeth. Who knows, if I hadn't met Mr Pal it may never have happened.

Only when we got back to Leonard's did he explain what he wanted to do with my hair. Cut it all off. I said no. It had taken so long to grow. I just couldn't bear it. But Justin made me see sense. Leonard was probably the most famous hairdresser in the world. He and Vidal Sassoon were always trying to beat each other in claiming the headlines. 'The chance to have Leonard cut your hair is a chance in a million.' So, fighting back the tears, I said yes. But first there was *Women's Mirror*.

The next day Justin and I went back to the *Women's Mirror* photographer for the head shots Susan Robbins had wanted. I suppose they used them. Somebody told me that they airbrushed my nose because the art director thought it was too bony. Anyway my hair was still long, shoulder length and rather brassy. Magazines, even weeklies, work several weeks ahead of publication and by the time it came out, those pictures were as dead as last week's newspapers. By then I had a new image. They could have discovered me, but they didn't. The day after that we went back to Leonard again and I was given the full works.

It took seven hours. First Leonard did a rough cut. Then came a scalp massage and conditioning treatments before I was sent upstairs to have highlights done by Daniel Galvin, Leonard's top colourist, who did my hair for years. And then his son Daniel junior took over. My hairdresser now is Michael Rasser of Michaeljohn, and although he didn't have anything to do with me that day, he was in the building.

Then it was back down to Leonard again for the finish. The final cut. Vidal Sassoon had been doing all these asymmetrical, geometrical cuts but what Leonard did with me was something radically different. No one else was doing hair like that. Leonard was so grand, with everyone bowing and scraping, he continued to terrify me. But it was so exciting. And when it was finished I loved it. From the moment I got up from the chair and the hair was brushed off my shoulders, and I was shown the back, with its wonderful little tail of longer hair, my life changed. Looking in the mirror at the back, as you do, I saw all these other faces looking at me, in a way no one had ever looked at me before.

The next morning it was back on the bus to Baker Street and Barry Lategan's studio and we did the head shots for the salon as planned. Years later Barry told me his side of the story. When he'd seen me that first day, he hadn't recognised any particular photographic possibilities, he said, but that as I seemed 'a very nice sort of person' and he knew I wanted to be a model, he thought, why not? and so he gave Leonard the go ahead. But when I turned up with the new cut he had the surprise of his life. 'I always find it difficult to explain what makes somebody photogenic. It's something certain people have. Through the lens of the camera you were a totally different-looking person. As much as you were just the same thin and gawky girl of two days before, there was this self-assurance, this natural elegance. And with the hair and the painted eyelashes which no one else was doing, I knew even while I was taking them that I had something special in the camera.'

The next thing that happened was a phone call from Leonard a few days later. The photographs were already up in the salon. As the best hairdresser in London, all the big names of the fashion media had their hair done by him. And Deirdre McSharry, editor of the *Daily Express* had been in having her hair done when she spotted me up on the wall.

'I don't know that girl,' she said. 'Who is she?'

When Leonard told her that I was just a schoolgirl, the girlfriend of a former colleague of his, she just said, get me her number. So Leonard called up Justin and said, there's this journalist who's very interested in meeting Twiggy. She wants to interview her.

The *Daily Express* was the biggest selling newspaper of the day. It was also the newspaper that I'd grown up with, with its daily strip cartoon of Rupert Bear. I was so excited. Though I had no idea what an interview was. Would it mean a job? So off we went again, this time to Fleet Street. The interview turned out to be a chat about me. About my family, what I wanted to do, those kinds of things. It was all very friendly and after we'd had a cup of tea I went downstairs and was photographed by the *Daily Express* photographer. I was wearing a skinny rib polo neck and a pair of bell-bottoms that I'd made. (If it didn't work out, I thought, the publicity for the trousers would be useful.)

Then we waited. Day after day I would read through the paper, page by page, column by column looking for a little mention. But nothing. It wasn't until about two weeks later, when I'd all but given up hope, that Mum and Dad came bursting into my bedroom, Dad waving a copy of the newspaper. It was 23 February 1966. He hadn't needed to look through it with a magnifying glass. The newspaper, a broadsheet in those days, fell open at the middle and there I was covering two full pages — what I now know is called a centre-page spread — including two huge photographs, Barry's head shot and the one the paper took of me in my bell-bottoms. Although I was as amazed as everyone else, I had no idea just how amazing it was. This was not the *Neasden Chronicle*. I didn't realise the impact of something like that in a national newspaper with the power of the *Express*. I remember kneeling on my bed with it spread out in front of me and in huge letters right across the page the banner headline: I NAME THIS GIRL THE FACE OF '66.

5

It didn't take long for us to realise that something extraordinary had happened. 93 St Raphael's Way, Neasden was soon under siege. Whenever he heard the crunch of footsteps on the gravel Dad would be out there shouting and waving a walking stick at the journalists and photographers creeping up the side. I got used to it amazingly quickly: life clicks in, the telephone is ringing. But Mum never did. She appeared to be coping, inviting journalists in for cups of tea, giving them all the 'proud cockney mum' quotes they wanted, but it was all an act. And I was too excited and busy to see. It must have been so traumatic. Shirley and Viv had both gone but she must have thought I would still be there for a long time to come. She didn't have a job to fill the vacuum. Her job had been raising us.

One thing was clear: no more making trousers. I was a model. The *Express* said so. But what next? Should I join an agency? It didn't seem likely they'd stick to their five-foot-eight minimum now. Strangely it was Dad who was against it. He still thought I was making a big mistake. 'But if I stop you, you might end up hating me.' He was just being realistic. He'd seen the other side from working in the film industry. Agents, he said, were only after your money. As for photographers, he trusted them even less than he trusted Justin. 'The only way

I'll allow you to do this,' he said, 'is if Justin goes with you everywhere.' So on the basis of better the devil you know, Justin became my manager. Someone had to do the bookings, negotiate the fees. Why not Justin who knew about these things? Or said he did. However mad it seems now, no one had any idea of just how much money would be involved. It hadn't happened before, except to pop stars. If you'd tried to orchestrate it you couldn't. It was the sixties.

As well as giving Justin and me the green light, Dad lent us £100 and his car, a turquoise Morris Minor, a classic now, with its lovely soft round curves. He also gave me a big leather portfolio bag. No wonder I adored him. He knew I wouldn't feel a proper model without one. As it turned out I didn't need it, being spared the usual traipsing around most models have to do.

I went from total obscurity to full-time working model in a matter of days. The first few jobs came through Barry Lategan. Talent is probably less important than luck when it comes to getting that first break and I soon discovered just how very important Barry had been. His lighting has always been wonderful. It doesn't matter how good you look like, with crappy lighting you won't get a good picture. Nowadays when I'm asked how to get into modelling, I say go to a good agency. If they think you've got something it's in their interests to make sure you get everything done properly. They won't mess you around. There are plenty of sharks around who will. And charge for the privilege. Young girls — and let's not forget we're talking about very young girls — must beware jack-the-lad photographers, managers and agents, who'll take your money as well as your picture.

In those early days I had no control over what was used. The magazine booked you, you got paid, and they picked the pictures. These were bread and butter jobs: *Honey*, *Petticoat*, even the older women's magazines. Not great lighting, not great photographers. But you had to do them to survive. *Vogue* barely covered expenses. It's prestige and always has been. Their line is that it's enough just to be in there. Advertisers will want you and pay through the nose for the privilege. In those days I seem to remember *Vogue*'s fee was £15. Photographers would often work for nothing.

One of my first modelling jobs was with Peggy Moffat, the extraordinary American who was Rudi Gernrich's model, the avant garde designer who did the first topless dress. She had this long face which she covered with a very pale base on which she used to paint whole patterns in yellows and greens. (I last saw her in about 1993 and she looked identical. The same haircut, eyes and white face.) But to that gawky kid in 1966 she was so kind. I couldn't have asked for a better teacher. My dress was very short, white and made of crochet, the new thing that spring. Until that shoot all I'd ever done was head shots where I just had to sit still (even that I find difficult. A natural born wriggler, me). I had no idea how models worked. All I'd ever seen was the finished picture in a magazine. There's always music in photographers' studios and as the booking had been arranged by Barry the music was jazz. Watching Peggy as she moved her head and arms, making shapes with her body, was completely captivating. She was so wonderfully sultry and sexy. And all for a knitting pattern. I soon picked it up.

It wasn't long before I got my first job abroad. Although Justin came everywhere with me in London, as my Dad had insisted (very unusual in itself and not liked by the photographers), Sicily was out of the question as the magazine weren't prepared to pay for his ticket. We didn't have the money. I had no idea of 'abroad', the furthest away I'd been was the Isle of Wight. We landed at night then piled into a mini van and set off for the hotel along the coast road. There were three models, the photographer, and the fashion editor called Mrs Munroe. She was very mumsy, Scottish and knitted a lot — rather appropriate as this was *Woman's Own*.

It was pitch black. Suddenly I look out of the window and see what looks like a fireball in the sky, so I start to panic. 'What's that huge ball of fire?' I shriek in best Neasden. The driver laughs.

'Etna, Etna.'

This means nothing to me. He tries again.

'Volcano, volcano.'

The penny drops and I start screaming.

'My God, my God, I want to go home.' It seems Etna belches out flames like that all the time, it's just that during the day you can't see it. But I thought it was erupting and this was The End. How I got to sleep that night I'll never know. I was convinced that by the morning the whole place would be nothing but a lava flow.

Soon I was working five days a week, often a twelve-hour day and I was young enough to cope. Not that anything was left to chance. Except at weekends I was in bed by half past ten. And anyway, I was exhausted. After Viv had got married the previous October I had moved into her old bedroom which was much bigger than my little boxroom over the front door. Dad had built her an enormous wardrobe which took up almost a third of it. It came from working in the film business — everything he made was always bigger than we needed. At the time we'd all laughed, but now it couldn't have been better. He said I could have my room like I wanted. So I had purple walls and heavy-duty lilac and purple striped curtains, like deckchair material.

My day started at seven thirty with breakfast of cornflakes, toast, marmalade and tea. I was used to an early start — I'd had to leave the house by seven thirty to get to school. My hair was short so I just washed it the night before. Make-up artists were rare in those days. So models did their own. I didn't wear any base so I had only my eyes to worry about. First I covered the lids with white. Then I drew a black line around the eye socket. This had to be perfect and if it wasn't right, off it came and start again. Then shadow on top of the line, then eye liner, then the Twiggy lines underneath and then the eye lashes. Three pairs. It took about an hour and a half. Justin would arrive to pick me up around nine and we'd leave by nine thirty, depending on where we were going.

We'd aim to be at the studio about ten although there would always be some faffing around before the shoot really got going. As well as the photographer, there would be an assistant and sometimes someone else doing the lighting. Then there would be people from the magazine: fashion editor, stylist or if it was an ad, someone from the agency. For a high-profile fashion shoot, like *Vogue*, there would be hair and make-up people around too. Unless you're on location fashion photographers shoot against a plain background, usually white — sometimes blue, grey or black — which is in fact a giant roll of paper supported on a huge frame, the reason photographers studios have such high ceilings. This paper acts as both wall and floor. They can light it evenly and as soon as the 'floor' gets marked or scuffed the paper just gets rolled down.

Some photographers would take Polaroids first, to check on the lighting. But not all. They each had their own way of working. Some would shoot a couple of rolls of film on each shot, others would go on and on. And I'm talking up to fifteen rolls which even then I thought was stupid. After all each film has thirty-six frames so if you haven't got the picture in the first two or three rolls, I thought, you're not going to get it now. The cameras they used depended on the shot. Mostly it was just standard 35mm SLR, but for beauty or head shots they'd go for large format like Hasselblad, though I must admit I've never had any interest in the other side of the camera. I take snaps.

It went on like this all day, with cups of tea to break the pace. If there were two of you it was less frenetic, but I usually worked alone. Lunch would just be a sandwich — going out was difficult because of hair and make-up — then it would start again and didn't stop till five or six, sometimes even eight. People don't realise how hard models work. It may not sound much but concentrating, always being 'on', prancing about as airy and twinkly at seven o'clock as you were at midday is exhausting, and close-up beauty shots where you have to sit still literally for hours puts real strain on your whole body. Not that I didn't adore it. It was like being in love. In front of a camera I seemed to get an extra burst of energy, like the feel of the sun on your face in spring.

Right from the start Justin and I had agreed to go fifty-fifty — like we'd done on the hipsters. Not that we ever put anything in writing. He was my boyfriend so of course I wanted him to share everything. I don't think Dad was happy about it even then. The company we set up was called Twiggy Enterprises. I was legally a minor so Dad and Justin were the directors, though I wonder now much Dad really knew about what was going on. I knew nothing. My job was just to stand in front of the camera and watch the birdie.

Looking back I realise I was incredibly pig-headed. Although I suppose Dad could have stood his ground, should have stood his ground, he gave in. It was just like with Mum. Because he loved her he thought that letting her have her own way was how to show it. A big mistake. But now I feel really ashamed. Like an old record I can hear myself goading him, 'You're old fashioned. You don't know.' What did I know? I was a teenager for goodness sake. I never even had my own cheque book. Justin would control everything. There were no credit cards then. If I needed money, I'd ask for £50 and he'd give it to me. Always cash. I'd put it in my handbag and I'd go shopping and I was as happy as a clam.

To this day I have no idea how much money I earned during this period. Justin seemed to have no idea what to do with the money, except spend it. Investing? What's that? He bought expensive cars and Cartier watches and Tommy Nutter suits. Sure I'd go out and spend money, but I'd go to Biba because that was the look that I loved. I didn't buy designer clothes. My father must have been churning inside. But he wasn't a business man, just very straight and not very trusting of Justin. 'Him and his bloody fancy cars and his bloody fancy clothes, where's the money going, that's what I want to know.' And he was right. But I didn't want to hear it.

Justin fell into the life of grandeur very easily. By the summer of 1966 the money had started coming in. At first it wasn't that much, a couple of hundred pounds a week. But by the autumn it was more like a couple of hundred a day. By the time we reached America it was more than that an hour. Model agencies had rates and basically they stuck to them (and all models except me were with agencies). Though even I never reached the level of today's 'supermodels' when a top model can get up to $12,000 a day doing the catwalk shows. There is just no comparison. Anyway, I never did cat walk.

Justin appeared to me at that time to be a clever negotiator. There were plenty of other models, he would say, but only one Twiggy. He'd just tell them how much and hold out till he got it. Then he'd spend it. Cars and clothes were his particular passion. He thought nothing of ordering ten or twelve suits at a time from Tommy Nutter, who was the first of the new-wave tailors to invade Savile Row. It was the same with the cars. During our seven years together he got through four Rolls Royces, one Bentley, one Ferrari Daytona, one Maserati Ghibili, two Lamborghini Muiras, one Porsche Carrera, one Iso Lhala, one Ford Mustang, one Trans-Am Firebird, two Aston Martins and one E-type Jaguar. His appetite was insatiable. Cars were an obsession. At one point he seemed to get a new one every two or three months, trading in whatever he had just bought when he saw something else glinting in the corner of the showroom, which was often run by one of his old mates. The E-type only lasted a week. With a top speed of 110 m.p.h. he didn't consider it fast enough.

Soon after the madness started, Justin moved into a flat on the corner of Ladbroke Gardens. First he shared it with a designer and a student vet. Then when they moved out, he gradually took the whole thing over. He never admitted it was a £9-a-week rent-controlled flat. He always said he'd bought it. All part of the image. He was utterly undomesticated so as soon as we had the money, he employed Glyn, round, camp and Welsh, as a manservant. Glyn stayed for two years. Others followed, though I never got on as well with them. But Glyn I absolutely adored. He had short squat legs and used to wear a pinny and go around with a feather duster. His favourite expression, said in his strong Welsh accent, was 'There's ee-vv-il'. We met him through a Portuguese restaurant we sometimes went to. (Restaurants were another, if lesser, money pit.) Glyn lived in and his job, apart from making us laugh, was to cook, clean up and generally mollycoddle Justin and, of course, take the dog out. We had a Tibetan Lhasa Apso called Doogle who looked just like a mop. The flat was on the top floor so Justin would put Doogle into a basket and lower him down into the garden to poo. It was hopeless. You can't treat an animal like that. I was always discovering the little presents poor Doogle had left around the flat. Then there were the cats, Daisy, Poppy and Buttercup. Justin bought animals for all the wrong reasons, because they looked pretty, or he thought they would go well with the cushions. Image was always very important to Justin. When we had a Rolls Royce, he got a chauffeur to go with it. At the time I thought nothing of it. Pop stars had Rolls Royces. David Bailey had a yellow Rolls Royce.

Why not us? The best times were not when I was with Justin, who just treated the Rolls as normal life, but when I went shopping with my sisters and we could all have a laugh. Shirley still remembers the day we went shopping in Harrods and left the Rolls with the chauffeur outside the main entrance. She was terrified we'd get a ticket. 'They don't put parking tickets on Rolls Royces,' I told her. It was several hours before we came back, yet there it still was, and like madam had predicted, no parking ticket, just a tenner to the doorman. Nothing to do with me, I might add. The chauffeur dealt with that.

What kept my name and picture in the papers and set me apart from other models was not so much that art directors or photographers wanted me, but that the media were constantly trying to explain my success. I was the first of the celebrity models. Jean Shrimpton had begun to turn the corner in Britain, and in the States it was happening with Penelope Tree and Lauren Hutton. However what these journalists actually wrote about the 'phenomenon' called Twiggy rang no bells with me. It was just a joke. According to one I had 'the calm appraisal of a child or a Martian . . . rare, strange creature, tranquil, composed, almost bloodless'. Or what about 'one half orphan of the storm the other purely aesthetic'. Whenever I saw this kind of stuff I just laughed like a hyena and carried on as before.

My laugh has always been notorious. At one point Terry Wogan taped it and used it for light relief in the breakfast show he did for

BBC Radio in the seventies. Leigh says the first time he ever heard my voice was that loop of my laugh on Terry Wogan. You'd think it would have put him off for life. Thank goodness it didn't. No one believes it's natural. But you've only got to spend two minutes with my sister Viv to see it is. Get the two of us together in a cinema or the theatre and it's hysterical. Everyone turning around and staring. Actor or comedian friends are always glad to have me at the first night of a comedy or a show because laughter is so infectious.

I went along with whatever Justin wanted, including my first record, the truly awful 'I Need Your Hand in Mine'. Not that they seemed to mind in Japan. When I went there at the end of 1968 it was Number One. I was never allowed to make a decision on my own. I never did an interview without him being there. He seemed so knowledgeable (and compared to me at that stage, I suppose he was) that it never occurred to me to question what he was doing and we were getting hit left right and centre. He managed to convince me that I couldn't do anything without him.

Just after my seventeenth birthday I was invited to the Woman of the Year lunch at the Savoy. When I found out it was women only and that he couldn't come with me I threw a wobbly. What about disguising himself as a waiter? Even Justin drew the line at that. I took to my bed. Even then the press didn't leave me alone; there's a picture of me lying there with a pair of rubber gloves on, to hide the rash brought on by the stress. But thinking about it now, what exactly was going on? If I really was so freaked out, having a tabloid photographer clambering around my bed wasn't exactly therapeutic. And the trademark Twiggy lashes were securely in place. No one could have got me to do it except Justin.

Justin was a great believer in not letting on to the media exactly what our relationship was. Part of the 'mystique', he said. They called him my 'manager, promoter and constant companion' and, of course, Svengali.

The Twiggy roller coaster was fast turning into a gravy train. And everyone wanted on. In September 1966 Justin and I flew to Tunisia, courtesy of Berkertex, a well-known dress manufacturer who were wooing us to launch my own label. Tunisia was the most exotic place I had ever been to, but no amount of sand and camels would have made me sign up when it turned out all they really wanted was my name on clothes already in the pipeline. Instead we chose a company who would let me have a real input.

Taramina Textiles made old-lady frocks and wedding dresses. The company was run by two brothers-in-law, Leonard Bloomburg and Sydney Hills. Leonard I really liked. Sydney terrified me. Not surprisingly the range was called Twiggy Dresses. The teenage market was something quite new to them which was great for us, as it meant no pre-conceived ideas or old stock to get rid of. Right from the start it was agreed everything would be things that I would be happy to wear. I was even involved in choosing the designers, Pamela Procter and Paul Babb who came straight from the Royal College of Art. Pam and Paul weren't that much older than me and I would go in two or three times a week to talk over ideas and designs. There was I, earning all this money, yet I remember so clearly sitting there with them in Great Portland Street and envying them what they were doing, what I had always dreamt of.

The press launch was at the beginning of November and Barry Lategan did the pictures. I loved that first collection and I think it still holds its own by the standards of the time. Most of it was on a direct line through Courreges via Mary Quant, but among the acid-drop colours and daisies was a discernible hint of retro, like the pin-stripe gangster suit I loved wearing and was often photographed in. It was there in some of the dresses too. In the *Daily Express* Deirdre McSharry described me as 'too young to have heard of Gertrude Lawrence but looking remarkably like her in a felt cloche.' That was the first time I had heard of Gertie Lawrence who would later become such a hero. Having discovered me less than a year before, it shows yet again how perceptive and ahead of the field Deirdre McSharry was and it's no wonder she became the first editor of *Cosmopolitan*. Despite representing the sixties, I have always felt I should have been around in the twenties. From the look, to the music, to the social atmosphere I'd have swopped the swinging sixties for the roaring twenties any day.

Amazingly that launch is the only time I have ever done catwalk modelling. In those days you didn't do both and the top girls were photographic models only. Given the fact that nothing ever fitted me (what you don't see in photographs is the bulldog clips and safety pins at the back) it's a good thing. But the Twiggy Dresses were made with me in mind.

Quite coincidentally I had been approached by Adele Rootstein, who was the first person to make shop window mannequins based on real life models. They were made of fibreglass and the sculptor had to add an extra couple of inches onto my bust. As the New York DJ said, 'Twiggy? She's got a pretty face, but from the neck down, forget it.' Soon they were in all the shops. It didn't bother me — by then I was living this strange hermetically sealed existence and rarely walked anywhere, and don't remember seeing them except in some publicity capacity. But Shirley said she felt very unnerved; going shopping and seeing your sister staring down at you gave her the creeps, she said. A little later came the wax Twiggy in Madame Tussauds. I hear it is still on display now.

Then in early December it looked like the balloon was about to burst. I'd never had bad publicity before but this certainly made up for it. 'TWIGGY BANNED BY FOUR LEADING PHOTOGRAPHERS' ran the headline in the *Daily Mail*. The Big Four were David Bailey, Terence Donovan, Terence Duffy and David Montgomery, and in those days they shared an agent, one David Puttnam, now Sir David

Puttnam, who went on to become one of Britain's most famous film producers and is (and has been for many years, I am happy to point out) a very dear friend.

According to David Bailey they were refusing to use me 'because Twiggy is too amateur in her approach'. Worse still, I was 'grossly unprofessional. I had her booked for an evening recently and her manager appeared and said that they were going out to dinner instead.'

'The trouble is that Justin de Villeneuve insists on being in the studio. Models will start bringing mothers next.' That was the Puttnam contribution. (How prophetic. Apparently that's just what Naomi Campbell did years later.) Next comes Justin saying he couldn't care less. 'These people aren't the top photographers. They don't like me. It's nothing to do with Twiggy . . . I admit we are amateurs and we don't conform. That's why we have enemies.'

He was right about it being nothing to do with me. I never experienced anything other than kindness and help from everyone I worked with, both models and photographers — and I don't think they were just being polite. I'd even worked with Terence Donovan, who tragically died recently and got on really well with him. The problem was Justin wasn't a photographer; he wasn't one of the gang. All the other major photographic models of the day had been 'discovered' by photographers. Just take David Bailey: Jean Shrimpton, Penelope Tree, Marie Helvin. The other top models of the time, *Vogue* and *Queen* models like Sue Murray, Jill

Kennington, Moira Swann, Grace Coddington and Celia Hammond (always so serene it was as if she was in some other place) — had all made their names through photographers. Whereas I'd come from out of left field from nowhere.

When I first started out, we had a composite made up, a selection of prints on one sheet of ten-by-eight photographic paper which we then sent round like a calling card. Possibly we didn't follow the standard etiquette. For whatever reason, it didn't go down well. Terence Duffy was horrible. Instead of just ignoring it he telephoned and said he didn't need to be told who to work with thank you and hung up. There had been something similar with David Montgomery who said I'd be a great deal better off if I just got rid of Justin. The trouble was, Justin might have been able to charm the pants off female fashion editors, but these were East End boys like him.

Obviously there must have been some kind of mix up over a booking with Bailey to have sparked the whole row off. But it can only have been a genuine mistake. Being punctual and professional meant everything to me and Justin. I'm convinced the piece in the *Mail* was just an excuse to stir things up. These photographers were their own little Mafia. They didn't like Justin and saw no reason to let him steal their thunder, or more to the point the cream off their coffee. It was the first time I'd seen the other side of the press, the side that wants to have a go. To be called unprofessional and amateur was so hurtful. And it did lasting harm. For a long time I would have nothing to do with any of those photographers, either for work or socially. Once, when we found we were at a dinner party with Terence Duffy, we just walked out.

For years David Bailey and I snubbed each other. Fortunately we're both grown-ups and have since worked very happily together, including a big campaign for American Express. It was shot in the eighties, when I was a bit more curvy than I'd been first time around and under a skimpy tank top I had a bit of a cleavage showing. But by the time the ad was used, my bosoms I was so proud of had been airbrushed out. What they wanted was the iconic flat chest. Modelling can be very tedious and the great thing about David is that he's so much fun to work with, he has you in fits of laughter. Thirty years on we can all laugh about that awful row and none of us remembers quite what sparked it off. But at the time it was devastating, because it's always so much easier to believe the bad stuff. And after all, Bailey, Donovan, Duffy and Montgomery were up there with the greats. I consoled myself by saying that they weren't the only ones. And they weren't. Other greats were just round the corner.

6

In the sixties Paris was still very much the shrine of fashion. And that first summer, while my friends were sitting in an airless hall in Kilburn sweating over their O-levels, I had a front row seat at the *salons* where the high priests of *haute couture* offered up their next season's collections. The razzmatazz was not limited to the catwalk; neither were the clothes. Everyone was dressed as if they were going to a gala. But then everyone was someone.

By then I had already been to Paris several times working for *Elle*. I'd met Guy Bourdin, a French photographer who was then very big in the fashion world, on my first ever *Vogue* shoot and it was Guy who suggested me to Helene Gordon-Lazareff, *Elle's* highly influential editor. In those days there wasn't an English *Elle* but you could buy the French one. And I did. It made no difference that I could barely understand it; it was the clothes that mattered. There was nothing like *Elle* in English. The choice lay between *Vogue* and *Honey. Nova* had only just begun.

Apart from anything else Guy had wanted to make things up to me. It had been my first booking for *Vogue* and I was so excited. Then, as now, to work for *Vogue* was every model's dream. In those days they had their own studios in the Hanover Square offices. I'll never forget that first visit to the holy of holies. From the receptionist onwards everything about it was intimidating. 'We work for *Vogue*. You don't,' were the unspoken words. As usual I'd done my makeup but I was a bit surprised that no one looked at it.

We go to a room off the studio scattered with shoes and the stylist tells me to 'pick some out'. The scowl she had obviously been born with lightens a tad as I try some on. 'It's so hard to find a model with small feet,' she says. Then into the studio. All I'm wearing is the shirt I arrived in, and the shoes. At the far end of the studio are two builder's ladders, with a plank between them. 'Climb up, please' Guy Bourdin tells me, after the introductions. I'm too scared to say anything, so just do what I'm told. But I'm completely mystified. Then into the studio comes this very elegant man. He and Guy walk towards me until they're directly underneath and I have to move my legs to stop my feet kicking this other man's head. And then I suddenly realise this is the photograph. I later found out that it was a feature on famous men. And in order to get a fashion angle some bright spark had come up with dangling feet wearing shoes they could credit. The only reason I'd been booked was that the shoes had been flown over from France and were too small for most English models.

Sitting up on that plank, swinging my legs as Guy told me to, I felt so humiliated. There was I thinking I'd made it. But I realised now that it wasn't me they wanted. It was my little feet. By this time the plank was cutting into the top of my legs and what with the pain and the humiliation I started to cry.

Guy hadn't noticed because he was looking through the camera at the famous man, who turned out to be Vidal Sassoon. But Vidal did hear me, or rather sobbing noises coming from above his head and he got Guy to stop and climbed up one of the ladders and handed me a handkerchief from the top pocket of his very smart suit. He had no more idea who I was than I knew who he was. I suppose I must have told them why I was upset. Guy immediately had a go at the fashion editor and refused to carry on. 'We've got the shot,' he said. 'Now go and tidy your eyes up. You've got a beautiful face, let me take some pictures.' He took a couple of rolls of black and white, and they were what got me the *Elle* bookings.

This time I was in Paris for the *Daily Sketch*. Readers back in Britain would be offered my views on the collections in the form of a letter to Mum. Now it makes me cringe; but I was only sixteen and didn't know any better. I lasted two days. It was the Balmain show that caused the stink. Monsieur Balmain himself was lovely to me, but his clothes were hardly innovative and Shirley Flack, the journalist whose idea the whole thing was, saw no reason to tone down what I thought. 'Twiggy's letter to Mum' appeared the next day. Balmain's clothes were fine for someone middle-aged like her, I wrote, but were old fashioned. *Quel Scandale*. I was immediately banned by the Chambre Syndicale that runs the *salons* from all further shows. To make matters worse Eugenia Sheppard, the doyenne of the foreign fashion press who wrote for the Paris-based *New York Herald Tribune*, chose to feature me rather than the collections. I remembered having spoken to this tiny little silver-haired old lady who everyone treated as though she were royalty but I had no idea what it would lead to. It did nothing to improve my standing with the Paris fashion houses but when her piece was syndicated by one of the wire services, it flashed across the world and I became international news.

The result was a call from American *Vogue*. Could I do next season's Paris collections? American *Vogue*, then edited by the legendary Diana Vreeland was, is and probably always will be the ultimate in fashion magazines. Taking the pictures would be the equally legendary Irving Penn, one of this century's all-time greats, although I have never thought fashion was what he did best. Perhaps I'm biased. The Legend took one look at the skinny scrap he'd been sent and said No. And to please come back in ten years' time. As it turned out it was more like twenty, when Tommy Tune and I were the toast of New York and *Harper's Bazaar* — *Vogue's* only real competitor in the States — had booked us, with Penn as photographer. Before we began I reminded him we'd met before, but it didn't appear to register. The intervening years had not improved him. Tommy's and my quest that afternoon became to make him laugh. The rest of the studio had a great time. But not the maestro. He kept asking me to close my eyes which, as Tommy pointed out, was a bit odd. ('Mr Penn, do you realise Twiggy's eyes are probably the most famous eyes in the world?') But this time I wasn't there as a model, I was there as a song 'n' dance, Broadway star, so I didn't give a hair what he thought. How the pictures turned out, I don't know. They were never used.

American *Vogue* had not been impressed by Penn's assessment of my potential. They knew what they wanted and they wanted me. The job was still on; Bert Stern would do it instead. Another coup. Justin was beside himself. His other passion, beside cars and clothes, was jazz and Bert Stern's documentary film *Jazz On A Summer's Day* was second only, he said, to the real thing. Another legend. By the time we met I was feeling distinctly nervous. I needn't have worried. From the moment we shook hands I knew it was going to be all right. Whereas Irving Penn had been old and gaunt, Bert Stern was sweet and chubby. And he laughed.

In those days cameras weren't allowed inside the *salons* for the shows, just artists with sketch pads who sat beside the catwalk quietly catching the essence of the clothes with just a few quick strokes of a pencil. Only garments that had been bought by American stores could be photographed and then only at night. During the day they were needed back to be modelled for individual customers and buyers. The ones who planned to buy rather than just look.

Haute couture is fashion at its purest. It has

nothing to do with getting ten rather than eight garments out of a roll of cloth, it's about sculpture, beautiful fabrics and stitching so fine you don't know it's there. In those days there was a much larger genuine market. Now the number of people who can afford to spend $8,000 plus on one dress is tiny. And with the growth of *diffusion* and ready to wear, there's no need. It's largely an exercise in publicity for what really generates the money: the perfume, sunglasses and, of course, the ready to wear.

It was exciting but weird sleeping most of the day and working all night. We would get there about nine or ten in the evening and work through till five or six in the morning when the clothes would be packed off home like fashion Cinderellas. Couture houses only make one of each design, fitted to the model who'll wear it. The problem was, as usual, my size. Catwalk models are very tall, simply because clothes look much better on elongated, slim, long-legged bodies. There are some that break the rule though not the mould. Kate Moss is a current example. She's exactly the same height as me, five foot six and a half. That year Pierre Cardin had a tiny model; Japanese, I think, and Ungaro did too. Otherwise it was back to bulldog clips.

Because big models have equally big feet even the shoes were enormous and I had to curl my toes up to keep them on, just like I'd done when I was little when Geraldine and I would dress up as princesses and ballet dancers in Mum's old dance frocks. The best part was wearing her high heels and we would spend hours clumping around. As this didn't do them much good, one Christmas I was given a pair of play high heels, plastic with little bows in the front and heels with twinkles in them. I adored them.

Being small always created problems. I remember a big fashion shoot a year later in New York where the stylist, a lovely woman called Polly Mellon, wanted me to wear a pair of gold lurex tights. But when I picked them up from the table where the accessories are kept we were just hysterical. They reached from the floor to the top of my head. It turned out they'd previously been worn by Veruschka, one of the great models of the day, who was a good six feet tall.

Back to Paris. Bert Stern's pictures were brilliant. What nobody knew was that half-way through the shoot I had fallen over in the garden of a public relations girl who had thrown me a party. While everyone else was schmoozing, I was playing out in the back with her puppy, fell over and twisted my ankle which meant a trip to the hospital and bandages. Somehow Bert contrived not to let it show, keeping the bad ankle either out of shot or hidden behind some carefully positioned object. The result was a triumph of lateral thinking. To go with the pictures was a huge up-beat profile by Polly Devlin who had interviewed Justin and me in Paris. There was nothing Svengali-like in our relationship, she said. But then she was an intelligent journalist writing in *Vogue*. Most importantly Diana Vreeland was delighted with the results. My next assignment for the magazine, she said, would be with Richard Avedon. The date on the magazine is 15 March 1967. It was exactly a year and a month since I had started out.

The horrible business with the four photographers in London in December had given us the push we needed to think seriously about going to New York. The call from Vreeland was the match that lit the blue touch paper. Working with Avedon didn't only promise to be the pinnacle of any model's career in an artistic sense, he was my passport to American advertising, which was where the money was. And then there were the Twiggy Dresses. The States was such a huge market, but difficult to break into. With me there to promote them, they had a much better chance. A lot to think about, a lot to set up and it all took time.

Bad publicity seems to be contagious and the next thing to hit was the *Sunday People* and an interview with Justin's wife Pam, saying that I was responsible for the break-up of their marriage. That was all rubbish but the worst thing was Mum and Dad. I had never plucked up courage to tell them Justin had been married. They didn't turn a hair.

In those days you needed a visa for America, and a full passport, which I didn't have. Like everyone else who needs one in a rush, this meant a visit to Petty France, London's Passport Office, a bleak subterranean hall the size of two tennis courts filled with literally hundreds of people queuing.

It's barely changed in the last thirty years. Around the sides are the counters where you hand in your form. Justin makes straight for the one grill that doesn't have a queue and in his poshest voice tells the man who I am, that I need a passport and that I'm in a hurry. The man explains that his grill is only for people who need a passport for work. Justin's eyes light up. Great. That's exactly what I need it for. We can't believe our luck: all these hundreds of others having to queue. We fill in the form and hand it back. He peers at it as closely as if it was a forged bank note. 'Date of birth, nineteenth September 1949. Is that right?' Yes, I say. 'Which makes you seventeen.' That's right, I say. His eyes glint behind his glasses and he opens a small book and starts writing in it. 'In that case,' he says, 'I'm afraid I am unable to give you a passport. You are a minor.'

I remember just standing there, thinking I'm not hearing this. Justin exploded. But we had a contract. With American *Vogue*. Glasses told us he didn't care who our contract was with. Justin gripped the bars. 'You don't seem to understand.' The man explained that he understood very well but it was the law and it was for my own safety. Something about the white slave trade. And it seems there actually is something called the Slave Act, dating from the mid-nineteenth century to protect young girls from all sorts of unmentionables. It would have been funny if it hadn't been so desperate. For once I couldn't see the joke.

So many things were riding on this trip. There

were the Twiggy Dresses. All nine of Taramina's factories were at that moment churning them out, ready for the American bonanza. We had enquiries from 150 outlets, but only if I was part of the package. Bert Stern had got ABC Television to back him to make a documentary on my visit to the States; which was even more extraordinary then than now. These days documentaries on celebrities are common. But then you very rarely got a prime time television documentary unless you were the Queen, the Beatles, or the Pope. Last but by no means least we'd landed a huge advertising campaign for Monsanto, a man-made fabric manufacturer, a ten-day shoot with a hot young photographer called Melvin Sokolsky. In these days of wool, cotton, linen and silk it's hard to believe that anyone could get worked up over man-made fabrics but in the sixties they were seen as the way forward. It started off with stockings (the NY in nylon stands for New York). In Britain there was Bri-nylon, Terylene, Courtelle and Crimplene. That March '67 issue of American *Vogue* has advertisements for Banlon, Arnel, Dacron, Alamac, Fortrel, Caprolan, Crelon, Crepeset, Cantrece and Antron. Plus Dynel for wigs and Shugor and Corfam for shoes. It was a huge market and millions of pounds and dollars were spent on promoting the different brands.

New York wasn't just a dream. It was an economic necessity Justin's remedy for everything was publicity so we called Shirley Flack of the *Daily Sketch*. As usual her idea had a twist. Another letter. Not to Mum this time, but to Prince Philip, who had recently been spearheading an export campaign. Why not write to him and explain the problem? So I did. He wrote back a very nice letter saying that he sympathised but there was nothing he could do although he had passed on my letter to Lord Watkinson, chairman of the export committee to the USA. In the meantime he suggested 'you might like to consider taking it up with a newspaper such as the *Daily Mirror*'. Which was all very funny as the *Mirror* was the *Sketch's* arch rival. Needless to say both letters were published and the result was a call from the head of the Passport Office. The law was still the law and I had to go to Bow Street Magistrate's Court with my parents and swear that I was going to America on my own volition and that Justin wasn't a white slave trader. I was handed a pink piece of paper, and that was that.

Most people's first view of Manhattan is across Queensborough or Brooklyn Bridge, but we flew straight in by helicopter from Kennedy Airport and landed on the roof of the Pan Am building. It took less than ten minutes. The madness had started the moment I arrived. I thought I'd got used to idiot questions from journalists in England. I hadn't even begun to appreciate what lay in store. 'What do you think of New York Twiggy?' they asked in all seriousness. I'd only just walked down the steps of the plane.

New York has the most exciting skyline in the world. In 1967 the World Trade Centre had not yet been built and the Empire State was still the highest building in the city; in the world. New York is now like a second home to me, but the excitement I felt that first time always returns when I see that skyline. From the street the differences in the buildings are less noticeable but from above it's a different story, like my personal favourite, the art deco Chrysler building topped with its stacks of silver helmets. It was several years before they stopped anyone landing in a helicopter on the Pan Am building, when the vibrations threatened to damage it.

Just like Americans' vision of London is Big Ben, black taxis and fog. Manhatten really is all the images you have ever seen about New York and then some. The sheer height of the buildings turns every avenue into a canyon, one side brilliant sunshine, the other deep shade. Billows of steam leak out of subway vents lit by these shafts of light, splintering down from the sky. Horns honk incessantly and the sidewalks are packed with people pushing and jostling their way through the city as if their lives depended on it. Yellow cabs and cops at every corner. And always the noise. Everyone talks twice as loud as in England. There's no sense of subservience. They all have a right to be there. As long as they're fast and keep moving. The excitement and energy are palpable, raw. New York is the gateway to America and it never lets you forget it.

Bert Stern had lent us his apartment on the Upper East Side. It was huge, but empty, two knocked into one. At that time he was married to a ballet dancer, with two children, but they lived in another of his many properties, a brownstone somewhere on the East Side. At first I thought it odd not staying in a hotel, but thank God we didn't. There at least we could have some kind of normality, some kind of privacy. As for the huge blow-up picture of me that dominated the bedroom, I suppose he imagined it would make me feel at home?

In terms of the NBC documentary, designed to be a day-to-day account of my trip to New York, nothing was invented. Bert planned to film only the genuine schedule, though as my major assignment was the Monsanto job, it was never going to be straightforward. Melvin Sokolsky was a young and hot photographer, and at the cutting edge of the fashion world.

It was the Beatle-like frenzy from the moment we landed at Kennedy airport that gave him the idea. A constant problem for fashion shoots is onlookers, particularly in very public places, which all too often means shooting at ridiculous times of the day or in the middle of winter. Making a virtue out of necessity Mel printed up two sets of twelve different black and white headshots of my face, lifesize, then cut them into masks with holes at the sides for the elastic for onlookers to wear if they wanted to stay in shot. As a new angle for an otherwise prosaic fashion shoot (Twiggy at the Empire State, Twiggy at the Statue of Liberty, Twiggy on the Staten Island ferry, etc.) it was completely off the wall — the whole concept later got Melvin and his art director awards from the advertising industry for innovation — and for Bert Stern and the documentary it was a gift, giving the whole thing a surreal edge which completely mirrored what was happening to me in real life.

One afternoon I was out shopping in Bloomingdales, more hip than Harrods and twice the size of Harvey Nichols but with all its chic and class. People had begun to follow me. It was very unnerving so we decided to leave. They followed us. When we reached the street we broke into a run, people shouting, 'I want your autograph'. But there were too many. In desperation looking for refuge we ran into a small, rather smart boutique on the sidewalk and asked the rather imperious looking assistant if we could stay there for a bit. Eventually she agreed. But she was not sympathetic. 'What do you expect. You should go out there, You're public property.'

Melvin's stylist was a girl called Ali McGraw. Two years later she leapt to stardom in *Goodbye Columbus*, and followed it with *Love Story*. She married Robert Evans, then head of Paramount but after making *The Getaway* with Steve McQueen she caused a great scandal by running off with him.

One afternoon a few days into the trip, we're all back at Melvin's studio on First Avenue, around 30th Street, when the door bell rings. Ali goes to answer it. Two twelve-year old boys stand there asking to see me. She's just shooing them away when the cinematographer on the documentary intervenes. It's okay, he says. Bring them in. It turns out that they've come from the Bronx or Brooklyn, and played hooky from school, just to meet me. So in they come, and apparently I was very nice and gave them two signed photographs. Apparently? Don't I remember? Well, no. But one of those small boys was called Steven Meisel and as he left Sokolsky's studio on the Lower East Side that afternoon, he told his friend that one day he was going to be a famous photographer and one day he would photograph me.

It took twenty-five years but he did it. In 1993 I was asked by Italian *Vogue* if I would break my self-imposed purdah of the last twenty-five years and do a fashion shoot with the hottest young photographer in New York, Steven Meisel, who had recently shot the famous the shrink-wrapped *Sex* book with Madonna. The pictures Steven and I did together for Italian *Vogue* graced the cover and eight pages inside and later we used them on my 1996 album sleeve, *London Pride*.

Over the years I was always being asked to go back to modelling, but after *The Boyfriend* I realised that if I was to be taken seriously as an actress, I couldn't do both. I still think it was the right decision. But times change and both Lauren Hutton and Isabella Rossalini have shown that it could be done. As a showcase Italian *Vogue* is hard to beat, always so classy. And, of course, I knew of Meisel: he was the Avedon of the nineties; so, why not? The shoot was to be in New York.

After the usual, 'Lovely to meet you' exchanges, he added, 'actually we've met before.' The usual surge of embarrassment flooded up. I meet so many people and I'm terrible with names. I must have met him a few years back, I thought, never imagining we were talking about a quarter of a century. And then he told me the whole story: how he'd forced his friend to come with him; how they found out where we were by ringing around and pretending they were journalists, which was pretty amazing in itself. He was only twelve. He even has a photograph of us together, which somebody took with the little camera he'd brought along. Fascinating how exceptional people are often so quirky.

In New York in 1967 it was soon apparent that we needed extra security. We'd brought along an old friend of Justin's called Teddy the Monk, as a bodyguard, but for all his East End 'bottle and lip' no one had anticipated the madness and it wasn't enough. Enter four bodybuilders. It turned out that Melvin's hobby was working out. So finding bodyguards he could trust wasn't a problem. They included Harold Poole, a former Mr Universe. His biceps measured the same as my waist. It was Harold who saved me from being trampled to death on Fifth Avenue. His size disguised a heart of gold. One evening he asked us to dinner at his apartment in New Jersey. The whole place had been decorated with tinsel (it was otherwise pretty run down) and he and his muscle-bound friends all wore little white pinnies while they were cooking. It was so endearing and sweet.

The trip to B. Altman's hadn't been advertised. But Twiggy in Manhattan was station to station TV and radio news. Radio shows were interrupted with bulletins about Where Twiggy Was Now. The famous hit songwriting team Lieber and Stoller were even then busy writing a song to commemorate my visit: 'I'll Remember You Twiggy'. No wonder I find it hard to believe that the person they were directing all this stuff at was me. All sorts of rumours were going the rounds, including one that I wasn't a girl at all, but a boy. But the quote that really seemed to hit the cute celebrity button was when I was asked if I thought my figure was the thing of the future. My reply amazingly made headline news. 'It's not really what you'd call a figure is it?' I was this gauche gawky thing. I just said what I thought.

One thing Bert Stern had set up was a TV interview with Woody Allen. He wasn't the famous name he is now, just an up-and-coming comedian, and a jazz friend of Bert's. We sat perched up on high stools in the middle of a big studio. No sofa to feel comfortable on. The second question into the interview was who was my favourite philosopher. I'm used to bizarre questions but this is a new one on me. 'I haven't got one,' I say, smiling. 'Oh, come on,' he says, 'everyone has a favourite philosopher.' 'Well, I haven't.' Then, desperate for help I added, 'Who's yours?' It was entirely innocent. I wasn't trying to be clever.

Woody: (taken aback) 'Ooh, I don't know, I like them all.'

Me: 'Who?'

Woody: (lost for words) 'Ooh, all the basic Philosophers.'

Me: (pushing) 'Who? I don't know their names.' My eyes were burning into his for help. There was an audience out there and I was feeling this big. It was like bear baiting.

Woody: (waffling) 'Like your Greeks, your Eclectics.'

Me: 'Yes, but what are their names?'

Having tried to make a fool of me one way, he tries again.

Woody: (cocky) 'I suppose you don't get time to read much, being a model.'

Me: (gormless) 'Read what? Books?'

Woody: (Patronising) 'The great literature. You know, Dickens, Thackeray.'

Me: (Dismissive) 'Oh yes. At school. We had to read them.'

At the end he said, 'Oh I can't interview her,' and fell off his stool.

At the time I felt so stupid, like when you're at school. Bravado hiding your embarrassment. But looking at it now I reckon it's him who's made to look the fool. And they did it to me all the time, asking what I thought about Mao Tse Tung, or the Vietnam War. What did they think they were doing? I was seventeen, a sitting duck. Needless to say I disliked him intensely at the time for how he'd treated me. And I don't suppose you'll be seeing me in a Woody Allen film.

What was real, what was set up? The lines were blurred. An example was a ticker-tape welcome in Fifth Avenue. That was set up I know, but who by? With Bert Stern filming everything it became difficult to separate out reality from fantasy. New Yorkers were as confused as I was. Merchandising came hot on our heels. Nowadays we're used to it, but then it was quite unusual. The big toy makers, Mattel's (who make Barbie Dolls) made us an offer we couldn't refuse. Twiggy Dolls in various costumes, Twiggy totes, Twiggy make-up bags, Twiggy lunch boxes with Twiggy Thermos flasks, Twiggy board games. Now they're quite rare. I've only recently begun to collect them. A pristine Twiggy Doll still in her box, circa 1967, recently cost me $400 at an auction somewhere in the mid-West of America. Though at the same sale a Barbie Doll of 1959 fetched $7,000, which puts me in my place.

It was Melvin setting up another Twiggy mask shot that must have done it. Masks were now disappearing as fast as the crew were handing them out. I'd been given a changing room at the top of the store and the plan was just to walk out of the main door onto Fifth Avenue, with carrier bags marked with B. Altman's logo, like any other tourist shopper. But the Twiggy masks on the street acted like tribal war drums. And anyway, a film crew in New York is like an accident on the motorway. Everyone slows down to rubberneck. Not that we knew until too late. All I had to do was walk through the revolving doors, and head straight for the car. No stopping for autographs; just long enough to let Melvin get the shots he needed. Bert's crew were with me. As soon as I came out of the lift I knew something had gone wrong. I could see Justin getting nervous and frightened and unable to do anything to help me. Looking at the documentary recently it's obvious this was the time he should have called a halt to the day's shooting. I remember trying to say something and finding I couldn't really speak, my mouth was all dry. The head of security for the store was saying, 'Don't worry, they'll separate.' But this wasn't the Red Sea and I wasn't Moses. They just kept closing in, pushing from the sides and from the front. I really knew things were bad when I heard one policeman say to another, 'We're never going to hold them back.' Outside they're chanting 'Twiggy, Twiggy, Twiggy', getting louder and louder as we moved forward, because there was no way back. It was absolutely terrifying.

At this point on the documentary the camera stops in freeze frame, my face contorted in fear. It wasn't a clever edit. Simply there was no more footage. The camera was knocked from the cameraman's grasp and broken. It was then that I screamed and Harold picked me up under his arm, bulldozed his way through a narrow gangway toward the limousine and pushed me in through the open window where I just cowered on the floor, hysterical. What probably just started as excited enthusiasm turned into something really very nasty, people rocking the car and jumping on the roof. I have never been so frightened in my life. Whenever I think about it, which is whenever I see a crowd, I thank God for Harold Poole.

It wasn't the last time I was to experience mass hysteria. It happened again, after the Johnny Carson Show. Because of the B. Altman scenario, I was told not to stop, just to make straight for the car. No autographs. But something had gone wrong, the car wasn't there. The autograph hunters were. Lots of them. Too many for comfort. This time we could turn round and go back. As the lift doors closed the mayhem had already started. Eventually we went down in the garbage elevator. According to the operator I'd really arrived. 'The only other person who uses this is Frank Sinatra.'

All I wanted was to go home. This wasn't fun any more. But then it wasn't a game. Money and contracts were more important than any individual, including me. And, as I was reminded, I still hadn't met Richard Avedon.

7

My only link to home was Justin and Teddy the Monk. As for phoning Mum and Dad, in those days you didn't just dial, it was a whole performance, through the operator and very expensive. I was always aware of how much things cost, a Neasden working-class childhood does that to you. I still go through the house turning the lights off. And although I'm lucky enough now not to have to watch what I buy at the supermarket, I can never resist a three for the price of two bargain. I rang once a week.

The madness showed no signs of letting up. People would even stand up and clap when I went into a restaurant. It had all the qualities of a dream: surreal and without logic. When you're in a dream, even the most ludicrous things seem quite normal. It's only when you wake up you realise how bizarre it was. New York was like that. The only thing that really got to me was when a girl, not much younger than I was, came to the apartment to do an interview for her school magazine. As it was Easter she brought me a duckling as a present. It was so tiny and so soft and I would lie back in the living room at the apartment watching non-stop television (in Britain then there was no daytime TV) while Jim Webb (the name this girl had given the duckling, after the man she'd got it from) would march up my front and snuggle down under my neck or under my arm because it was warmer there. It's no exaggeration to say that I was besotted with that duckling. I wanted to take it everywhere and would be very upset when I had to leave it in the flat. It shows what a state I was in. But even I realised I couldn't keep it, so through one of the bodyguards we arranged to take it to a farm on Long Island. But the day before we were due to go, I came back to find poor Jim dead. We think he was accidentally squashed by the cleaning lady. I was completely beside myself. The next day Justin went out and bought me a kitten, which was pretty stupid. Whatever happened I wouldn't be able to take it back to England because of the quarantine laws. At least that survived. I gave it to the girl who had given me the duckling.

Diana Vreeland had a reputation like Coco Chanel in her heyday. Going to meet her was like going to meet the Queen, though I don't think I realised at the time quite how much influence she had. She looked just like her photograph, almost witchlike, with this white face, an incredibly big nose and black hair, really scary. Even the people who worked with her were terrified of her. But to me she was lovely. The first time we met was in the *Vogue* office, which wasn't too daunting. Later I went to dinner in her apartment and that was something else. It was incredibly over-decorated, all mirrors, plush and gilt, and definitely not somewhere a girl from Neasden could really feel comfortable. Like many Americans she was over the top, and would go on about how she ‘adored’ me. I don’t know about that but I know I probably owe most of what happened in New York to her. Avedon was only the beginning.

I first became aware of Richard Avedon through his photographs of Jean Shrimpton in American *Vogue* which was one of the magazines that Mr Vincent, the hairdresser I worked for, used to take. Plenty of photographers make clothes look beautiful: for Avedon it’s people. Even with Bert Stern I’d come across as innocent and cute. Avedon made me look like a woman.

Although Melvin Sokolsky was innovative, most fashion photographs in those days were rather static. Richard Avedon was the exception. His pictures were all about movement. Dick — as everyone calls him — started the thing of getting you to leap and jump through the air with shutter speeds just slow enough to faintly blur flying hair or a swirling skirt. I was young and I could do it, and I’d learnt a thing or two about working with the camera by then, so that first session wasn’t the last; he used me a lot. This sense of movement was also achieved in other ways. Photographers I’d worked with before would generally leave the lighting alone once it was set up. But Dick had an assistant who would follow him around with an umbrella light. As he himself was always darting around like a little imp, each frame looked entirely different.

The hairdresser he worked with was Ara Gallant, a true artist. Even though I had this little short hairstyle, Ara would do amazing things, like weaving hair through it to give me ringlets. It would take hours but you never saw the join. He was a law unto himself and wore the most outrageous clothes, black from head to toe, from a big black cape to a French sailor's cap covered in badges which he never seemed to take off.

Avedon's studio was always a happy place to work. I know he has a reputation for being arrogant but I never saw that side of him at all. It's probably just professional jealousy — the deal he has with Versace is reputed to be worth $5 million a year. And he is a genius, of that I have no doubt. Of all the thousands of photographs I did in my four years of modelling among my very favourites are a set he did in 1968. Called The Four Seasons, they are headshots, shot in black and white, hand tinted and quite extraordinary.

For that first shoot in New York, Avedon wanted a headshot with one of the world's rarest diamonds on my forehead. It was huge, lemon-coloured and shaped like a teardrop. I had just started to put on my make-up when I noticed this sweet elderly lady sitting in the studio. I thought she must be somebody's mother. To my astonishment (and later Avedon's) I found out she was from the jewellers. The diamond and a gun were in her handbag. Although there were other security guards, she was the only one allowed near me. They were there to protect her. She followed me everywhere, presumably in case I swapped the real thing for a fake, or was robbed.

Although Avedon is physically small, not much taller than me, he is like a reservoir of unrestrained energy, which you feel is only just held in check like a released cork in a bottle of champagne. In those days he had this sculpted helmet of black hair; now it's silver. He was always incredibly tanned which gave his eyes behind the glasses an even greater intensity. I remember thinking at the time that there was a touch of Fred Astaire about him. I didn't know then the Fred Astaire role in the fifties' film of Gershwin's *Funny Face* was based on Avedon.

From New York we went on to Los Angeles and more razzmatazz. My first Hollywood party set the tone. In the usual way of visiting celebrities, I'd been asked who I wanted to meet. In New York I'd asked to meet Cassius Clay, later Muhammad Ali. But he'd just been indicted for something, so that was vetoed. (Not that I cared. It wasn't my idea but ex-boxer Justin's.) So I said Sonny and Cher, who had just hit Britain with 'I've Got You Babe'. And in the way of Hollywood, they were prevailed upon to host a party for me. Their house was the usual palace up in the Hollywood Hills. Half the faces there meant absolutely nothing, but even I recognised Robert Mitchum, Tony Curtis, Peter Sellers, Kirk Douglas and Marlon Brando.

Suddenly there's a vroom-vroom that's closer than it should be, and across the grass, completely ignoring the car park, comes this E-Type jag. By now everyone is staring. Then out jumps Steve McQueen, a great pin up of mine at the time and within seconds he's asking me to dance. 'No thank you,' I said. I was just too shy to say yes.

America is crucial to international recognition. Every pop star knows it, from the Beatles to Oasis. John Lennon once said the Beatles were, 'Just a band who made it very very big, that's all.' What made them very big was America. I'd gone there as a famous model; by the time I left I was this famous person. They even sent pictures of me in a time-capsule into outer space. Imagine it, in thousands of years' time aliens will break open these things and they'll see me. What will they think? 'Weird looking women they had on earth in those days'? or 'There's one just like us. Just the wrong colour. Though her eyelashes are the same.'

America taught us a lot about exporting. Just before we left New York the Twiggy Dresses arrived. In one afternoon we did $1 million of orders. How many of them actually came good, however, is another matter. Rather than organising a franchise, we had exported the dresses themselves. Yet another big managerial mistake. Because no American manufacturer was behind us, pirated copies were soon everywhere and nobody lifting a finger. It was just like the merchandising. Even though Mattel were huge in the States, even they were powerless against the pirates and consequently we were ripped off right, left and centre.

By the autumn we were better organised and as part of a franchising deal to Germany, Justin and I went to the medieval town of Bremen where the manufacturers were based, to meet the press. Glyn and our secretary Nina came with us. After a TV promotion, we set off for the Black Forest where they'd arranged for us to stay, Justin and I in a sports car somebody had lent him. Word gets around. After what seemed like hours of driving through forest we drew up in front of a creepy looking castle. 'There's ee-viil.' Glyn didn't like the look of it at all. I don't think he can have come on many trips with us, because while we were waiting for the massive gates to open, he kept grabbing my arm and saying in his up-and-down Welsh accent, 'Ooooh, Twi-g-g-y. Ooooh. Is-n-'tt-itt po-shsh.'

When the gate finally opens there's this man standing there, in full William Tell kit: black leather boots, lederhosen, green loden cloak, slicked-back hair, two red setters and a very serious expression. By now Glyn is shaking with fear. I know because I'm clutching his hand to stop him from cracking up. In we go. More members of the reception committee, lined up like a firing squad. Still no smiles. Even I begin to get the heebie-jeebies. Justin is in his travel-weary-man-of-the-world mode. If you get scared, he tells Glyn, you can always bang on our door. By now it's very late, so we just go to bed. Suddenly I hear a shriek to wake the dead. Out we rush. A gibbering Glyn is pointing at the wall. 'Over here. Over here. Look, look.'

He was pointing to a wooden shield on the wall. I didn't speak German any more than Glyn did, but one word loomed out as if it was written in blood. Frankenstein. I clutched

Justin and Glyn clutched me. He was by now hysterical. He refused to sleep in his room, so Nina agreed that he could sleep on the extra bed in her room. Fear is contagious and I wasn't used to sleeping with no noise. At home there was always the North Circular; at Justin's there were the regular sirens of the ambulances that used to race up and down Ladbroke Grove regularly through the night. I could cope with all of that. But here there was nothing but owls. It wasn't till the next morning when our host, all smiles now, told us how the house had been in his family for generations and turning it into a hotel was the only way they could afford to keep it going. His wife did the cooking. The family name was Frankenstein.

The way Twiggy Dresses worked was that we got a royalty for every garment sold and while it was going I think we made quite good money. But — and I know I must sound like a stuck record — I never knew what I earned. I was more interested in the clothes. In the end we did get completely screwed. And it was because I was more interested in the clothes that we discovered the scam.

Over the three or so years we were in business, buyers from all over the world would go into the Great Portland Street showroom where models would show the stock and they'd make their orders: thirty of this one, twenty of that one, and so on. One day — it must have been sometime in 1970 — I went into one of the stockrooms to look for something. Not a room I'd ever been in before.

As I'm looking through the dresses for the one I want, I suddenly notice the labels. They all say 'Miss T'. It must be a new line, I think. I was really stupid. So I take this dress back out to Justin and say, look, here's a dress with one of my new labels.

Sydney or Leonard — I can't remember now which of them it was, went white. What they had been doing was filling half of an order under the Twiggy label, and the other half as Miss T — which Justin and I were nothing to do with. At the bottom of the case they packed Twiggy labels for the buyers to sew in. A huge row broke out. They tried to talk us round, but it was the end. Leonard and his wife Pearl had become friends, or so I thought. I used to go to their house for dinner. And that's why I was upset. It wasn't the money. I felt I'd been betrayed. But that was still in the future.

* * *

Models advertise clothes but there is no limit to what famous people can advertise. A whole new world was opening up for me. Cars and models have always been seen as natural advertising partners. And with the sort of coverage I was getting, I didn't need to advertise a car for it to get publicity, I just had to drive it. Well that's what Ford must have thought when they gave me a Mustang on loan late in 1966. But of course I couldn't drive. It was gorgeous. White with blue upholstery. They'd delivered it to me on my seventeenth birthday and I immediately went out and got a provisional licence, though it was two years before I passed my test. In the meantime Justin took the wheel and happily informed everyone that the car was his. I realise now it was a metaphor for our relationship. How he hated not being seen to be in the driving seat in whatever he did. Ford were not pleased when they read this in the papers and soon set the record straight. But it made no difference to Justin. He still claimed it was his. It was the same with so many things. Although it's over twenty years since we split up, it irritates me that he still seems to bracket himself with me. He wrote a book in 1986 which is a testimony to his reinventing mentality, changing fact to wishful fiction on nearly every page. He is presented as the author of what I thought was a dreadful musical mainly about me. He even claims to have invented the Twiggy painted-doll eyelashes. Does it matter? Yes, I think it does. I didn't pick modelling. It picked me. But I picked up the ball and ran. He was the lad who got lucky for a time.

A provisional licence was enough to let me do an advertisement for the Mini, which was then known as the Mini Minor and just taking off. Me and the Mini were perfect casting. The location was the forecourt of the Carlton Towers Hotel in London.

As the cameras rolled I'd come out of the hotel, say 'I love my Mini', then climb in, start up and drive off. So. Roll camera, *action*. Lots of smiling, into the car, start up, put it into gear — but it won't go in. Of course the guys all think it's me. I get out and let them try. Still nothing. Up comes the bonnet. A bit of tinkering. Try again. Nothing. By now it's major panic. The clock was ticking and they couldn't get another car the same colour in time. Enter the cavalry, or rather Shanks's ponies. In the finished ad you see the Mini disappearing out of shot. What you don't see is my shoulders heaving with laughter and ten guys pulling me on ropes.

In the end I not only got paid, I got the car. In the ad I say 'my car' and when it was sent for approval by the advertising authority they asked the advertising agency if I actually had one. The answer of course was no. They only agreed to let it be shown if the car genuinely belonged to me. So I had to take it. In 1967 a mini cost about £600. Eventually it got passed to Dad and finally to Shirley. But I did genuinely love my Mini. Later I had one custom built that I took my test in. A Mini de Ville, dark purple automatic, sun roof, beige leather interior. I should have kept it. Carly would love it. But for me the most important thing in a car is safety. I love driving and I love driving good, safe cars. But cars as status symbols, no. I saw too much of that with Justin.

And he drove them so hard. That summer we had driven down to the South of France with some friends in the lovely grey Rolls Royce we had then, and coming home it started to make funny noises. But Justin wouldn't stop. Just kept going. We never took the ferry, but, as usual, drove it on the plane and flew from Deauville to Lydd in Kent, which you could do in those days, then home to Neasden. When we came down in the morning the entire engine was sitting on the road.

* * *

That autumn we had a call from a Mr Nagashima. He would like to arrange for me to go to Japan. He had done it for the Beatles and he could do it for me. When we eventually met, Tatsuo Nagashima, or Tats, as he liked to be called, was a shock, well over six feet tall, unusual in somebody Japanese. He was from a very wealthy family and had been educated in America. But I said no. It wasn't just Japan; I didn't want to go anywhere. It was very basic. That first trip to New York had seemed never-ending. Then I'd gone back to the States for a coast-to-coast tour for Yardley. By then we thought that franchising was the way forward. My idea had been to have a range based around how I did my make-up. But they wanted the old Twiggy; Yardley made eye-paint kits and 'Twiggystix' eye-pencils and false lashes. But I was using purple and red lipsticks and my eye make-up was similar, colours that Biba were then producing. Worse Yardley were putting out eye-shadows in pastel green and blues. Yuk. Just stuff they couldn't sell which by putting my label on they thought they could get shot of. I hadn't worn eye-shadow like that since my dressing up-days with Geraldine. You can't con people like that. In any case I was moving on. Chicago, St Paul, Cincinnati, Minneapolis and Washington ending in Montreal for Expo 67 where we had the high profile Prime Minister Pierre Trudeau's bodyguard to protect us. The tour had been exhausting and my heart wasn't in it. Now I was back and all I wanted was to be home with Mum and Dad. Most girls at eighteen would have jumped at the chance of leaving home. But I hadn't gone through the weaning process. It just happened so young for me.

Justin was mortified when I said I wouldn't go to Japan. ('But you can earn all this money.') There were the Twiggy Dresses to consider, he badgered. I told him I didn't care. No amount of money was worth not being with Mum, Dad and my friends.

'What if we could take our friends with us and if we asked a silly sum of money and they said yes, what then?'

I agreed, convinced they would say no. We thought of a number and doubled it, and added eight first-class return tickets. They offered us cash. I couldn't believe it. But I couldn't get out of it now.

By the time everything was arranged, it was November and the miseries of the Yardley trip were a long way away. We flew to Tokyo via Stockholm. With us came the Twiggy Dress designers Paul and Pam, our secretary Nina, our accountant, Monty Coles, a photographer, and of course Teddy the Monk. It was a long flight; nineteen hours. By the time we arrived I was exhausted. We went down steps from the plane onto the runway and we had to walk through hundreds of Japanese photographers, all of them shouting 'Triggy, Triggy'. Tats had started as he meant to go on. They were terribly polite but I was terrified and I burst into tears. Although most of them were no bigger than me and certainly wouldn't have touched me it took me back to the B. Altman thing. Triggy in tears. Straight to the front page.

We were staying at the Tokyo Hilton, where you could choose to stay Eastern style or Western style. We chose Eastern and it was like being on another planet. Now I wouldn't dream of going anywhere I hadn't read about but then I knew nothing. Absolutely nothing. The rooms were very spacious and traditional, with cushions to sit at a low table and instead of beds there were mattresses on the floor. I'd never heard of a futon, let alone slept on one. And ladies on call to give you a massage. I'd never had a massage. I'd never had sushi or sashimi either; the very thought of raw fish was so disgusting I didn't even try. (Silly me. Now we're sushi and sashimi addicts.)

Compared with my usual schedule Japan was like a holiday. In three weeks I only had three jobs. First was a commercial for Toyota cars. As well as being paid they gave me (and shipped back) a one-off sports car. Like Ford they didn't know I couldn't drive. But I sat in the driving seat, waved the key and smiled, which was all they wanted. Then came an ad for Choco Flakes, where I had to sing. (The awful pop record I'd made in 1966 had become Japan's Number One.) And finally a fashion show for Tokyo Rayon, yet another man-made fabric company, at the Budokwai Stadium where the Beatles had played two years before.

When we'd arrived at Tokyo airport, the hippie phase was just beginning and both Justin and I were wearing smelly Afghan sheepskin waistcoats embroidered with flowers. My hair was now quite long and I wore it parted in the middle and pinned back from my face with flowers. The flower-power era had arrived and with it psychedelia and drugs. Not for me. I might have had the trappings, smelling of patchouli, with satin trousers from Granny Takes a Trip, a wonderful shop in the King's Road. But that was it. Never any drugs.

The stadium was full. God knows what they were expecting to see, it wasn't as if I was going to sing. All I had to do was walk down a specially constructed catwalk, do a twirl then walk back up again. Even the clothes were my own Twiggy Dresses. Top Japanese pop groups provided the music. One band sang Beatles covers in Japanese. But what had us all in hysterics was what they were wearing. They'd obviously seen the newspaper photographs of our arrival but hadn't been able to work out exactly what we had on — but knowing it was 'the look' did their best to copy it. They'd managed the suede waistcoats but in the absence of sheepskin, stuck cotton wool balls on instead.

Backstage, about half-way through the show, a tiny man came up to me holding a string of pearls, very twenties and very long, about two yards. Everyone was bowing and scraping, even more and lower than usual, a sign of extreme rank. This was Mr Mikamoso of Mikamoso Pearl Company himself. Justin had done a last-minute deal. If I would wear them, they were mine. So I did, though I had to wind them round several times so as not to trip over. Later I used them as belt. But one day in London the string broke when we were in a restaurant — everyone in the place was soon on their hands and knees trying to find them. So I had to stop wearing them. They're called black pearls but are actually grey and sadly far too valuable to wear. They are absolutely beautiful but they now live in a bank vault, part of Carly's inheritance.

In America I had been treated like a freak. In Japan I was treated like a royal. Everyone everywhere bowing, so kind and eager to please and make me welcome. My every wish their command. Once I said I wouldn't half like a cup of ordinary English tea. With milk. And sugar. It was rush hour. But that wasn't going to stop them and, with a full team of twelve motor cycle outriders, the Twiggy cavalcade sped through Tokyo to a colonial-style hotel on the outskirts of town. We even went through red lights. All for a cuppa. I was so embarrassed. The most moving experience was being taken to a Kabuki theatre in Kyoto where I was taken backstage to meet the star. It was like going into a temple: candles everywhere and the overpowering smell of incense burning. It was more an audience with a deity. I got the feeling he was a cross between John Gielgud and Buddha and I did feel very honoured.

Not all my tourist experiences were successful. At one restaurant, I was handed a bowl containing a Japanese delicacy. Then I saw it wriggle. It was a fish and was live. You were meant to slice it and eat it. They had to carry me out. The Tea Ceremony was less grisly than embarrassing. The star of this drama was Paul Babb. Although he had come along in his Twiggy Dresses capacity, Paul was great company: very tall and gangly; someone who could always see the funny side of things. Because there were so many of us, we were spread out along a long table. Each of us was allocated our own Geisha to serve us. They all wore these amazing kimonos, fabulous colours and embroidery. But most bizarre was the thick white make-up they wear, like old-fashioned grease-paint. And of course that hair is a wig, with the gauze and the glue perfectly visible. Not madly attractive.

Anyway, along come all the delicacies and different teas, the music is playing and it's all very charming. Then suddenly I look across at Paul, who's sitting opposite me and his face is contorted in what I take to be pain. I quickly look at his Geisha to see what's up and can't believe my eyes. She's smiling at Paul and has completely black teeth. Out comes the Twiggy laugh which sets Paul off, then everybody else.

Afterwards I was mortified. It turned out she was the top Geisha. The teeth weren't rotten or anything, they were just stained as a mark of her superiority and great beauty.

Much of Tokyo, even then, felt no different from anywhere else. But the two days we spent in an old hotel in the mountains, two hours away, made up for it. This time it was just Justin, Teddy and me. We drove through a landscape that came straight out of National Geographic, with wonderful little villages where all the women still wore full Kimono. As it was autumn the colours were absolutely gorgeous. Mount Fuji itself was about the only thing in Japan that didn't give me VIP treatment and remained shrouded in mist the whole time we were there. I'm glad I'm not royal. Although I only had a taste, to be fêted and fawned upon all the time must be in the end a daunting ordeal.

Back in London it was time to say goodbye to Neasden. I had managed to salvage some of the Japanese cash so Dad and I went house-hunting. Mum wasn't really up to it. We found a lovely one-off thirties villa right on the Thames at Twickenham, white with blue shutters. Dad, being careful Dad, thought the one on the other side of the road would do just as well. Not being bang on the river it was cheaper. But this time I held out. It wasn't too big, just four bedrooms, nice kitchen, and spacious, and it had a lovely garden leading down to the River Thames with a huge willow tree trailing in the water. Looking across the river all you could see were fields. Very beautiful. And there was enough DIY to keep Dad happy.

In Japan Justin had been given a posh camera, a Pentax, and it became his latest craze. First he found the studio in Charlotte Mews, and when the office above became vacant he moved in.

In any case with Glyn and the animals, not to mention his suits, the flat in Ladbroke Gardens was just not big enough. What really clinched it was having a garage for all the cars he kept buying. The up-and-over door was painted with a life-size traffic warden standing in front of a giant 'no-parking' sign. During his Lamborghini phase a mechanic would be round every Saturday to tune it. I tried never to be there because of the noise.

A journalist once described the studio in Charlotte Mews as 'an absurd and splendid monument to pop art and the sixties'. Upstairs was comparatively normal. That was where the office was and the kitchen and where we ate. Though nothing was ordinary. Even the chairs were by Mr Freedom, a friend of ours otherwise known as Tommy Roberts, who made everything from work-clothes to furniture. I remember I had a pair of Mr Freedom dungarees. And the walls were covered with pop art murals and Walt Disney cut-outs. But downstairs was extraordinary. For a start it had no windows. You never knew if it was night or day or winter or summer.

At the time it seemed like a magic room. It was all done out as a Bedouin tent. Justin said it took 6000 yards of material. I think that was yet another of his exaggerations. Being a photographer's studio the ceiling was very high. It was psychedelia gone hippie. The whole place smelled of joss-sticks and the sides were draped in beautiful Indian hangings and mirror work and screens. Somebody said it looked like something made by Bill Gibb, the brilliant designer of exotic clothes, who I had just got to know. And subconsciously he was probably one of the influences. Barbara Hulanicki was too. But if I had to describe the look now, I'd say it was like something designed by Bakst, the Russian painter, for ballets like *Scheherazade*.

To reach the studio you had to go through the garage past electrically operated mirrors which moved. Whenever Shirley came to visit we'd have to turn them off as they made her feel sick. She was the only one we ever allowed to sit on a chair, which we'd have to bring down from upstairs. Everyone else had to sit on the mountains of cushions that covered the floor and half crept up the walls.

All in all we were there about four years and inevitably things just got added on. Behind the hangings for example were some of Brian Robbins' kinetic sculptures and large op art paintings by Jon Brunner. (So-called because they often looked like optical illusions.) It was through Jon that we met Stewart Grimshaw, who would become very important in my life, a stalwart friend who is always there whenever I need him. Jon and Stewart were the friends we drove down to the South of France with that time when the Rolls packed up. We met them through Keith Lichtenstein who used to run a restaurant called The Casserole in the Kings Road. We only ate in when we had people for dinner. I felt a bit like this thing that Justin loved presenting around. Anyway, we were regulars and the walls of the restaurant were used as an exhibition space by young up-and-coming artists. Justin had always been into modern art and fancied himself as a collector. One night we were there he fell in love with this one particular painting. It was abstract and very geometric, Op Art, I suppose, as opposed to Pop Art, which Justin also liked. The artist was a young American called Jon Brunner, and we arranged to meet him. Jon's studio was south of the river, close to the Old Vic theatre. He and I hit it off immediately. He was very thin, very intense and painfully shy. That first time we met he could barely speak to us. It turned out he was sponsored by Simon Sainsbury, who was the man who saved Covent Garden: before Simon stepped in the wonderful eighteenth-century fruit market was about to be turned into a multi-storey car park. Simon introduced us to Stewart Grimshaw, another restaurateur, who ran a restaurant on the Fulham Road called Provans. Before Stewart and I met my only theatrical experiences were Norman Wisdom and *My Fair Lady*, which Mum and Dad had taken me to when I was about ten. We sat up in the gods and I just remember thinking how small they all were. There was certainly no sense of *Oh, I'd like to do that*. But Stewart was my introduction to legitimate theatre. And I loved it. The National Theatre on the South Bank hadn't yet started up, but the Old Vic was already fulfilling that function. I started at the top. He would take me to matinées and that season the company at the Old Vic included Laurence Oliver, Robert

Stephens, Maggie Smith and Jeremy Brett. Yet another door to yet another world. I had never done anything like that with Justin. And as he wouldn't let anyone else near me, I had no way of finding out. But I was growing up, changing. Which is why it was obvious I was going to have to get away.

8

Late night movies are a godsend. As any actor will tell you, three hours on stage every night leaves you with the adrenaline still pumping and it's hard to wind down. There's something so romantic about a black and white film late at night. Leigh and I both have a passion for them. Some are old favourites, others are completely unknown but there's usually something to recommend them; even if they're dreadful you can have a good laugh. But I often have that sense of déjà vu. Half-way through I'll realise I've seen it before. The chances are I probably have.

Mum had always been a great picture-goer. Her favourite actors were Errol Flynn and a Canadian called Lee Paterson, who always made thrillers. The trouble was that for some bizarre reason that I've never understood, she liked to see the end of a film before the beginning. I suppose it's like people who read the last pages of a book before the beginning. Madness to me. Especially if it's a thriller. In those days you could stay in the cinema as long as you wanted; at least you could at the Neasden Odeon. God knows what other people must have thought. She wouldn't do it any other way. It didn't matter what the film was, we'd always go in half-way through and sit through the interval munching our sandwiches then watch the first half of the film. At the time I didn't see anything strange about it but it's little wonder I got confused.

My adult film education began with Philip Jenkinson. In the sixties and seventies he was very well known, always talking about films on television on arts programmes like *Late Night Line-up* and *Film Preview*. But what really interested him was old black and white movies and he had this amazing collection of old films which he had saved from destruction when studios were chucking them out, or doing swaps with other studios. When I got to know him he had over 2000 films, most of them rarer than gold dust.

We met Philip at the film director Ken Russell's house in Ladbroke Square, just round the corner from Justin's flat. I can't quite remember how we met Ken and his wife Shirley. It might have been through Bill Gibb the dress designer who also lived in Ladbroke Gardens and who was a friend of Shirley's. Billy and I met in the most normal way, like neighbours do. It was snowing and my Mini was stuck and he offered to give me a push. Anyway, it wasn't long after I had come back from that first trip to America in the spring of 1967 when we first went to have supper with Ken and Shirley at their house at 23 Ladbroke Square.

I can see that house so clearly. It was on a corner, Victorian, five floors and completely wonderful. I had never been into a household like it. This was Notting Hill, buzzy and bohemian. It had a huge effect on me and it was a wonderful release. Until then I'd always liked modern things. Just like Mum and Dad: if it's modern it's good. Suddenly going into this house was a revelation. For a start it wasn't conventionally neat. It was full of wonderful things, from a stuffed parrot (which Oliver Reed eventually burnt in a drunken rage) and Shirley's collection of Staffordshire pug dogs. I remember thinking this is how I'd like to live and this is how I'd like to be. Instead of the kitchen being hidden out the back, it was the first room you come to after the front door. It was the heart of the house and took up the whole of the ground floor. There was no carpet or lino, just sanded and polished floorboards with a moth-eaten Bengal Tiger rug. And the kitchen units weren't hidden at the end but ran half-way down one side of the room and there was a sofa and a pine dresser with wonderful copper saucepans hanging from it. My Mum with her working-class kitchen and everything hidden away would have had a fit. But as Shirley Russell pointed out, why should she miss all the fun while she was cooking? And of course in the middle there was this massive old pub table where we would eat huge suppers of spaghetti bolognaise or shepherd's pie or casserole and baked potatoes and bottle after bottle of red wine. It was love at first sight. All of them: Ken because he was so eccentric, like a big kid — in my world fathers were fathers, they didn't do silly things; Shirley because she was completely lovely and the only person I'd ever met who was as obsessed with clothes as I was; and all five of their children, Xavier, Alex, James, Victoria and

Toby (cast in order of age). Xavier was about eleven and Toby was about two. And they were so happy then. The perfect family.

Ken and Shirley became really good friends. For three years we saw each other at least once a week when we were all in London. Looking back we must have been a strange foursome. Yet somehow the chemistry worked. When it was our turn we'd usually go out to dinner, either to one of our favourite restaurants, like San Lorenzo, Julie's, Mr Chow's or Stewart Grimshaw's restaurant Provans. On Saturday afternoons we'd pile the little Russells into the Rolls and go shopping on Kensington High Street, either to Biba or Mr Freedom. It was such fun being part of this wonderful family. We even went up to the Lake District where they had a cottage and would take the kids roaring round the tiny twisty roads in the Lamborghini. Imagine, a Lamborghini in Borrowdale. Even Justin, who boasted of doing over a hundred miles an hour down Bond Street couldn't get a lot faster than thirty. The hills were alive with the sound of brakes. Ken was just as mad but at the other end of the spectrum of speed. He had a black and white thirties Rolls that he used to drive with the hood down and blare out classical music to the mountains. Coming back we'd arrange to meet up at motorway service stations but we'd always get there hours before them. Once, not long after we'd met, we'd just come back from some jaunt or other and the children were round in Justin's flat and I was in the kitchen making tea when Victoria asked

Justin, 'Where has your Mummy gone?' Justin was completely puzzled. Only later did he realise she meant me.

Being entertained at the Russells was unlike anything I have experienced before or since. Organised chaos. About once a week they had these film shows. Philip Jenkinson and Ken had known each other for years. Philip had been the cameraman on Ken's early films which he made before he started working for the BBC. They'd started these films shows way back then, once a week going to each other's houses. In those days there was no such thing as late-night television. Old films were limited to Sunday afternoons. And that meant one a week. The chance to see these amazing archive films was something you literally could do nowhere else, so the house in Ladbroke Square was always filled with fascinating people. I remember Melvyn Bragg was at the first film evening I went to. I think he and Ken were working on the Debussy film, one of the series of composers Ken did for the BBC arts programmes *Monitor* and then *Omnibus* which followed. His work on these programmes had already marked him out as the *enfant terrible* of British television. Before I met him I knew his name but I think the only one of his films I'd actually seen was the one on Elgar. But in 1968 they repeated all of them, ending with the one I loved most, the last one he made, *Song of Summer*, about Delius, which starred Max Adrian and Christopher Gable. Ken used the actors he liked over and over again. It was like a theatre company really. These wonderful films in this series have become classics, quite rightly. And I will never forget his Isadora, played by the wild and wonderful Vivien Pickles.

The way it worked was we'd see one film first and then go downstairs for supper which had been cooking while we watched. By then the children had all gone to bed. Or were supposed to have done. But pretty soon they would creep down and there they'd be, sitting on the stairs looking at the big white screen flickering at the end of the sitting room which took up the whole of the first floor.

It was full of Art Deco and posters of the Russian Ballet but also pieces of pop art. They had this pianola with a collection of rolls of old music which you just put in and played. But it worked like an ordinary piano as well although the only person I ever saw play it was Paul McCartney. The furniture was a mix of incredibly beautiful things from Victorian side tables to Ray and Charles Eames furniture, including the 'egg' chair Ken later used in *Tommy* that Ann-Margret sat in and, of course, the pinball machine itself.

I had never seen anything like these old movies before and I was hungry for more. When Justin moved into Charlotte Mews in 1968 the studio made a perfect projection room, so I asked Philip if he could come and do the same for us. And he did. Just out of the goodness of his heart and because it's his obsession. He showed us everything. We worked our way through all the great directors: Eisenstein — *Ivan the Terrible* was my favourite; Lubitsch; Erich Von Stroheim — it was the first time I'd seen Marlene Dietrich; and then Hitchcock of course. *Rebecca* completely entranced me and I immediately went out and bought the book which is still one of my favourites. What really fascinated me was how things were done. While everyone else just shut up and watched, I was always butting in and asking questions or would collar Philip at the end. Like the poisoned glass of milk in *Suspicion* that seemed to glow. How did Hitchcock do it? Philip knew because he'd asked Hitchcock himself. It was a specially hollowed-out glass with a bulb in the bottom. Then the great female stars, Greta Garbo in *Ninotchka* and *Camille*; Rita Hayworth in *Gilda*. Claudette Colbert in *Midnight* and Katherine Hepburn in just about everything. Then there were Philip's pride and joy, the early silents, which were extraordinary. He made up a tape of music of the time to accompany them. I remember Myerow's *Faust*, and *Vampyre* by Carl Dreyer and of course good old *King Kong*. There was a thirties version of Dante's *Inferno* with this amazing sequence in hell, all mystic and swirling mists. The only thing that touched it was the great battle between the workers and the aristocrats in Fritz Lang's amazing feast of art deco, *Metropolis*, made in 1925 and which I made Philip show again and again.

People assume that because I was a model, my friends were people in the pop music world. But apart from one or two exceptions, it didn't happen.

One of my few friends in the rock 'n'roll world is Paul McCartney, who I met through Ken very early on. Ken always used unusual people in his films, people who weren't trained actors, like Christopher Gable who was a principal with the Royal Ballet until Ken cast him in *Song Of Summer*. And he had come up with something he thought he could do with me. It was from a William Faulkner story called *The Wishing Tree* about a magician and a young girl and he wanted Paul to do the music, so he arranged for us all to meet over lunch. I was completely beside myself. I was still only seventeen and the Beatles were at the height of their fame. They were the biggest thing that had ever happened. Only four years before I'd been one of those screaming girls at Finsbury Park Astoria, the only time my Dad ever shouted at me, really shouted at me. Finsbury Park was a long way from Neasden and although Jennifer and I went on the train, Dad said he would pick us up. But after the show we'd gone through to the stage door, so I wasn't where I'd said we'd be. So he just sat in the car out front waiting as these hysterical teenagers poured out, and getting frantic when he realised we weren't there. When he finally found us, these simpering teenage girls all crying, he was so angry. It must have been so scary for him. Now I'm a parent myself I realise how frantic he must have been, and that his anger came out of fear.

So four years later and there I was about to have lunch with my idol. I was so nervous.

Working with Avedon was nothing compared with lunch with Paul McCartney. All I kept thinking was I've got to behave properly. I can't go gooey. I recognise it in Carly now. Having crushes on people is something everybody goes through. She's had crushes on people who she's eventually met through Leigh and me. Like Ben Elton who she's always absolutely adored. By chance she had just finished reading one of his books when we invited him over for dinner. I suppose she must have been about fifteen. When he arrived I introduced her. She was her usual chatty, friendly self and didn't show anything of what she was feeling, but half-way through talking to him she went down to her bedroom, screamed into a pillow and pinched herself just to make sure it was really happening and then came back, completely calm as before. When I told Ben that she was a fan, he was thrilled. The next day all his books arrived by special messenger signed 'to Carly'. On television he can come across as quite caustic. But he's not. He's a gentle, nice man. And really talented, clever and funny.

Paul was the same to me that day. So kind. It seems stupid to call someone like Paul McCartney ordinary, but that's what he is. Ordinary but extraordinary. Shortly after that meeting, the six of us arranged to have dinner. Paul was with Jane Asher in those days. We went to the White Tower, a very smart Greek restaurant, to talk more about the film and he just started thinking up songs while we were sitting there, tapping out tunes with a fork on wine glasses which he'd just filled up to various levels with water.

We didn't see much of each other in the early days because he was busy touring and being a Beatle. A few years later, after he'd broken up with Jane, he rang me and said, 'Listen, I've just got back from New York, and I've met this wonderful girl, she's American and she doesn't know anyone over here. Do you mind meeting up with her and maybe go shopping or something?' And I said absolutely. And I remember we went shopping in Knightsbridge. Linda had Heather with her, her little girl from her first marriage, who was only six, and then I took them for lunch at San Lorenzo. When Linda first came over the fans and media were horrible to her. They gave her so much stick. It was just sour grapes pure and simple. She's a really good lady and over the years has been a fantastic friend to me and Carly and later Leigh and Ace. She's a very special person and we all adore her. Their kids are amazing, very together and very normal and I've known them since they were born. The McCartneys are proof that money and fame don't have to muck people up. It's all a question of attitude, of family values. I so admire them. They seem to have got things right.

In life things don't happen in a straight line. There are so many layers. So much dovetailing. At the end of 1967 I was already beginning my new look. And although skirts were generally still short, the maxi was beginning to push out the mini, in the magazines if not out in the streets.

Barbara Hulanicki was making long coats. There had always been a twenties air about Biba, with the potted palms and bentwood hatstands; now the clothes were following suit and the hatstands were draped with feather boas. I stopped wearing short skirts more or less completely around October 1967, my hems were all around mid calf. And I pushed my growing hair into my favourite brown beret with the growing bits sticking out underneath in fluffy curls. I had been very influenced by Garbo and Katherine Hepburn in all those wonderful thirties films I'd now been exposed to. They had an enormous effect on my new look.

We were still in touch with Justin's artist friend Bryan Robbins and I think it was him who told us about the Erté show at the Grosvenor Gallery. Erté is probably best known now for the illustrations he did in the thirties for *Harper's Bazaar*. But he was also an amazing costume designer. His real name was Roman Tirtoff; Erté is just the way his initials, R. T., are pronounced in French — *Air-Tay*. He was Russian, born in St Petersburg, but moved to Paris when he was twenty-one in 1912. By the twenties he was designing for the Folies Bergères and later for the Ziegfield Follies in New York — amazingly flamboyant show costumes with fantastical headresses, all ostrich feathers, a bit like a showbiz Aubrey Beardsley. He even worked in Hollywood for a while. I'd heard his name before I knew his work. I was in Biba's one day and somebody said that I looked like 'Erté's sketch book come to life'. So when I met him it was a real thrill. He was tiny, like an elf, but so elegant, never without a handkerchief in his breast pocket, straight out of one of his drawings. And having been so long in the States his English was wonderful and very precise and we just chatted away without any problem. It was somebody at *Queen* who came up with the idea of a Twiggy/Erté makeover.

If there was just one word to describe an Erté woman, it was vamp. And that's what I wanted to be. We did the shoot just before I left for Japan. This time there was no Ara Gallant to weave his magic in my hair so Erté just used his imagination. One of the stylists was wearing a long string of pearls, another had come wearing a white fox-fur stole. Against the white of the fur, Erté went mad with my eyes. For once I didn't do my own eye make-up and the result was pure Erté, a rainbow ranging from green on my eyelids to red on my cheekbones. I should have got him to sign it.

We had just got back from Japan when Eric Asterick, owner of the Grosvenor Gallery, who had been responsible for Erté's recent renaissance, suggested Justin and I might like to go along with them to the theatre to celebrate his seventy-fifth birthday on 23 November. It was a revival of the fifties musical *The Boyfriend* which had just opened at the Comedy Theatre to good reviews, though I can't remember feeling very enthusiastic. But it was Erté's treat not mine. It didn't take me long to change my mind. It blew me away. It was just so funny. Afterwards we had dinner at the Savoy. Erté leant over. 'My dear Twiggy,' he said in his lovely half-Russian, half-French accent, 'I think you should do something like that.'

About a week after this, we went out to dinner with the Russells at the Artiste Assoifee just down the road in Notting Hill. We hadn't seen them for months as they'd been out of England filming the Tschaikovsky feature, *The Music Lovers*, so we had a lot of catching up to do. At some point in the evening, I started to tell them about this wonderful play we'd just seen. *The Boyfriend* had had its first production in the fifties at the Players Theatre underneath Charing Cross arches in London and, by one of those amazing coincidences, it turned out Shirley had been involved. One of her teachers at Art College had been the costume designer. And by the end of the evening after many bottles of champagne, Ken had become very excited. 'We should make a film of it,' he exclaimed. 'I've always wanted to do a musical. You'll be Polly and I'll direct.'

He'd had a few. More than a few. So I didn't really take it too seriously. Ken's enthusiasms had the tendency to fade the morning after the night before. But not this time. He phoned soon after breakfast.

'Well? What do you think?'

'What about?'

'*The Boyfriend*. You and me.'

'Brilliant, but there's just one little problem, Ken. Actually three. I can't sing, dance or act.'

His reply was immediate.

'Don't worry, we'll send you off to class.'

The Wishing Tree had come to nothing. *The Boyfriend* would now be our next project. Ken's first two feature films, *The Billion Dollar Brain* and *Women in Love*, had been made for United Artists so naturally he took the idea to them. They were all for it. But it turned out MGM had bought the film rights from the author Sandy Wilson in 1954. And MGM wouldn't sell. Over the years they'd tried and failed to film it. The script was always the problem. MGM will always be known as the studio that brought the world the great Hollywood musicals of the forties and fifties. They were the obvious people do it, so Ken then suggested he do it for them.

From the start Ken knew that a filmed version of Sandy Wilson's musical wouldn't work on its own. *The Boyfriend* is a loving pastiche of the 1920s, very stylised and each of the characters too much like stereotypes to work on film — which is probably the reason all previous attempts at screenplays had failed. Nobody quite knew how to bring it to the screen. Then Ken's mum phoned. Her local amateur dramatic company were doing *The Boyfriend*, she said; would he like her to get tickets? Ken's mum is very sweet and usually Ken would have just said thank you for thinking of me Mum, but no thanks. This time was different. 'It'll be a hoot,' he said, 'we've got to go.' So that weekend the four of us trotted off to somewhere in Essex, met up with Ken's mum and took our places in the local town hall. It didn't help that the chairs were the excrutiatingly uncomfortable wooden folding kind.

It was quite possibly the most amazing production of *The Boyfriend* that has ever been staged. Ken spent the entire time with his handkerchief stuffed in his mouth to gag his laughter. Thank God he wasn't sitting next to me. But when the heroine Polly Browne began singing the number about her being 'seventeen or thereabouts' I was just shaking. The leading lady was at least fifty and Tony, the Boyfriend himself, was not much younger. I felt dreadful about it later. They must have been so excited to have us in the audience. They might not have known who Ken was but everyone would have recognised me.

And that's how he got the idea of a rather tacky rep company putting on a production of *The Boyfriend* and tying it in with his *hommage* to all those thirties Busby Berkeley musicals. But a pastiche of a pastiche? I was worried it might have been too corny. I needn't have been. Hollywood has a greater affinity to corn than Iowa, and Ken's 'Hollywood-film-director-sees-seaside-show, fantasises-about-how-it-would-look-on-the-silver-screen' was tailor made. MGM loved it. But it would be a year before we got the green light. The first problem had been the rights. Second was the female lead. Twiggy might have been a household name as a model but this was a part for an actress, singer and dancer.

It wasn't only MGM who didn't think I could do it. The star was not entirely convinced herself. It was Ken who was sure. He obviously recognised something in me and it became an obsession. The more people said no, the more he stuck to his guns. It was extraordinary really. As for me, I was so young and green and I trusted him. I should have been trembling in my boots. I think I was infected by Ken's passion. I don't think I ever sat down and calculated, *this is my lucky break*. I had always gone along with what other people had believed. Now Ken was my mentor. And that was no bad thing. Ken was always ready to admit he too owed everything to his mentor, Huw Weldon, who was in charge of *Monitor* and later went on to run BBC television itself.

But perhaps it wasn't such a shot in the dark. Not long before, the ever-innovative Melvin Sokolsky had been at it again. This time it was an ad for Diet Rite Cola, one of a series where they had famous skinny people saying they drank it because they liked it, not because they wanted to lose weight. And as I was probably the most famous skinny person in the world, Diet Rite wanted me. I refused to go over to America, so Melvin came over here. It was shot in Wembley. It was to be a jazz age spectacular. I was dressed in classic Dietrich style, with white tie and tails. And, like Dietrich, I had to sing and dance. I had always loved dancing, moving to the music, and often in fashion shoots that's what I'd do. For the *Monitor* documentary on David Bailey I am doing just that, dancing to Martha and the Vandellas' 'Jimmy Mac'. But it was just totally freestyle dancing. I had never had to learn steps that had been choreographed, that had to be rehearsed and repeated. But Mel thought I could and brought over the choreographer Grover Dale to teach me. It was the first time I realised how hard dancers worked. We shot during the day, because the other girls were all in shows. And when I was ready to collapse by the evening, they'd just be setting off for the night job.

My tail coat was made by Mr Fish and the set was a thirties nightclub with me on a catwalk, singing to the tune of 'Yes Sir, That's my Baby', 'Yes Sir, I'm not on a diet, That's not why I buy it, Just got the taste that's right for me.' Just singing was nerve-wracking enough. Then came the word from above. It was too American. They wanted cockney. That was incredibly difficult. It's not just the accent that's different, it's the rhythms as well. And for all my reputation, I'd never spoken the sort of music-hall cockney they wanted anyway. Like everything Melvin did, it was a very stylish ad. Sadly it became the victim of a health scare over cyclamates, the sugar substitutes used in those days, and it was pulled. They had to change the recipe for the drink and when the ad was eventually released they'd put this huge banner saying 'NO CYCLAMATES' across most of the screen and all you could see was my face and my feet.

In order to get me up to scratch even for that short sequence, Grover Dale had to teach me the rudiments of dance. He was incredibly patient and we became firm friends though I don't think Mel had let on that I was such a complete novice. It didn't matter. I was hooked.

By the time *The Boyfriend* was a real

possibility rather than just a dream I had been modelling for three years. I could have gone on for another ten or even fifteen. But you can only do so much. You stand in front of a camera, and do what you do and that's it. Although it was fine for a while, it was a cul-de-sac. The Diet Rite ad had shown me a way out.

9

In the meantime my life as a model went on, though I no longer did the bread and butter work. There was no need. Increasingly I just worked with Justin; he could always sell photographs of me, so we could always get bookings. In hindsight I realise there is no way *Vogue* would have hired Justin de Villeneuve to do a set of photographs otherwise. *Vogue* had their own A list of photographers. But when *Vogue* wanted to book me and I said 'yes, as long as you get Justin to do the pictures' — it was a *fait accompli*. He had been very clever in getting Barry Lategan's old assistant Chris Killip to be his assistant and light for him. By that time we knew that everything is in the lighting and Chris was the best. And Justin could afford the best. We had only got back from Japan at the end of 1967 yet by February 1968 Justin had his first spread in *Queen*, the Valentine issue. Three months between getting a camera and hitting the big time. He did take some good pictures so he must have had some sort of an eye. But after we split he never did it again. That was the end of his career as a photographer, as far as I know. Even in an exhibition he had quite recently there were mainly only old pictures of me, I'm told.

The film evenings didn't let up, they just upped tempo. Now the focus was on musicals. I'd always loved the RKO Fred and Ginger movies, but Philip Jenkinson's collection went further back, and included all the Busby Berkeleys, like *Forty-Second Street* and the *Gold Diggers* series. The storylines are pretty much all variations on the 'goes out a hoofer, comes back a star (or married to someone seriously rich)' scenario. But everything else was amazing. Dazzling kaleidoscopic patterns shot from above with just chorus girls and a huge imagination. All I ever seemed to say was, 'How do they do that?' Philip had met Busby Berkeley and had spent a week with him when he was in England. So I learnt everything second hand from the horse's mouth. Busby Berkeley was a completely self-taught dancer which is perhaps why he broke so many of the rules. Lesser mortals could choreograph dancers; this man choreographed the camera as well.

I became obsessed with tap and could watch it for hours. And even though I hadn't started doing it myself, I was already learning by watching. In *You Were Never Lovelier*, Rita Hayworth was so beautiful and so perfect and seemed to dance so effortlessly. But if it came to a contest, in my book Ginger Rogers wins. Although she never got quite the acclaim of Astaire, she really was an amazing tap dancer in her own right — just to keep up with Fred, let alone to put all that style into it. I think I only realised this when I started to do it myself.

In May 1968 Rita Hayworth was one of the five Hollywood stars whose identities I borrowed for a *Queen* shoot that Justin photographed. The others were Theda Bara, Greta Garbo,

Marilyn Monroe and Ginger Rogers herself, in top hat and tails, which was used for the cover. The others were head shots. Leonard did the wigs and Jon Brunner did the styling. Another photographer friend of Jon's, Steve Lovi, did the lighting and it was his idea of using old-fashioned tungsten like they would have done in the thirties that gave those pictures their sense of period. I still think they are absolutely gorgeous.

Like a lot of talented photographers Steve Lovi was keen to try his hand at moving pictures. And working with us gave him the chance to direct. Granada TV had agreed to put up the money for a documentary, *Twiggy in Russia*, and we had put together a Romanov-inspired collection: white knee-length boots, Cossack trousers, everything in white. Steve and the crew had gone over in advance for their recce and we were all set to go. Then in early May we got a telegram saying our visas had been refused. We couldn't understand it. Things seemed to be opening up behind the iron curtain. They were, but too quickly for the Russians, it turned out. In Czechoslovakia the Prague Spring had begun; communism was giving way to 'socialism with a human face'. That night on the news we heard the Russians had moved their troops to the Czech border. In August they invaded. It would be another twenty years before the iron curtain finally came down. We did the shoot in Sweden instead.

Paul McCartney had agreed to write us a song, but in all the confusion we'd forgotten about it, until one evening a few months later we were all together in Mr Chow's and we reminded him. To everyone's amazement Mr McCartney started belting out 'Back In The USSR' which later found its way onto the Beatles' *White Album*

Paul had always written songs for people other than the Beatles. 'World Without Love', which Christopher, my first boyfriend, had given me just before he opted for a scooter rather than a girlfriend, was a McCartney song. Soon after I met him, when he was still with Jane Asher, we had gone up to Liverpool to stay with Paul's father and stepmother in the house Paul had bought for them in Heswall, on the Cheshire side of the Mersey. Over supper he told us he was on the look out for new singers. 'Did you see last week's *Opportunity Knocks*?' I asked. *Opportunity Knocks* was the talent show hosted by the late Hughie Green. I'd been watching a few days before and had seen this young girl who sang like an angel, called Mary Hopkins. Paul hadn't seen her. And if she didn't win the viewers' vote, he wouldn't. So we all sat round the dinner table that night and wrote postcards voting for Mary Hopkins. In the end we must have done over a hundred. Very naughty. Then we had a week to wait. It was all so exciting. She won, of course — not that it had anything to do with our cards. It was a landslide. Immediately after the show Paul called and said he thought she was brilliant. The next day he sent a car down to Wales to fetch her. He found her a song called 'Those Were the

Days' which he produced. And it went straight to Number One.

* * *

As part of my cinematographic education, I was also becoming a connoisseur of really bad musicals. Philip was going through everything he had for Ken to get ideas for the fantasy sequences for *The Boyfriend* and Shirley for costumes. There was one called *Moonlight and Pretzels* with one scene of a long tap dance with ten chorus girls. The whole point about the chorus is that they dance together. Not here. One is always out of step. Even when you can tell it's a different set-up because the camera angle is different, there's this same girl out of step. It was hilarious. We kept playing it again and again. You just couldn't believe nobody had spotted it.

The costumes were always gorgeous. It was the height of the depression and films like this were just spinning a little web of dreams. In *Fashions of 1934* there is a huge gondola and all the girls rowing it are dressed in ostrich feathers. They used a wind machine and a thin sheet of velvet on the studio floor and it looked like water strewn with roses. There are literally thousands of ostrich feathers. There can't have been a fully covered ostrich left in the world.

I was still obsessed with clothes and whenever we went round to Ken and Shirley's I would always go up to look through her latest finds.

Her workroom was next to their bedroom but the clothes were all over the place. 'Look at this,' she'd say. 'I found them in a shop in Hemel Hempstead,' and pass me a whole box of cami-knickers. At the end of filming *The Boyfriend* she gave me a wonderful dress made in France around 1815 as a thank you. It's really a museum piece, exquisitely beautiful made of white voile muslin, hand embroidered with a train. I think it's finer than a similar one in the Victoria and Albert Museum's costume collection. Shirley thinks it may even have been worn by the Empress Josephine. I wore it at the premiere of *The Boyfriend* in Paris. Sadly it's too small for me now, but perfect for Carly.

Shirley had trained as a fashion designer but now she was a fully acknowledged costume designer and she and Ken always worked together. In Ken's films the look and the period details are always perfect, thanks to Shirley, and she always got her inspiration from the real thing if she could.

In those days you could still find fabulous things in street markets and second-hand shops. Shirley once found a Fortuni dress. I have never found anything so amazing, but I was a compulsive second-hand clothes browser even before I became a model. It was Louise, Justin's brother Tony's girlfriend, who started me off. Until I met her no one I knew would have dreamed of wearing somebody else's clothes, no matter how much they'd been washed or dry-cleaned. People didn't do that. A hangover from the Depression when to have to wear second-hand clothes was the ultimate humiliation. The first thing I got was a wonderful racoon coat. Dad bought it for me for £3 in Portobello Road. Long before I hit the headlines, I was photographed in it in the Kings Road in 1965, as an example of what London's young people were wearing. I even wore it for my interview with Deirdre McSharry, the journalist on the *Express* who kick started the whole crazy roller-coaster.

I'd never dream of wearing real fur now and I feel really guilty about having worn it in the early days. I am totally against anyone wearing fur coats. Fur should stay on the backs of the original owners, the animals themselves. My only excuse was my youth and ignorance of the facts. In those days green issues and animal rights generally weren't things anyone thought about. Over the past twenty years I have tried to make up for this callow disregard by helping to campaign with organisations such as Lynx, who had a huge impact in raising awareness both among designers and the buying public. Although they achieved so much, Lynx are sadly no more. Their role has been filled by PETA, People's Ethical Treatment of Animals, who are doing wonderful work and whose remit is much wider. But for the trade in animal skins to stop completely, the problem has to be addressed not just by charities but by the general public. Until wearing fur is seen for what it is, stupid vanity pure and simple, it's not going to stop. In this day and age with such wonderful fake furs there is just no excuse. I don't really believe in violence but if I see a woman in a fur coat, certainly in an exotic fur coat, it's all I can do not to hit her.

The Boyfriend was shot over the summer of 1970. MGM had finally agreed to Ken's package in mid-1969, by which time he was shooting *The Devils*, based on a play by John Whiting written in the sixties but about seventeenth-century nuns in France who believed they were possessed by devils. Lots of scope for manic debauchery. One day towards the end of shooting, Ken asked if we would like to visit the set. It was the perfect opportunity to see how he worked, he said; indeed how the whole thing worked. Then he had another idea. What about being extras? There was a big scene coming up. 'Nobody would know it was you.'

We would be credited as Nigel Davies and Lesley Hornby. Justin was all for it. Me less so, but as usual I went along with what he wanted. I was dressed as a male courtier, in a wonderful seventeenth-century costume, looking like Louis XIV. Justin looked outrageous in a silver wig and high-heeled shoes on wedges ten inches high, making him tower over me at six foot eight. Once I got on the set I was petrified, not to mention embarrassed. Though Ken was right. No one did recognise me. At that time I didn't know anything about the script, but it soon became apparent that this wasn't a BBC costume drama. And when Ken began rehearsing a scene where nuns start ripping their habits off, that was it. I declined to reappear. Justin of course stuck it out.

The delay in the start of shooting *The Boyfriend* was crucial. I had to learn to sing and dance from a standing start, doing in nine months what normally takes years. I began my dance lessons with Terry Gilbert, Ken's choreographer. For tap he sent me to Gillian Gregory at the Dance Centre in Covent Garden, because he wanted me to get used to dancing with other people. I was terrified because even though it was only a beginners' class these were mainly professional dancers just adding something new to their already considerable repertoire. And, as usual, I was very conscious of being me. There weren't many of us to start with, but as Christmas got nearer and word spread that *The Boyfriend* was up and running, the class mushroomed as every dancer in London wanted in.

I took to tap like a duck to water. Gill was wonderful and never lost her patience with me or any of the others. In the meantime Justin was determined to do his bit. It was right at the beginning of video and he had bought an incredibly expensive (and heavy) camera. He would stand there and film me, tap-tapping away back at the Charlotte Mews studio, routine after routine, then when I couldn't move another step we'd play it back supposedly to see where I was going wrong. For music we'd use the soundtracks from Fred and Ginger musicals which were available on record, which conveniently had all the taps in as well. A favourite one was The Piccolino from *Top Hat*.

At the same time Ken thought I should do a ballet class to get myself really fit. Being thin doesn't necessarily mean fit, and in my case it definitely didn't. I soon discovered I had muscles I didn't know existed. It took just one class to prove it. This was a one-to-one, but it was so tough that by the end I just couldn't move. Then I heard that Gill also did a ballet class, so I tried her. But she couldn't stand all my grunting and groaning. ('You're the noisiest pupil I've had in my class.') She suggested a jazz class instead, because it included ballet exercises as part of a warm-up routine which 'helped separate the different parts of the body'.

Half-way through my labours of Hercules, Christopher Gable, who Ken had cast as Tony, the Boyfriend himself, arrived. I knew Chris already; we had met round at 23 Ladbroke Gardens. He was one of Ken's stable, and after playing Eric Fenby, Delius's amanuensis, in *Song of Summer*, went on to be in *The Music Lovers* and *Women in Love*.

Ken and Chris were close friends. Until *Song of Summer* Chris was principal dancer at the Royal Ballet. It's hard to imagine it now but part of what makes Ken so extraordinary is that before he turned to directing he too had been a ballet dancer. Unlike Chris who had done it since he was a kid, Ken didn't start until he came out of the RAF where he'd done his national service. It was the film club projectionist at the RAF base where he was stationed who had turned him on to ballet. Boris had been a dancer and gave Ken the bug. After he left the

RAF Ken trained for three years, but starting at twenty-one he didn't have much of a chance. Although he did spend a year with the London Festival Ballet, from then on it was downhill. His swan song was in the chorus of *Annie Get Your Gun*, along with another unlikely dancer, Robert Carrier, who later discarded pirouettes for cooking pots.

And he's never forgotten it. Ken says dancing is like riding a bike. From time to time when we were shooting *The Boyfriend* he'd suddenly launch into a ballet routine on the set. It was mostly just to ease the tension I think. Ken was no longer the slender young dancer he once might have been and prancing around in the fell-walking plus-fours that were his usual outfit he looked like a deranged robin, a sight enough to diffuse the most difficult situation, and would always succeed in making us all laugh.

Although he was a brilliant ballet dancer, Chris had never done tap so he and I learned together. Luckily we got on really well. We just seemed to gel; great for the film, but it didn't suit Justin at all. For the first time since we'd met, there was something in my life he wasn't a part of. I'm not sure how useful the video business was, I now believe it was him trying to retain control. When he was behind that camera he became a real martinet. Telling me to do this, do that. It was the first time he'd ever been like that with me. Then in March Tommy Tune arrived, which was only going to make things worse.

In Chris and me Ken had his young lovers. But the original *Boyfriend* script had a young American, a slightly off-beat character. None of Ken's regulars fitted the bill except Murray Melvin; but he wasn't American, nor a dancer, and Ken had him earmarked for one of the other roles. Otherwise casting hadn't been a problem — Max Adrian, Glenda Jackson, Bryan Pringle, Brian Murphy, Vladek Sheybal, Georgina Hale; they had all worked with him before. One day Ken was wringing his hands when I suddenly remembered a dancer I'd seen on television on my last trip to the States, called Tommy Tune. Neither the name nor the guy was something you'd ever forget. I had been watching a half-hour musical variety show called *Dean Martin's Gold Diggers* when on to the screen came this extraordinary but wonderful-looking man with jet black shoulder-length hair, doing this amazing tap dance. I'd never seen anything like it. Quite different from Astaire or Kelly. At six foot six Tommy's body is as loose as a string puppet. His legs have a life of their own and because of them he's developed a style like nobody else. And that face and that smile. I was mesmerised. I remember watching till the end of the programme. I mean who is this person? And it came up 'performed and choreographed by Tommy Tune'. And then I put it out of my mind as you do. I just remember being knocked out. Now was my chance to put a bit of luck somebody else's way. Ken was interested. If there's a choice he'll always go for the extraordinary rather than the normal.

Because for years and years he had refused to fly, there was no way he would go out to see him. But by phoning around we managed to get some film sent over. As soon as he'd seen it Ken phoned me.

'Love him.'

Unbelievably Tommy Tune is his real name. He was born to Mr and Mrs Tune in Wichita Falls, Texas. Tommy is a real Texan and sounds like it. He tells the story of the phone ringing and him picking it up and an English voice saying, 'Hello, this is Ken Russell,' and Tommy thought it was a friend, a wind-up. Tommy had just seen *The Music Lovers* so he knew exactly who Ken was. 'I'm doing this film of *The Boyfriend* with Twiggy and we want you to play the American in it.' He still thought it was a wind-up.

Of course, Tommy was knocked sideways. He was a hoofer — and when did a hoofer in real life get a chance to 'go out there, kid, and come back a star'? He says he will never forget the first time he ever saw me. We were rehearsing in a British Legion hall somewhere around Hammersmith in west London. And as he walked in, I was in a backbend. I remember meeting him vividly. As I had seen him before on that TV show, I thought I knew what he looked like and I shouted out, 'Blimey, it's him.' But in real life he was so much more everything: a foot taller than me, and so skinny. We had that link too. Someone later wrote about our performance in *The Boyfriend*: 'Every movement of Tommy's marionette body is echoed in miniature and rounded detail. It's a lovely double-take.' We were soon like brother and sister. And a quarter of a century on, we are still very close.

I also had to have singing lessons with Peter Greenwell, the film's associate music director. At least I could read music, which helped. Just doing the numbers from *The Boyfriend* for nine months would have made me stale, or driven me mad, so we got all the sheet music we could of the twenties and thirties. I had always been able to sing in tune, but the lessons helped my breathing and pushed me four notes higher up the register.

For all his 'I knew it all along', Ken seemed to be impressed by how I was doing and Shirley told me later that he would come back and tell her that he was 'enchanted' at my voice. In the original script 'A Room In Bloomsbury' was my only solo. My other two numbers were duets with Chris Gable. Ken decided I was good enough to take on more, which was better than any praise and made all the hours I'd put in worthwhile. 'Exactly Like You' was one of the songs I had been practising on. It was originally sung by Ruth Etting, for me the greatest torch singer of all time. But sadly whoever owned the rights wanted too much money. Then MGM, whose picture it was, said we could pick something from the catalogue. As MGM dominated Hollywood musicals in the forties and fifties the list was amazing. In the end I did two: 'You Are My Lucky Star' and 'All I Do Is Dream of You', both from *Singing In The Rain*. But my favourite is 'Lucky Star', which in the film I do into the mirror. It's a really simple shot, but it has a lovely period feel and Ken did it beautifully.

In the spring, before shooting began, Ken wanted to take me through the new script he'd been writing holed up in the Lake District. Like the wonderful madman that he is, he'd said, 'Oh, don't let's meet in a boring office, let's have lunch in Brighton.' The real reason was so we could go on the Brighton Belle, this beautiful old steam train which was then under threat of closure, and soon afterwards it was axed. It was the English equivalent of the Orient Express — although the luxury and romance of the journey lasted not much more than an hour. Everything was painted brown and gold: there were no normal carriages, it was like one big dining car, and on the way down we started as we meant to go on with a proper English breakfast. It was a lovely day and I'd never been to Brighton so we did all the touristy things. First we wandered around the Lanes, window shopping for antiques, then we had lunch in a favourite fish restaurant of Ken and Shirley's called Englishes, very old fashioned with red plush seats. After lunch we strolled along the pier to have a look at the camera obscura and finally we did the Brighton Pavilion, the Prince Regent's rococo extravaganza which was so much more extraordinary than I'd ever imagined from photos.

By the time we got back to the station I was feeling a bit peckish. It was a good ten minutes before the train was due to leave. Shirley was buying a book so I asked Justin for a shilling to get a bar of chocolate from a slot machine. But there was something wrong with it. The tray only came half-way out. I tried putting my fingers behind it to get it out that way, but then one of the rings on my fingers got caught in the mechanism, so I called Justin who was still standing on the platform talking to Shirley, to get him to help.

By this time Ken was already in the train, leaning out of the window and telling me to hurry up. 'I can't. I'm stuck,' I shouted back. And I was. I couldn't get my hand out. At first he didn't believe me. Then looking pretty cross he came out. But the drawer was completely jammed. No matter how they tugged and pulled nothing happened. By now there was smoke coming out of Ken's ears. The thought of missing his return dinner on the Brighton Belle had made him apoplectic. All I could do was say pathetically, 'I'm sorry.' At first it was hard not to laugh and I had to be careful not to catch Shirley's eye. But as time went on my sense of humour went AWOL. Ken was beside himself. Inevitably a crowd was gathering with people saying everything from 'It's *Candid Camera*' to 'Somebody call an ambulance.' Then one little old lady in the front shouted 'What she needs is a bar of soap.' Shirley finally found the woman with the keys but even they didn't work. Eventually, after being jammed for one and a half hours, a porter with a crowbar had to wrench it open. But the Brighton Belle had long gone. We had pleaded with the guard to hold the train, but it was no use. It had chuffed out of the station and our special dinner with it. The next train to London was a stopping train with not even a buffet. The atmosphere was awful. Nobody dared speak. It was only when we were nearly half-way back to London that I plucked up the courage to ask, 'Anyone want any chocolate?' I cannot repeat what Ken told me to do with my bar of Dairy Milk.

The Boyfriend took eighteen weeks to film, split between Dad's old studios in Elstree and location in Portsmouth where Ken had discovered an old theatre that was waiting to be demolished. I'll never forget the first day of shooting. It was the first time I'd ever had to speak words that weren't my own. And it was truly terrifying. Here I was with all these proper actors and I was so scared I just remember thinking this is insanity. Nothing I'd done before had prepared me for it. The only thing I was comfortable with was the camera. I just had to put my trust in Ken.

Thank God my first day was with the lovely Max Adrian. The film script takes the form of a play within a play. Just like those old Hollywood musicals: the life backstage runs parallel with what's happening out front. It helped that this was a real old theatre. My character Polly (Polly Browne in the show) is sweeping the stage and I look through the curtain and I say 'Blimey, there's more on the stage than there are in the bloomin' audience.'

And I survived. More than that, I blossomed. Everyone was so helpful, especially Georgina Hale and Max and lovely Murray Melvin, and of course the girls in the chorus, who had to put up with a lot. I adored them all.

Only one person was horrid to me. I overheard him saying — loud enough for him to know I could hear — 'how do you expect me to act with that 'thing'. She's not trained.' I was so shocked. The only other time something similar happened was when I was in Los Angeles during the time of madness. I visited a film set and everyone was doing the usual chant of 'Twiggy, Twiggy', when suddenly this lone, very English theatrical voice resonated at the back. 'Twiggy Go Home.' It was the wonderful comedy actor Lionel Jeffries. Afterwards he apologised and said he only said it as a joke. Apparently during the war in England they used to say 'Yanks Go Home'. Now I would understand but at the time it really stung and I left the set in tears.

For me making *The Boyfriend* was a very happy time, particularly the six weeks we spent in Portsmouth. Chris, Tommy and I became inseparable. We called ourselves the Three Musketeers. Our favourite hangout was the Chinese restaurant round the corner because the hotel food was pretty terrible. Films don't always have big budgets and *The Boyfriend* was made on a shoestring. Directors don't usually join the actors after the day's shoot. They've got their next day's shots to sort out and rushes to see (the unedited film that's been shot that day, what the Americans call 'dailies'). Ken was no different, though like many directors he didn't allow actors to see the rushes. He used to, but some time before he'd done a film and this actress had been wonderful the first week, then went downhill. He didn't know why. Towards the end of the film they were having a drink and she said, 'I was so glad you let me see the rushes because after the first week, I realised I was playing it wrong and I was able to change.' He says he could have shot himself. I don't know if it's the same now, but from that day on he never let any of the actors see the rushes.

It was Tommy's first time in England and he adored it. The three of us must have looked hysterical: Tommy six foor six; Christopher looking like a Greek god, with his hair bleach-blond and curled for the part; and me, this funny-looking thing.

Dancing is a stressful business and there can be a lot of jealousy. But not with Tommy. He was as un-prima-donna-ish as real talent can be. Shirley had such fun exaggerating his height, doing all those things you're not meant to do if you're tall, giving him very narrow, vertical striped trousers and clingy tights when he was dressed as an elf and really high-heeled shoes. She made him this amazing skyscraper hat. Not everything was exactly in period. After all, as Shirley said, what was the period and what was the point? She was quite happy to 'monkey about'. Most of it was twenties but there was one dress that Shirley found, a beautiful satin cross-cut slipper dress that was more thirties, more Fred and Ginger. It fitted me like a glove so I had to wear it.

Poor Shirley's wardrobe room was right at the top of the theatre. I don't think anyone can have been up there in years. It was full of cobwebs and dust and if a costume fell on the ground it was a nightmare. The clothes we wore 'on stage' and in the film fantasy sequences were all made by wardrobe. But the clothes we wore as our backstage characters were as much as possible originals put together from Shirley's finds, like my golfing jumper, which she'd bought somewhere for 3/6d (17p), a wonderful long lined cotton jumper with zigzags in pink, mauve and black, in incredibly good condition. Shirley had found it years before *The Boyfriend* was ever on the cards.

Not that everything was sweetness and light. It never is on a film set. Frustrations in front of the camera get taken out somewhere else. The first thing that happened was that the choreographer left. I'd spent nine months learning to tap and now everything seemed to be ballet. It was all right for Christopher, of course, but even he saw it wouldn't work for Tommy and me. The trouble was that the choreographer was a ballet choreographer. Wonderful in his own field, but not right for this.

Justin had managed to get himself billing as Associate Producer. I don't know what it was that finally tipped Ken over the edge about Justin. Justin didn't tell me and I wasn't privy to all their rows, although I used to catch snippets from Ken. But he couldn't take Justin's continual interfering. For four years Justin had got used to telling photographers, and everyone who came anywhere near me, 'do this' and 'don't do that' and he still saw himself as the puppet-master, making all my decisions. Already by now I was beginning to feel a resentment. And Ken, quite rightly, was having none of it. It wasn't long before Justin was banned from the set.

10

Manipulative he may have been, but I think in his own way Justin really did love me and there is no doubt his possessiveness did in certain ways protect me. I was such an innocent, if he hadn't been around, who knows what might have happened. Everyone knows about photographers and models and it could so easily have gone terribly wrong. The wrong photographer, the wrong crowd. One model I met a few times died of an overdose not long after I stopped modelling. The pressures to stay at the top once you've got there are horrendous. I could easily have been led down the wrong road. There were a lot of unscrupulous people around at the time. I never came into contact with drugs. Asthma had put an end to Justin's dope-smoking days, and by the time I met him he didn't even smoke cigarettes. Though I did. (How I regret it now) Gitanes. I loved the smell of them and I thought I looked ever so sophisticated. Justin only drank champagne. A taste he shared with Mr Russell.

As a result I was never part of Italian film-maker Antonioni's *Blow Up* school of modelling. No orgies, no drugs, very few clubs and parties. I hated being recognised, hated being stared at. And I was, the whole time. Always on show. The only people I felt comfortable with were friends, people who knew me. That's largely still true today. I hated large parties even then and still do. Some people treat you like you are public property. Once in the early days we were invited to a society party. When we arrived the hostess took me by the arm. 'Twiggy, I want you to stand here by the fireplace so all my friends can see that you really do wear your skirts that short.' It made me feel like a performing monkey. Needless to say we left.

Long term, Dad was probably right to insist Justin looked after me. But he made me too dependent on him. He never let me do anything by myself. Not a shoot. Certainly not an interview. And because I was so young he led me to believe that if he wasn't there something awful was going to happen. He was like a policeman, a one-man protection racket. Without my even being aware of it I was being suffocated, stunted even. I had no chance of finding my own feet, of learning to cope on my own. On that level I was as young as I looked. About twelve. It wasn't until working on *The Boyfriend* that I began to think there was anything unusual in this arrangement.

There's always this feeling of euphoria about the first day of shooting, a psychological punching of the air as if to say 'We've Done It'. Of course it's just a mirage. So many things can go wrong on a film set and if they can, they will. My first run-in with Ken Russell was over my hair. I'd been growing it ever since the summer of 1967, so by the summer of 1970 it was wonderfully long. I'd had it trimmed but it still reached half-way down my back.

How I loved it. Short hair is all very well but there's no versatility. Now I could play with it for hours, put it up, curl it, leave it hanging straight down. Ken didn't understand. 'Get it cut,' he said. During rehearsals I started parting it in the middle and plaiting it into earphones which Shirley said she thought I might just get away with for period.

'Get it cut.'

What about a wig?

'Don't be silly. It's only hair.'

And of course he was right. I said I'd do it, as long as it wasn't layer cut, because it's easier to grow from one length. There was nothing to do but call in Leonard. More problems. Shirley had organised Vidal Sassoon to do everyone's hair. He was better with period cuts, she said. All his geometric cuts were based on the twenties. So down came Vidal's right-hand man, Roger, and chopped mine all off along with everyone else's. But the next day I crept back to Leonard who spent three hours reshaping it. Roger was certainly a good hairdresser, but Leonard knew my hair and my head much better. He'd been doing it long enough. But it wasn't just loyalty that made me stick to him. Now that I wasn't actively modelling, we had been looking at other projects and one of these was a joint venture with Leonard, a salon called Leonard and Twiggy which had just opened in Sloane Street. If it got out that arch rival Vidal Sassoon was cutting my hair it wouldn't do the new salon any good at all. Anyway, I felt comfortable with Leonard and I trusted him. In the end Leonard cut mine and

Daniel Galvin, the brilliant colourist who did my hair on that first fateful visit to Leonards came down every few weeks to do my colour. Although I agreed that cutting it was right for the role, I still had this obsesssion with my hair being long. The day shooting ended I started growing it again.

* * *

Justin still saw himself as the final arbiter of what I did or didn't do. In the script Tommy does a dance in this big racoon fur coat. On the final cut he turns his back to camera and it zooms in then pulls back to reveal a fur rug (a grander version of the moth-eaten old tiger skin that used to skid over the kitchen floor at 23 Ladbroke Square) with girls lying on it in little satin teddies and nylons and all a bit saucy, like Mr Russell likes. And Ken wanted me to be one of them. Justin said No. Whether I would have done it if Ken had asked me himself, I don't know. But Justin had already told him that I wouldn't and that it wasn't my image and when Shirley handed me a pair of little round John Lennon glasses to wear at the beginning of the film, I was really upset. I thought they made me look dreadful. I hadn't realised that was the whole point. They were only there as another of Ken's film in-jokes, to be pulled off in true Hollywood 'Take off your glasses Miss Jones' style when Tony discovers how beautiful Polly really is. What's even funnier is that I really got to like the look of those glasses and soon took to wearing them in real life.

The only major row I had with Ken was when he told me he wanted to put my face on the centre of a spinning record for one of the Busby Berkeley routines. 'Only if they organise a special shoot,' Justin said. With him naturally taking the portrait. He wasn't going to have some crap set photographer taking the picture, he said. So that's what I relayed to Ken. Sensing that this might not go down very well I had another idea. 'Can't we just use a still of the film?' I remember him going absolutely berserk. Whether at me or because it was Justin interfering I don't know. I left the set crying and went back to the hotel. I just lay on my bed and howled. Then the phone rang. Ken. And not saying sorry. He was so furious he couldn't get his words out straight. He just kept shouting at me down the phone. He was incoherent and I was hysterical. I can't remember now what happened with that bloody picture but the next day, he was fine. He even came to the hotel to apologise. But I felt terrible. I felt that I'd been naughty and I'd let him down. And over what? A bloody photograph, that Justin insisted he shoot.

Justin couldn't be there all the time in any case. There was the office in London to run, other projects to push on like the restaurant we hoped to get Erté to design. But like so many other things it never got off the ground. And by then Justin was trying to build up a stable of other people to manage.

At the beginning when he did come to the

location in Portsmouth he was always chipping in. After Ken banned him from the set he only came down at weekends. And when he left on Sunday night I remember the wonderful, if guilty, sigh of relief. The truth was I had a much better time when he wasn't there. I know now that it can happen with any film or theatre company and can be disastrous for relationships. If you're in a relationship that you care about you have to be so careful. Because you do become like a family and it takes over your whole life. When Leigh was doing Oberon in *A Midsummer Night's Dream* for the Royal Shakespeare Company in 1996 he walked around our flat rehearsing incessantly, talking in rhyming couplets. If you are a happy married couple — a couple that want to be a couple and come through — then you have to allow the person who's doing the work to drift into that world for a while. You have to allow it. Even if you do feel excluded you mustn't let it get to you. It only becomes dangerous if it goes into the next phase. Leigh and I are both very aware of the dangers. And if you stay aware, then that's the best you can do.

Romance can be a problem and affairs with on-screen/on-stage partners do happen. You're working with your emotions, so it's a risk. Justin was never jealous that way of Tommy, although we became as close as you can become with somebody without having a sexual involvement. He was like the brother I never had. Tommy wasn't a threat and I think Justin knew it. But Christopher was a different matter. Ken adored him and I adored him. It was no more than that. Our relationship was completely innocent. But for Justin that was irrelevant. It was just part of the power struggle. The battle of wills.

Adding to Justin's antagonism toward Chris was the fact that he'd been cast in the first place. Justin had wanted David Essex. This was when David was just a tousle-haired pop singer, long before *Godspell* or *Stardust*, before he had done any acting at all in fact. David had been tipped the wink by Terry Gilbert, the choreographer, who'd suggested he came along and learn to tap. He did the classes for three months. When it came to the audition, which Ken conducted in his traditional fur coat, David was only half-way through his number when Ken called out the equally traditional 'Thank you. Next.' When Justin asked what was wrong with him, Ken said, 'Not enough experience.' In his role as associate producer Justin thought he had a right to some say in the casting. It turned out well for David, however. A few months later he scored a big success in *Godspell*.

With hindsight I find Justin's jealousy of Chris particularly rich: I later discovered that while I was working my butt off in Portsmouth, he was carrying on with two different females, one in London and one in the country, a conveniently situated pit-stop half-way down to Portsmouth. But whatever lay behind Justin's gripe, Tommy, Christopher and I were really really close and he didn't like that. I suppose he saw the beginning of the split, though I don't think at that time I was aware of it. He was my manager and he looked after my life and I was fond of him; although I'd known in my heart for some time that I was no longer in love with him. The reason, I suppose, that I refused his offer of marriage so many times. Also I found myself wondering about the money side of things. Why wasn't he investing? Why wasn't he looking after me in this way? Questions I should have been asking myself a long time ago. I suppose I was growing up.

Anyway, cut, mix, dissolve. Back in Portsmouth there were the usual high jinks that happen on location. One little scandal was a fight that broke out involving Barbara Windsor, who played Hortense, the French maid. There were all sorts of rumours about how it started, that someone punched Barbara and Barbara punched back. Or vice versa. It involved another girl in the cast and one of the boys. All hell broke loose. It got hushed up of course. The press never got wind of it. I just remember being amazed that things like this happened. And I have to say that night it was terribly exciting. Running in and out of everyone's room to find out who'd hit who with what, where and why was a big buzz. High jinks on a film set. Such fun. Although twenty isn't that young, I'd led this funny cosseted life. Those years from fifteen to twenty are incredibly important. Going out with different boys. All the things you do at college. And I missed all that. Both the joy and the pain. I was this thing on a pedestal.

The fantasy scenes were all shot in Elstree. Being back in London was a real downer. No more jolly evenings in the Peking Duck, or whatever it was called. Every evening after the wrap the Three Musketeers would go their separate ways. The off-screen dramas continued as usual. The worst, or best in terms of black comedy, was to do with the plane, which was a direct lift from the first ever Astaire/Rogers musical *Flying Down To Rio*, where all these girls appear to be tap-dancing on the wings. It was originally choreographed by Hermes Pan, who I later got to meet.

Obviously the plane wasn't real but a wooden mock-up, and the night before the shoot Ken tells the scene painters he wants them to paint it silver overnight. The next day he arrives to find it painted all right. But white. They couldn't find any silver paint on the lot, the gaffer explains, so he thought white would do. Ken's face nearly explodes.

'Do you know who I fucking well am? I'm the fucking director of this fucking picture. Send a man out now and get some tins of silver paint.'

The poor guy came back later that day with a van full of tiny egg-cup sized pots of silver paint. All he could find in the whole of London.

I didn't have to go on the plane, which is just as well. In those days you couldn't fudge things on computer like you can today. Because it had to look as if they were really flying it was strung up really high, about forty feet I should say, and all the girls who had to get on it felt terribly seasick: they couldn't have fallen off because their seventies-cum-twenties boots were attached to the wings but, because they were strapped into them and were supposed to sway about, the boots really cut into their ankles. But it was nearly mutiny that day. The things we do for art.

One thing I had insisted on from the beginning was 'putting in the taps'. I hadn't realised until I started watching musicals that the noise of the taps are put in later. It wasn't always like that. The taps in the early musicals weren't nearly as pronounced. Philip explained it was an invention of Fred Astaire's, although Gene Kelly always claimed it was his. After the film was in the can, Fred would dub in the taps, in the same way that you dub dialogue, using special shoes with solid silver taps on a paving stone which the crew would bring in and set up in front of a mike, while a rough cut was screened in front of him. And he'd do it all over again — and again, and again, and again until it was right. He must have been impossible to work for. Such a perfectionist. Even when he wasn't working he would do two hours tap dancing every day. Anyway, I had seen for myself how much better it was with the taps added. I was determined to do the same. And I did. Just the same way, although the taps on my shoes weren't silver.

Once the film was over, Justin immediately took control of his asset again. Because of the continuing row between Justin and Ken, we didn't go to the press preview or the final party at Claridges, a really great sadness to me. I adored Ken and Shirley and the whole cast who'd been so wonderful to me. I should have been there. The final party of a film — and this was my first ever film — is such a major thing. It didn't just spoil it for me but for everyone else as well. If he didn't want to go, fair enough. But to forbid me to go was completely unfair. I should have broken it off then. But somehow I just didn't have the courage. He kept insinuating that there were dark secrets that I didn't know about. The row with Ken ended in time for the Royal Premiere. But only at the eleventh hour. Ken and Shirley just turned up the night before at Charlotte Mews and it was kiss and make up and the next night we all went to the premiere together in a wonderful white Rolls Royce Phantom. Though it was never the same. Something had gone for ever.

This was the first time I had done a royal line-up, but by no means the last. The person who enjoyed it most was, of course, my Mum. And to have Mum, Dad, Vivien and Shirley there was just wonderful. Princess Anne had obviously done her homework and in the interval we talked about my dancing lessons. Everyone else was drinking champagne. Both she and I stuck to Coke. She was a great improvement on her aunt Margaret who I once found myself sitting next to at a dinner party given by The Marquis of Dufferin and Ava. For the first half of the meal Princess Margaret completely ignored me and then when she'd got bored talking with her other neighbour, she finally turned to me and said, 'And what's your name?' She must have been the only person in the country who didn't know. At that time I must have had one of the most famous names and most recognisable faces on the planet. 'Well Ma'am,' I said, smiling sweetly, 'My real name is Lesley Hornby but most people call me Twiggy.' Her Royal Highness took a long drag on her Nth cigarette of the evening, puffed a long column of smoke out and said 'How unfortunate' and turned away.

The London premiere was not the first time I'd seen the film. I'd been to a screening, which was just misery. Not having seen the rushes I had no idea what to expect and felt sick with nerves. Nothing I had done before had prepared me for this. It was mainly for the cast and because the jokes were all so familiar and we were all so terrified, each watching our own performance, we sat there in the dark like a row of tombstones. No one was laughing. Not even me. And it was supposed to be funny. I was convinced it was a dud. A flop. A bomb, as they say in Tinseltown. Which just goes to show what I knew. The full charity premiere audience told a different story. I was sitting just in front of Princess Anne and a line of mine about having Shippam's Paste (a fish sandwich spread) at the Palace had her laughing along with everybody else. The relief.

The notices were generally good. Alexander Walker, who generally hated everything that had Ken Russell's name on it, said I was 'actually surprisingly good. Her determination to succeed matches the role so touchingly, that you find yourself getting warmly protective of her and longing to take her hand and guide her through the traffic that's thundering down Ken Russell's 42nd Street.' Which was nice. It showed too that he had spotted Ken's main source of inspiration, although not all reviewers did. Glenda Jackson as the star who sprains her ankle (pure *42nd Street*) was Bebe Daniels, not Rita Hayworth, as some newspaper had it. Even her dialogue was word for word. But then Ken was perfectly happy for people to see what came from where. It was 'homage', not plagiarism. The *Times* described *The Boyfriend* as 'Twiggy's metamorphosis from a giggling, gawky girl of 1966 into a capable, talented actress.' So the caterpillar had finally made it into a butterfly. Though to counter this, Donald Zec, the *Daily Mirror's* critic, described me as 'thin as a well-picked frog's leg, flat enough to post through her own front letter box'. Don't call us, we'll call you.

Next stop America. In true US style, *Time* Magazine gave me a three-page splash. *Newsweek* said I was 'an overnight success . . . when Twiggy sings 'I Could Be Happy With You', tears of unrequited love streaming down her cheeks, she touches our hearts, a precinct that parody can never reach.'

My own heart was in a right old tizz. The perpetual flutter of excitement when you first fall in love. But not for a man. For the life. There hadn't been a road-to-Damascus moment of revelation, but it was just a feeling inside me that had been growing and must have started about mid-shoot. I remember telling Justin, 'This is what I want to do.' Yet when I think how easy it would have been to chicken out . . . To not do it . . . Perhaps it just shows my lack of knowledge about what could happen. Doing *The Boyfriend* was like walking the plank blindfold. Imagine how easy it would have been to fail. Yet I honestly don't think it ever occurred to me that anything could go wrong. It wasn't a question of being brave. I was like a child in the hands of her father. I trusted Ken implicitly.

I loved working on the film more than anything else I had ever done. It was like finding a door into a magic garden that you feel you knew was there all along. Now all I wanted to do was learn. I wanted to go to dance classes, go to singing lessons. I wanted to act. What I did not want to do was to go back into modelling. I wanted to get other acting parts. I just wanted to do it. I also knew it was going to be a huge thing for them to accept me. From what had happened on the set of *The Boyfriend* with Mr Horrid, I was only too aware of the stigma of being a model. And I knew that if I tried to do both, carry on with modelling and trying to act, it wouldn't work. There was still the huge prejudice that models were pretty but stupid and I was blonde to boot. And you know what they say about blondes. I must have known I had to make a decision. But in the end, like most really important things, it wasn't a hard decision to make. It was like being let into a toy factory. Besides which my heart and inner self knew it was right. Going with your instincts is something that grows stronger as you get older, but it's something I've always done. I've learnt that first impressions are usually right.

As for me and Justin, *The Boyfriend* had been

a weaning-off period. Suddenly he wasn't there every day. I had learned that I could survive without him. Now I was back I could feel the claustrophobia. I was like a canary in a gilded cage. Until the cage was taken away I didn't even know I hadn't been free. It wasn't that he'd been cruel. Just that I'd allowed myself to be manipulated by him. We were still physically together but emotionally I wasn't and that made me feel guilty.

I was looking for the out really.

In the meantime it was promo time and California. All the usual razzmatazz. All the usual suspects. At one dinner I was sitting next to Barbra Streisand and was wearing a lovely Alice Pollock mid-calf bias-cut dress in flesh-coloured satin with little cap sleeves and lace panels down the front. 'What a pretty dress,' she said. 'Is it your nightie?' Her next question was equally diplomatic. 'You were wonderful in *The Boyfriend*. Were you dubbed?' But I liked her anyway.

But the best question of that trip was the usual greenhorn-comes-to-Hollywood 'who would you like to meet?' This time there was no hesitation. Fred Astaire. There's always been this thing about Astaire versus Kelly. But although Gene Kelly was equally as talented as a tap dancer, for me Astaire will always have the edge. It's the style. Fred Astaire is the epitome of the word. Everything he did was so right. Even down to the way he used to tie belts around his trousers. He was so innovative. And as for his professionalism, he did most of those dances in one take. They'd just set up the camera and off he'd go. Complete magic.

We were at MGM, home of Hollywood musicals. It's now Columbia TriStar but the original buildings are still there, from the old Colonial-style offices and the sound stages behind, to all these strange little bungalows without windows dotted around where all the greats had waited for their calls, from Clark Gable to Judy Garland, and of course Fred Astaire in *Band Wagon* and *Funny Face* during the Arthur Freed era. It was all very exciting for me. Although I'd done this film, and even done it for MGM, it had all been shot in England, so I hadn't actually been to the big studios.

As soon as I said I'd like to meet Fred Astaire, the publicity guy's face fell. He'd been hoping I'd want to meet some hunk who they could have done a whole publicity thing with. 'That's a bit difficult,' the PR guy sighed. 'Because Mr Astaire is retired now and he's a very private person.' I wouldn't have dreamed of disturbing his privacy. But they'd asked me who I'd like most to meet and he was genuinely the only one. So that was that and we left to go back to the hotel.

Later that evening the phone rings. The publicity guy again. He has 'a really great surprise'. It turns out there had been an older lady in the office who'd overheard the whole thing. She had been working at MGM in the fifties with the Freed unit and after we left she'd called Fred herself. The result? 'Mr Astaire would like you to come to tea.'

The house was on San Ysidro Drive, a beautiful thirties mansion, not overly big as some of them (most of them) are. The butler let us in and Ava, Fred's daughter introduced herself. ('Lovely to see you, Daddy's just coming.') And then I heard a step outside the door and the door opened and I swear my heart stopped as Fred Astaire himself walked across the room. That wonderful walk, that famous walk — and it is a great walk. And he looked wonderful. He was wearing a grey flannel suit, a pale blue Oxford shirt with a gold collar pin, a faded pink knitted tie and the palest of suede shoes. So often when you meet people — heroes — it can spoil everything. You build it up in your mind into something that can never be, but he was just so charming, very softly spoken and modest — just like he is in all those films that had become my Bible. What do you say to someone like that? In fact he was very easy and we were soon chatting away. Later I heard from Ava that he had phoned her that morning and begged her to come over for 'moral support' as he was 'going to meet Twiggy'. 'I'm terrified to meet her on my own.' He couldn't have been as terrified as me. The whole afternoon was a delight. It's a dream to meet somebody you adore and to find they are just as adorable as you had hoped. Although there was a butler-type person around, Fred would never have dreamed of not doing the things a gentleman should do for a lady; opening the door, standing up when she comes into the room, taking her arm. We've lost a lot of that. It's become the fashion for some women to snub men who show them this kind of courtesy. More fool them I say. One of the reasons I fell in love with Leigh was that he's like that. A complete gentleman.

The next time Fred and I met up was about a year later. By this time he had seen *The Boyfriend* which he admitted he wasn't thrilled by. But he was very kind about me and my dancing. We had rung to suggest dinner. And he said he'd love to, and would it be all right if Hermes Pan joined us. 'He says he'd love to meet you.' I couldn't believe it. Hermes Pan is one of the great choreographers of all time. And divine, so funny and so sweet. He was about ten years younger than Fred but seeing them together was bizarre. They looked so alike, they walked alike, they talked alike. They did all those great musicals together so of course it was only to be expected.

We had gone up to the house on San Ysidro Drive for drinks beforehand. When it's time to leave for the restaurant he says we'll all go in his car. And we all pile into the Rolls Royce. He explains that as his chauffeur had died the year before he'd be driving us himself. It was a terribly sad story; this man had been with Fred for forty-four years and because he was like one of the family Fred couldn't bring himself to replace him. So Fred's sitting in the front and we can only talk through the funny old intercom and as we pull away Hermes tells us that to his knowledge this is the first time Fred has driven on a real road (not a film set) for forty years.

'We'll be all right,' Hermes said cheerfully.

'It's an automatic.' So it was a bit stop-and-start as we made our way down the hill into Beverley Hills and to the restaurant in Rodeo Drive.

The food was Polynesian, which was then very fashionable. There's a typical drink called a Maitai, which is basically rum and pineapple juice which you drink out of a hollowed out pineapple, and it comes with all the paraphernalia, little paper umbrellas and things. It's the sort of drink you see in holiday brochures. Anyway, it seemed very glamorous and fun to little me. 'Ooh, I want one of those,' I squeaked when a tray of them went by. So Fred said, 'OK, I'll have one too.' So we all did. Although I stuck at just the one, the guys didn't. These things are quite strong and you've got to be careful. And it turned out Fred wasn't usually a drinker.

By the time we leave everyone's very jolly. Not drunk. Just very happy, and he's parked a few blocks down and when we leave the restaurant and we're walking down Rodeo Drive, Fred Astaire starts to dance.

It's the only time in my life that I wished I'd had a secret video or film camera. He was humming some tune as he did this little tap dance, ending with a double pirouette, landed on his knees, put his hands out to the skies and said 'Hollywood I love you' and it was just magical. At that time he hadn't danced for quite a few years. He was just doing straight roles and in fact he had point blank refused ever to dance again. So to actually see those twinkling feet in action was one of the most extraordinary experiences of my life. He wasn't drunk but the rum had obviously loosened him up and he was feeling good. We all were. When we got back to the car we were all giggling and laughing and I said, 'Can you imagine somebody driving down Rodeo Drive and saying, 'Do you know, that looks like Fred Astaire dancing down the street. No. It can't be.' '

The saddest thing was that he couldn't come to see me on Broadway. It was ten years on, in 1983, and he was too ill. Of course we invited him. But he sent us a lovely note. It's a shame because I think he would have loved it. The finale was a tribute to him. Mind you I think Tommy would have had a blue fit knowing he was out front. It was bad enough doing it in front of Ginger Rogers, which we did. But Fred Astaire, now that would have been scary. I think our feet would have gone rigid. Hearing that voice. 'Work, get those taps. Every beat.'

I stayed in touch with Fred over the years that were left to him; and Ava and I did too. She was about six years older than me. She had a rare skin complaint which meant she couldn't take the sun, so during the California summer she would live in London. Later she and her husband moved to the west of Ireland. Sadly when Leigh and I went there a couple of years ago they were away. But I can quite see the appeal of living in that country. It was my first time to the west of Ireland and I was completely captivated. It reminded us both of how life used to be, the pace, the warmth of the people.

Ava is a really nice lady. When we opened

in *My One and Only*, she gave Tommy one of Fred's old shirts, which was amazing for him. I thought he was going to faint. And she gave me the most beautiful hand mirror that Fred's sister Adele had left her when she died. True to form I burst into tears. 'You can't give me this,' I said. But she insisted. It is completely beautiful; silver, twenties, and one Adele had obviously had before she married, when she was still dancing, because the initials on the back are AA. Adele had been Fred's first partner but she gave it all up when she married into the English aristocracy. Ava says Adele was quite a girl and very funny and would embroider naughty cushion covers in her castle in Ireland. I didn't only have it with me to bring me luck. It is the perfect dressing room mirror. And I used it every night to make up.

When people say to me, 'what was it like living through that amazing time?' the truth is that when it's happening to you, you don't think, God this is amazing. It's only in hindsight. But Fred Astaire was different. Every moment I was with him I was always aware that he was one of the most extraordinary people I would ever meet in my life. I was sad when he died. But he lived a really great life and left a legacy that will live as long as there is music and people to dance.

11

Justin wanted the same role in my film career as he had with my modelling. But the film world is a big boys' playground. The games he had played with photographers and magazine editors cut no ice in Hollywood. I remember in one interview we did at the time he was quoted as saying: 'Modelling is hateful to us now.' That royal 'we' says it all. In any career there are times when you're hot and times when you're not. After *The Boyfriend* I was hot. Over the next few months quite a lot of offers came through. But Justin wanted to be in there. He wanted to be the producer. But they didn't want him as producer. Quite understandably. A svengali? I don't think so.

I can remember knowing that it wasn't right but not knowing how to cope with it or deal with it. I can remember that feeling I had then, a deep discontent. I had to split and I didn't know how to do it because I didn't want to hurt him, I was still fond of him and we'd been through a lot together. All those things you go through when you know that you want to get out of a relationship, but can't see how. It was doubly complicated for me. He wasn't just a boyfriend, he was my manager. He made sure he ran every aspect of my life.

In the meantime Tommy and I were already planning something of our own. In 1973 the sixties were finally over. Reality had set in with the oil crisis and three-day working week in Britain. Escapist entertainment always thrives in times of economic gloom and we thought a Fred and Ginger kind of thing would have a real chance. Tommy's partner, a man called Michel Stuart (pronounced Michael), came over from New York and together we worked at developing a storyline and routines which were right for us. It would be set on an ocean liner, as so many of them were, and our working title was 'Gotta Sing, Gotta Dance', after the Gene Kelly song in *Singing in The Rain*. But we didn't know what we were doing. We thought we could do it on our own, but we couldn't. And, of course, Justin was right in there, both in terms of the script and trying unsuccessfully to raise the money.

If I hadn't been so committed to Tommy, perhaps I might have plucked up the courage and just taken one of the film offers and run. But I wimped out. I thought, *I can't put the spanner in the works now*. So we just went into heavy rehearsal. And that's when I learnt to tap properly, an intensive year of working with Tommy Tune, the best teacher in the world, so I can't say I regret it. If I hadn't done that, would Tommy have had enough confidence in my ability to take on something as huge as Broadway with me? I don't think so. So we hired a studio and a pianist, and three times a week for nearly a year we worked till our toes bled. Or mine anyway. Tommy's were made of steel. But again I didn't know just how hard it would be. One swallow does not a summer make; one film does not an actress make.

We needed to raise three and a half million pounds. And we really thought we could do it. Tommy and Twiggy were a great combination, weren't they? All sorts of big name people seemed to agree. Or said they did. Justin happily went around saying that Paul McCartney was doing the title music, that Ferdinando Scarfiotti, art director on Visconti's *Death in Venice*, the surprise hit of the year, was to design it. In the full blaze of publicity he even flew to LA in a misguided attempt to try and interest Buck Henry, after *Catch 22* the hottest writer in Hollywood, to do the screenplay.

Justin's version of events was fuelled by an imagination that increasingly seemed unrelated to reality. In an interview in *Vogue* in 1971, he told Polly Devlin 'I want her to play Joan of Arc. I see a huge array behind her, banners flying, like a medieval Renaissance painting, Twiggy with a sort of medieval pre-Raphaelite look, all in black and white and with really heavy rock music.' Then I chip in.

'I think it sounds awful. I want to play Tess of the D'Urbervilles.'

At least I was beginning to find my own voice.

'Now the balance has shifted,' Polly Devlin wrote, 'and Twiggy is the strongest figure in the partnership, the surest, very cool and together, while Justin, slightly out of breath, hurries along.'

The time away from Justin had given me the distance needed to see him as others saw him.

In that interview you can hear him pushing the self-destruct button. Justin is quoted as saying:

'I knew I would be a success. I didn't know how or when but I had this instinct. Like I know I'll direct a film one day. I don't think I'm that clever, but I know it will be good. It's a matter of having common sense and taste. And I know I have taste and think I have got common sense. I'm very down to earth, but one thing that makes me nervous is that I have become used to luxury. I feel I can't exist without it. I'd be devastated if I found myself penniless. Oh, I'd survive but I like being able to do what I want to do.'

It was the actor Jeremy Brett, who I'd met during his season at the Old Vic, who had given me Thomas Hardy's *Tess of the D'Urbervilles* to read. I think he had just done it on the radio. 'You should play this,' he said. Once I started to read Tess I literally couldn't put it down until I'd finished it. It is the most wonderful story and I was completely devastated by what happened to her. Tess starts out with the best of intentions and is honest and true and in the end is destroyed by the actions of the two men who claim to love her. Jeremy was quite right. I was twenty-two and it was perfect casting.

I immediately gave it to Ken. It turned out to be one of Shirley's favourites. Once again the rights were tied up. David O. Selznick had them from way back when he had planned to film it with Jennifer Jones and Joseph Cotton. Never done. But in six years it would be in the public domain. At that time copyright ended fifty years after the death of the author, which was 1928. 'We've got to just wait it out,' Ken said. So we waited and waited but the very day copyright ceased, it was announced that Roman Polanski's *Tess* was already in production. It nearly broke my heart. For all those six years I never gave up hope. It was my passion. I couldn't bring myself to see it for ages, I was just so distressed it had been done and that it wasn't me. In the end I just had to steel myself. I went ready to hate it but I loved it. I thought Nastassia Kinski, who played Tess, was fantastic. As for Alex D'Urberville, played by an English actor called Leigh Lawson, I thought he was brilliant. He could feed me strawberries any day. Little did I know.

Many years later when Leigh and I were living in Los Angeles, Nastassia and her then husband Quincy Jones, the brilliant musician turned record producer, came round to dinner. She had been only seventeen when she did *Tess* and had never spoken perfect English before, with or without a Dorset accent. Which is remarkable when you watch the film. Her accent is Piddlehinton perfect. She was very pregnant I remember, and very tired. But Quincy, who's a great guy, was on a roll and telling stories of life in Chicago when he was a boy and how they were so poor his grandma used to catch rats and make them into a stew. By midnight, Nastassia wandered off to find the loo. After ten minutes I said I'd better check to see if she was all right. Next door to the cloakroom was our office and there she was, curled up on a day bed, fast asleep. So I covered her with a blanket and we left her until it was time to go. Which was about four o'clock in the morning. She was breathtakingly gorgeous, even more beautiful in the flesh than on screen. People are always asking me who I think is the most beautiful woman around today. For me, it's Nastassia Kinski.

The only money Justin had managed to raise for *Gotta Sing, Gotta Dance* was £75,000 from a friend of his, Terry Knight. Terry had hit the semi-big time when he managed a band called Grand Funk Railroad. He now lived in the Bahamas and a neighbour was Commander Ted Whitehead, the man who became famous for the Schweppes advertisements, who also turned out to be a director of Cunard. Somehow we went on a three-week all-expenses-paid cruise on the QE2. Publicity for them, a jaunt for us: Southampton, New York, Bermuda, then home again. We should have known the Bermuda Triangle spelled disaster.

Amazingly I'd never been on a boat before. We always flew everywhere, even with the car: Lydd to Deauville. It should have been a jolly little crew that set sail that May: Justin and me, Tommy and Michel, Jon Brunner and Steve Lovi, but truth be told, it was pretty grim. The reason it was so agonising was my state of mind. Although the QE2 was amazing and huge, for me at this time it was claustrophobic. However wonderful it was dressing up for dinner every night and sitting at the captain's table, I couldn't get off. I felt bad about the others. My inner torment was affecting everyone. Even Tommy's relationship with Michel was being put under pressure. Tommy and I had become so close in *The Boyfriend* and quite simply Michel was jealous of what we had. But we just wanted to continue spending time together. Two big kids. The only happy times for me were the hours Tommy and I spent tap dancing hour after hour on a wooden deck with nothing on the horizon except endless sea and sky. Pretty amazing, and the taps sounded great. No Justin, no Michel. Nothing to cloud the view. Otherwise it was just an endless round of Monopoly, jigsaws, dressing up and falling out.

That autumn in 1971 Tommy, Michel, Justin and I were invited to spend the weekend in the country. In 1966 Granada TV had done the first documentary on me. The director was someone called Henry Herbert and he was adorable and very kind to me. One day soon after shooting, he asked Justin and me to dinner at his house. It was a very dressy do and I had the place of honour on his right. At one point he said something to the waiter clearing away the plates and this man said, 'Yes, your lordship.' So I shrieked, 'Did you hear what he called you? He called you your lordship.' Henry just smiled. I carried on digging my little pit. 'Why did he do that?' 'Because that's who I am. Lord Pembroke,' Henry replied sweetly. I wanted the floor to open.

Anyway, Henry — the thirteenth Earl of Pembroke now that his father has died — is lovely and we have kept in touch over the years. His big passion is tap dancing and he has actually got a pair of Fred Astaire's shoes. So when Tommy and I were rehearsing Henry would sometimes come and watch. Which was why we were all invited down that weekend. At that time his father was still alive so he wasn't living in the big house, Wilton Place, but in the dowager house in the grounds with his then wife Clare and their children. But still pretty posh. For Tommy and Michel it was amazing. Here they were, in England, the guests of an English Lord, at the English Lord's country seat. They could hardly believe it. And it would be nice for Zaradin, Justin said.

Zaradin was a beautiful blond Afghan. When Justin left Ladbroke Gardens, Doogle retired to a life of leisure in the country and I have no doubt heaved a huge doggy sigh of relief. Unfortunately Zaradin all too quickly took his place. We just saw this puppy one afternoon and bought it. Really stupid. Justin said he would look good on the velvet cushions. But Afghans are not lapdogs, they are nutcases. He was fine until he was about year and a half but then he started snapping. Because of course he needed as much exercise as a greyhound. I used to spend hours in Regents Park trying to catch this bloody dog whose idea of fun would be to let you get within an inch of his lead then run off. Great game.

Once we went up to Scotland to stay with Billy Gibb and his parents on their farm in Aberdeenshire. We'd just arrived and Zaradin had been let out for a bit of a run. Suddenly we heard this squawking and we ran out and it was just like a cartoon. They kept chickens and somehow Zaradin had got into the wooden chicken house and the poor birds were hurling themselves out of the windows. Feathers everywhere. One demented creature was running for its life, with Zaradin in hot pursuit, snapping at its tail, feathers in his mouth. He didn't actually kill any of them but I wouldn't be surprised if some of them didn't have heart attacks. It took us three hours to get him back.

Back in Wiltshire, as soon as we crunched up the drive of Henry Herbert's estate, I began to get nervous. The house is, of course, amazing. All Persian silk carpets and pale sofas. At the beginning we kept Zaradin with the family Labradors out in the boot room. But he'd been used to being with us and leaping around the cushions in the studio, mollycoddled and spoilt to death. So he started crying. We were all sitting round, having tea after our walk and Justin said confidently, 'Let him in, he'll be fine. It's not as if he's not housetrained.' Which he was. With us. In the flat.

So Zaradin comes bouncing in. And everyone's on these sofas and I'm opposite them facing an archway through to a connecting room so I can see Zaradin trotting around, sniffing everything, as dogs do. It's a new house, lots of exciting smells and he's having a great time. Then suddenly I see him go into the crouch position on the polished parquet. And I freeze.

It wasn't the first time he'd done it in

public. Once when we were having dinner with the Russells at a restaurant called Julie's in Notting Hill which was done up as though it was a private house, Zaradin performed in the fireplace. There we were, all dressed up for a lovely evening out and wonderful food, standing round the fire with our glasses just chatting when he did it. Right in front of all these people. Talk about not knowing where to look. So Justin dived forward with a couple of napkins and scooped it up. It was so embarrassing.

Now this time, at Henry's house in Wiltshire, it was my turn. Although the class system does exist in England, actors and entertainers seem to be outside all that. You get accepted. So it's not the people you're freaked by — people are people — it's all the rest of it. Take butlers, for instance. What do you call them? It's the famous knife and fork thing — which to use when you're faced with a table-top full of them. I remember the panic the first time I was faced with an artichoke. At home we'd never even had corn on the cob. So what, I wonder, transfixed by Zaradin, is the etiquette for dealing with a dog crapping on eighteenth-century parquet. Although I'd worked with Henry, and been out to dinner with him a couple of times, I didn't know him that well and it was the first time I'd met Clare, his wife at that time. I was just praying, please don't turn around.

All I knew was I'd got to get the dog and the dog doodoo out without anyone seeing. I happened to have a large grey suede handbag, with a flap. So, as casually as I could, I asked,

'Where's the nearest loo?'

Clare points to the door. So off I trot, taking Zaradin with me. I'm praying they won't turn round, that they'll just stay where they're sitting. So I get mounds and mounds of loo paper and make my way around to the room beyond the arch. I know I can get to it through another door. Thank God they're still all talking and don't see me creeping in, and anyway I'm pretending to look at the paintings. Then, when I'm half hidden by the sofa, I look and wait for the right moment and scoop it up into my handbag. Then I wander nonchalantly back to my place and sit there with this stuff in my handbag. I should really now go back to the loo to flush it but I think if I excuse myself again they'll think I'm ill. So I sit for a good forty-five minutes with this dog crap in my handbag.

Later when I told Justin and Tommy and Michel, they got hysterical. To this day I have never confessed to Henry and Clare. We still had the rest of the weekend to go and they would have been nervous wrecks every time Zaradin walked into the room.

Increasingly I was meeting more and more people without Justin and realising that there were other people out there who were lovely and who I enjoyed seeing on my own. Justin could be quite funny and quite amusing. And it must have been hard for him, meeting all these people, knowing it was not because of him, but because of me. It's a problem all celebrity couples face. A wife can completely lose her identity and a husband can feel utterly emasculated and if the individuals concerned can't cope with that, their marriages or relationships haven't a hope of surviving happily. On the surface it didn't seem to bother Justin (although he always liked to get his name in print) but looking back I think he probably thought he was as well known as me. I think he truly believed that.

In January 1972 I heard I had won two Golden Globes Awards for *The Boyfriend* (these awards are given in Hollywood by the Foreign Press Association and traditionally precede the Oscars). The first was for Most Promising Newcomer. And one for Best Comedy Actress. Just being nominated is honour enough. To win them, especially the one for comedy, meant so much to me and was just unbelievable. But time was running out to capitalise on *The Boyfriend*. The train moves on.

By now we'd come to a dead end with *Gotta Sing, Gotta Dance* and Terry Knight's money had all gone. Ava Astaire had come across a book which she thought would be brilliant for her father and me. Fred was very keen to do it and had already started talking to Jack Lemmon who owned the rights. It was called *The Colours Of Evening*, about the platonic relationship between an older man and a young girl. But no sex, no dancing, no singing. No go.

When the script of *W* arrived I was pretty desperate. Twiggy Dresses had gone down the pan and I was still determined not to go back to modelling but I needed to work and I had to get away. It wasn't Mr Russell and it wasn't Mr Astaire, but it was an offer. It was Hollywood. And this time no talk about Justin being a producer. *W* was a psychological thriller. It was produced by Mel Ferrer and the director was Richard Quine, who directed *How To Murder Your Wife* in 1965, a big big film with Jack Lemmon, Virna Lisi and Terry Thomas. Richard had been married to Kim Novak and was very high profile. The script was OK but that's about it. We started shooting in the spring of 1973, in Malibu, California. Justin came along too, of course, but he had learnt his lesson and stayed well away from the set.

In retrospect what happened was inevitable. I fell in love with my leading man. Michael Whitney was tall, dark and handsome. He was also twenty years older than me, though it was a couple of years before I found that out. At the time he admitted to thirty-eight. He wore a cowboy hat and cowboy boots and talked in a mid-west drawl, although he in fact came from up-state New York.

I was absolutely terrified about what I was feeling and what it meant. My knees had gone wobbly a couple of times over the past eight years but never like this. Michael played my husband, so we'd be doing all this intimate stuff on set during the day (nothing sexual, just being close) and then it was back to the hotel and Justin. Sometimes the three of us would even go out together in the evening and it was agony. Just agony. I didn't know what to do. By the end of the film I knew that Michael felt the same way about me, and so I told Justin. I had to. Not only because it affected him but because of all we'd been through. I couldn't deceive him. It's not in my nature.

Justin had always been terrified I'd run off with somebody. But I'd never had the chance, I was working so hard. I did form very close friendships, like Tommy and Christopher. And I did have schoolgirl crushes, but I never did anything about them.

W came to an end and Justin and I came back to England. I had never been so unhappy. In fact I don't think I had ever known what real unhappiness was before this. So the summer passed and I found myself listening to tear-jerker country and western songs. I think Justin was hoping that it was just a screen romance, which like holiday romances generally fade as soon as real life clicks in. But it didn't.

First was an assignment to do for *Vogue* with David Bowie. I'll never forget the shock when I first heard my name coming over the radio in David Bowie's unmistakable style in his song 'Drive In Saturday' from the album *Aladdin Sane*. It must have been around 1972. I was sitting sewing in my bedroom in Twickenham, when suddenly I heard him sing, Twig the wonder kid. Or thought I did. But because I wasn't really listening, I thought, No. I must have misheard. When the chorus came around, there it was again, Twig the wonder kid, and I thought, Blimey. I remember being absolutely bowled over and of course I rushed out and bought it. I had always wanted to meet him. Like the Beatles, David Bowie is an original. Several originals. It's hard to imagine the history of rock music without all his various incarnations.

We had heard Bowie was cutting a new album, so Justin and I had put the idea to *Vogue's* London editor Bea Miller. We were both seen as these two androgynous creatures. But I was a girl and he was a boy.

He was recording in a studio outside Paris. It was pretty amazing — one of those places where you stay and everything is laid on. I was really quite nervous, as I was a huge fan and as starstruck as anyone else would be. *Ziggy Stardust* is one of my favourite albums; every track is completely different and completely brilliant. He immediately put me at ease. He was everything I could have hoped for and more, witty and funny and incredibly bright; into films, directors, literature, art. Thank goodness for my belated film education. The pop world can be very egotistical and to meet someone who didn't just want to talk about their latest record was a breath of fresh air.

We had no idea what had been planned. To this day I don't know what input Bowie had into that now famous image, the two masked faces on the *Pin-Ups* album. Bowie's was basically Aladdin Sane, minus the lightning stripe. The Thin White Duke was still gestating. The problem was I had just come back from California and was as brown as a nut while Bowie looked like he'd never seen the sun. So they had this idea to whiten my face down — leaving my neck and shoulders brown and bare — and colour Bowie up. Anyway, the result was fabulous.

Back at *Vogue* the circulation manager was less than thrilled. 'We can't have a man on the cover of *Vogue*,' he announced. I couldn't believe it. I told him that David Bowie was possibly the only man in the world you could credit the make-up on. One of the traditions in magazines is that on a cover, the make-up is always credited. But it's all a joke. If you think 'Oh, that's a lovely lipstick,' nine times out of ten it won't be the one named inside, it'll just be out of the model's or make-up artist's box of tricks. In modelling what you see is not always what you get. It's all done by mirrors: safety-pins and airbrushing.

Bowie was as knocked out by the picture as we were. As Justin owned the copyright Bowie said 'while they're pissing about arguing' he'd like to use it for the cover of the album he was recording. In the end *Vogue* never used it. Pathetic really. But perhaps that circulation manager did us all a favour. *Pin-Ups* sold millions of copies around the world. In fact as a Bowie album it's a bit of an anomaly, with him singing cover versions of his favourite sixties' songs. It was some contractual deal he had to fulfil with his record label and the Spiders From Mars: Mick Ronson, Trevor Bolder and Woody Woodmansey. He never worked with them again. Bowie and nostalgia make strange bedfellows. But it's still out there. Now on CD. Strange to think that it's possibly the most widely distributed photograph ever taken of me, and yet it was done right at the end of my modelling career. And it was the last time I worked with Justin.

Although Michael triggered the break, I hadn't been emotionally happy with Justin for years. Now the pretence had gone. But where did we go from here? The tension was dreadful. Justin suggested a holiday. And just to show there were no hard feelings he went out and bought a brand new Porsche. He made me feel so guilty that I didn't put up a fight. Mara and Lorenzo Berni, who still run one of the best restaurants in London, San Lorenzo, very sweetly lent us their holiday house in Forti di Marmi on the Italian Riviera, Lorenzo's home town. By then we were all really close friends. Mara is a real mother earth figure. A real Italian Mama, very loving, and I adore her. She and Lorenzo look like Anna Magnani and Marcello Mastroianni. Although they've lived in England for thirty years, they're still as Italian as the day they arrived.

We had been to the house with them in happier times. Perhaps going back was a mistake. What made it worse was Justin's insisting we drive there in his new toy. The drive to Italy is long enough anyway, twenty hours door to door at least. And being in such enclosed quarters with someone you don't want to be with is just horrendous. We argued constantly. Anyway, it was no good. I was in tears the whole time, and so was Justin. I just wanted out. Not next week, not next month. Now. So Justin phoned Stewart Grimshaw and God bless him he caught the next plane down. A true friend. He and I flew back to London together, leaving Justin to drive back alone. By the time he got back to the studio I had cleared out. Taken what little I needed and bought my ticket to LA. It was all done so quickly that I left half my life in Charlotte Mews. Clothes, pictures, scrap books. (Big sigh.) I just didn't care. I just wanted out. For Justin's sake I had agreed to a joint press conference. It was pretty awful. As I saw it, without me he had nothing and I felt sorry for him. He wanted the world to know that I had agreed that for the time being he would continue to handle things for me in England. It never really worked but he remained as my manager, at least on paper, for another three years.

Nobody was very surprised. Dad didn't bother to hide his relief. And, like you do, it wasn't long before I began to hear about what had been going on all these years. All the other women, I had had no idea. When we split, I blocked him out of my life. I just closed the door. I had to. Justin went to bed for a week.

12

I was only twenty-three, but I had already done the tedious London/LA haul dozens of times. It's long enough anyway; this time it seemed never-ending. I went through every emotion I had ever known and some I hadn't. The canary had opened the door of her cage and flown. But her wings were still clipped. And it was scary. Michael met me, gorgeous and tanned and tall in his cowboy boots, looking like Marlboro Man. It was like I was in a film and this was the happy ending. I'd booked into a hotel — it seemed the right thing to do, but other than that I'd made no plans at all. Although Michael and I had spoken on the phone, it was nearly three months since we had last seen each other and a part of me was terrified it just wouldn't be the same when I saw him again. But it was.

The late September weather was beautiful and we took off up the Californian coast in his beaten-up dark blue Stingray Corvette driving north along Highway One. This was my first time in the States not working. No limos. No press. Just Michael and me, the car and the sea. He wasn't wealthy but he knew how to look after me. The Pacific coast was amazing — like Cornwall crossed with Mallorca but ten times bigger. Big Sur is all mountains, crashing sea, mist and amazing skies. Spectacular and very romantic.

When I was little I remember asking Mum, 'When do you know if you're really in love?' And her saying, 'When it happens, you just know.' And as the days turned into weeks and the weeks into months, I knew that this was it. All qualms about what I was doing had completely disappeared. The man I adored adored me. What could be more wonderful? But as time went on I discovered that Michael's love was the possessive kind. Which is fine as long as it doesn't strangle you. And that was part of his demon. He was a Scorpio and obsessive about the key things in his life: the theatre, acting, plays, me and later Carly. But I didn't know that then and just luxuriated in this new-found happiness. It was so long since I had done nothing. I felt so healthy and relaxed, I even began to put on weight. I didn't care that I wasn't working, or that Michael wasn't working. Unless you're a big Hollywood name I knew there are always going to be times when things are quiet. I was happy just being the two of us. The future could look after itself.

A few months later I flew back to England to do some publicity for Singer, the sewing machine people, who I'd done a deal with to promote their knitting machines with Twiggy knitting patterns. I'd discovered knitting machines even before I did *The Boyfriend*. Skinny knits only look right if they're really skinny and I could never get them small enough, so I had begun to make them myself. I'd found that with a little imagination and a knitting machine, anything expensive boutiques could do I could do better. Better fit and cheaper. I loved designing — clothes or knitwear. Although my early dream of becoming a designer never materialised, this way I could put some of my ideas into practice, and I also designed and made things for friends which they loved. One-off Twiggyknits.

While in London I did a guest spot on *The Cilla Black Show*. Although I'd sung and danced in *The Boyfriend*, that was playing a part. This was being me. The next thing I knew, the BBC offered me my own series, to be called *Twiggs*, which is what my friends call me, and the series was set for the following summer. When I flew back to Los Angeles, Vivien came with me, for a holiday and to give Michael the family once over. And of course he charmed her, as I knew he would, though the holiday part was less successful. Poor Viv. So much for 'It never rains in southern California'. The day after we arrived there was a terrible storm and it never stopped raining the whole time she was there.

Michael sold his Stingray and we bought a Porsche. It was the first time I'd driven a car with a gearstick. What a car to learn on, and in America, home of the automatic. I'd passed my test in my automatic Mini in November 1968 shortly after the move to Twickenham, which gave the press another opportunity to express their amazement at my ability to do anything except stand pigeon-toed in front of a camera. 'TWIGGY PASSES TEST' headlines, like it was major news. But I have never forgotten the wonderful feeling of freedom that finally being able to drive on my own gave me. Freedom and anonymity. Justin had loved cars, but I love driving which is different. I don't really mind what car I have as long as it's solid, comfortable and powerful enough to get you out of trouble. And I'm told I'm a good driver, by which I mean safe. It all stems from the years of 'Thirty miles an hour, Norman' directed at my Dad from my Mum in the back seat.

Mum's proviso was probably quite sound. When I was a still a baby the family went on holiday to the Isle of Wight. Dad left the car, a little Standard 8, on the mainland to be serviced and we picked it up on our way back. There was a hole in the bodywork over the back wheel which you could peer through and watch the road rushing past. Years later I can remember fighting not to sit next to it, as it was terribly draughty and in the winter really cold. Anyway, Mum, as usual was in the back. Suddenly Viv shrieked, 'Look, Dad.' And there, bouncing down the road in front of us, narrowly missing an old lady on a bike, was a car wheel. Nobody thought it could be anything to do with us, because we were still bowling along. But it was. The back wheel by the hole had come right off. By now our car was listing to the left but everyone was so busy watching this wheel careering merrily along, they didn't notice we were tipping and the carry-cot with me in it was half-way through the hole. It probably wouldn't have got through, but when Mum eventually noticed, it was tipped right back and I wasn't strapped in. A minute more and I wouldn't have

Me as a baby at Willesden carnival. I came third in the beautiful baby contest.

Mum shortly before I was born.

Barry Lategan's first photo of me, in February 1966.
(© Barry Lategan)

The Boyfriend, 1970.
(*Metro-Goldwyn-Mayer Inc.*)

An early picture of me and Michael, by Barry Lategan. (*© Barry Lategan.*)

The Twiggy look, with my famous eyelashes.

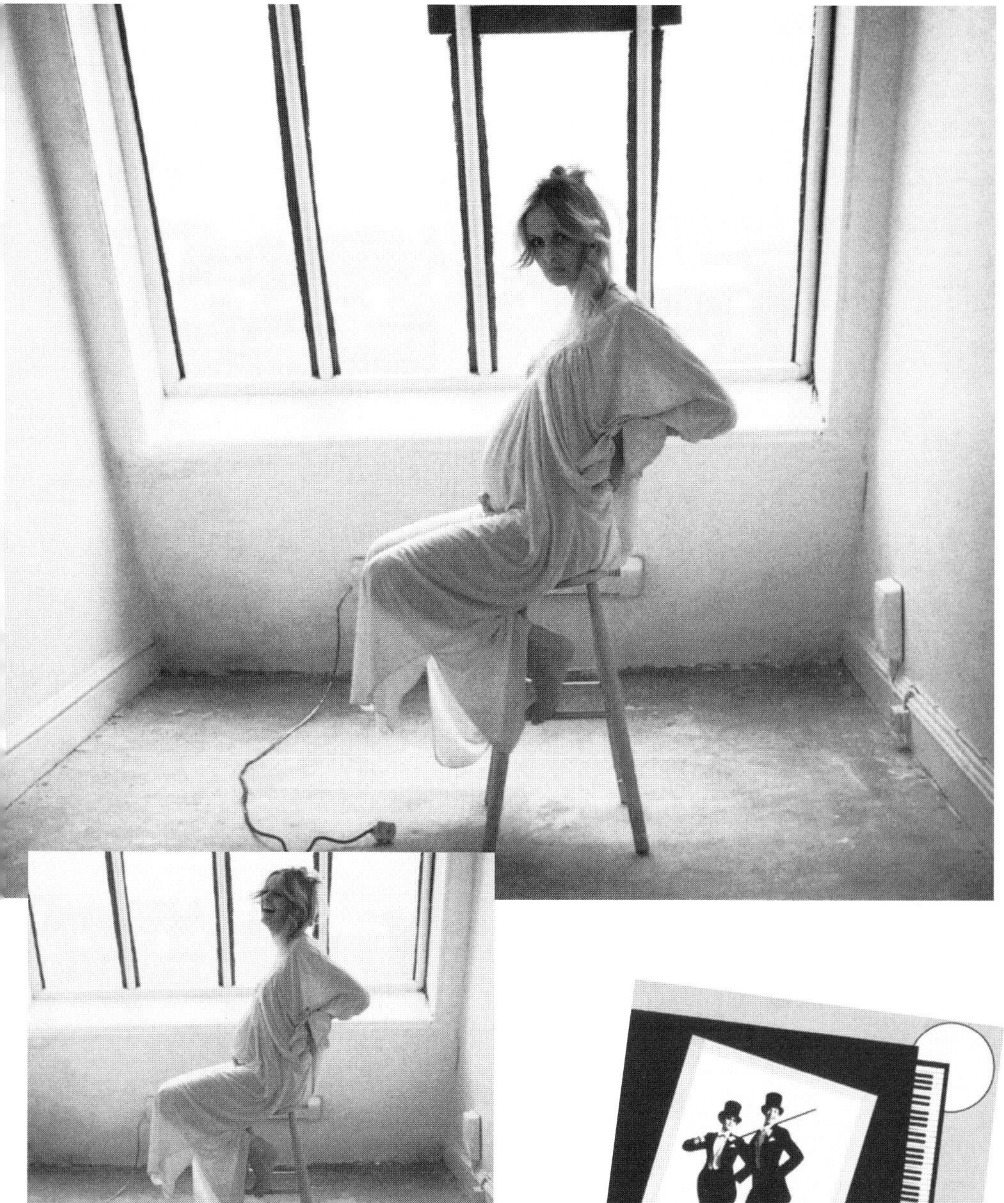

Me and Carly, aged 8 and a half months – I'm in a Bill Gibb dress. Taken by Norman Parkinson.
(*© Norman Parkinson*)

My One and Only – the finale was our tribute to Astaire and Rogers.

This was taken by Francesco Scavullo in 1983.

The Great Day, in Tony and Jen Walton's garden in Sag Harbor, Long Island. *From left to right*, Tony, Mary Frampton, Neville Shulman, me and Leigh, Carlotta Florio, Peggy Burke, Peter Firth and Hal Lindes. 23 September 1988.

Me and Leigh on our wedding day.

On location with Robin Williams in Jamaica on Club Paradise.

Happy families with the McCartneys – me, Paul, Leigh, Carly, Linda, Mary, their oldest, and James, their youngest.

Carly and Ace, aged 14 and 17. (© *Alistair Morrison*)

Carly and me taken by the wonderful Barbara Hulanicki.
(© *Barbara Hulanicki*)

My favourite picture of Leigh, taken by Brian Aris.
(© *Brian Aris*)

Carly and me at a premiere in 1995.
(© *pic photos*)

One of my favourite photos, taken by John Swannell in 1985. (© *John Swannell*)

Another Brian Aris work of art, taken in 1996. (© *Brian Aris*)

made nursery school, or anywhere else.

Cars and Hornby family legends seemed to go together. Shortly after the move to Twickenham Mum and Dad went off for a week's holiday on their own to Swanage in Dorset, scene of their courting days. As well as never sitting in the front, Mum would never talk on a journey, too busy concentrating on the road ahead. And with a maximum speed of thirty miles an hour, it was a long drive for poor Dad. But he chatted away anyway. Being deaf in one ear, even if Mum had said something it would probably have gone unnoticed.

Five hours later they reach Swanage. But it's not to Mum's liking. She remembers now she'd preferred Weymouth. So off they go again. Half-way there Dad pulls into the car park of a public toilet and asks Mum if she wants to go too, but she says no. After he's disappeared into the gents, Mum has a change of heart, gets out of the car and goes into the ladies. Dad returns, gets into the car and drives off. From time to time he points out some pretty scene. He doesn't question the silence from the back. It's the norm for Norm. Eventually he comes to a level crossing, halts, and says, 'Look at this bloody traffic Nell.' And turns round. No Nell. Total panic. Realising she must be back where they stopped, he does a three-point turn on what turns out to be a one-way street, shouting, 'I've left my wife behind.' They must have thought he was mad. He eventually gets back to where he left her. No Nell. More panic. He's just about to drive off when he spots Mum calmly waiting at a bus stop nearby. He pulls the car up. She opens the door, climbs into the back and Dad drives off. Not a word was said and they went happily off to their holiday.

* * *

In June I came back to England for my TV series *Twiggs* and stayed with Mum and Dad in Twickenham. It was lovely to be home again. The schedule was fairly straightforward. Two weeks spent putting ideas together then straight into the first of the six planned shows, rehearsing Tuesday through Friday, then recording on Saturday in front of an audience. Two weeks in, on the first day of the first rehearsal for the first show, a strike of production assistants was called. I can't remember now what it was about. But it had everyone's support, though nobody thought for a moment it would last seven weeks. But it did. It was a total nightmare. All we could do was rehearse and record some of the guest spots, doing song and dance routines. When the strike finally ended, there was only one week left in the studio. Six days to do everything else, all the chats with the guests and all the songs I sang live to mike. Remembering and performing two songs a week is one thing. Remembering twelve was desperate.

The attitude of the British tabloids didn't help. They hadn't taken to Michael who came over to join me. It was as if they thought they owned me and had the right to tell me who I should be with. They kept on about the age gap and the fact that he was married. That was true. And I'd always known it. But by the time we met on the film *W*, he and his wife had been separated for two years, and until he'd met me he'd had no reason to get divorced. Muckraking journalists even tried to make out he had a 22-year-old son. All complete fabrication.

The only good thing was because everything had to be done so quickly in that final week. I had no time to get nervous. In the end we only got four shows done, rather than the six planned. Against all odds they went down well enough to be repeated the next spring and a further series was scheduled for the following summer. For me it was some kind of coming of age. I felt I'd somehow proved myself. Other people thought the same. Would I be interested in doing *Cinderella* on the stage?

Although I had been on a real stage before — the old theatre in Portsmouth that we used in *The Boyfriend* — this would be my first time doing a real show, with a real audience, night after night. I said yes, but only if it was a proper old-fashioned pantomime. Pantos had become so smutty and tacky that by the early seventies a pantomime was the last place you'd take children. Once again Lady Luck was waiting in the wings. The director was Frank Hauser, who for years did exceptional work at the Oxford Playhouse, which he ran. So it was to be a proper production. And Frank agreed we should do a theatrical, stylish fairy story. Even the inevitible TV stars (Harry H. Corbett and Wilfred Brambell, then huge names because of their series *Steptoe and Son*) had proper parts to play (very appropriate: The Broker's Men). My ugly sisters were Roy Kinnear and Hugh Paddick. With Nicky Henson as Buttons, it was a great cast.

The show opened with Cinderella in her rags asleep in front of the fire because I'd told Frank, 'If I'm not on the stage when the curtain goes up I'll be so scared, you'll never get me out there.' It was a very happy show. The star for me will always be Roy Kinnear, who played the horrible ugly sister whose life's work is to make Cinderella as miserable as possible. But his best running gag was one the audience never knew about. To go with his outrageous frock, Roy had this outrageous red wig and every night he'd dress it up differently to try and make me laugh. He was so naughty. But wonderful, not like dreadful Wilfred Brambell who was as miserable and misogynistic in real life as he was in *Steptoe* with never a kind word to anybody. How lovely Harry H. Corbett put up with old misery-boots, I'll never know.

I always looked forward to that first moment of seeing Roy in his wig. Sometimes it was all I could do not to collapse in a heap on the stage. The nearest I came to that was with Joyce Grant who played my Fairy Godmother. Unlike Roy's antics, this was for real. I knew there was something wrong the moment she walked on. Something about her eyes. Only when she got closer did I realise what had happened. She'd managed to put her false eyelashes on upside down and was completely unaware. Instead of curling upwards, down, making her eyes look like they were being clawed by miniature garden rakes. I thought I was going to die trying not to laugh — just something as silly and insignificant as that is enough to set you off on stage.

* * *

Roy Kinnear was one of the funniest men I have ever met and I loved him. Whenever I see him now in an old film it makes me so angry because he should still be around. He was killed doing a horseriding scene on Dick Lester's film of *The Four Musketeers*. To die from an accident in life is one thing but to die for a bloody film or the telly . . . I will never understand why actors endanger themselves as they do. It's madness. Even a broken ankle or arm can put your career in jeopardy, and the film, and your family. But somehow Roy was persuaded to do it. He was very round and probably not very fit and he couldn't ride and they put him on this horse and he was very frightened and he came off. He didn't die immediately. They took him off to hospital — but this was in the wilds of Spain and the hospital was miles away. I don't know what he died of, what was on the death certificate. But one way or another he died because of doing that scene. There was quite a scandal about it at the time. A tragedy that shouldn't have happened.

I loved doing *Cinderella*. All that stuff with Buttons and the children yelling out wanting me to marry him and not the Prince. That was one bit of the panto that wasn't traditional: the principal boy was a boy. Usually it's the female star of the show, from the days when people got a kick from an upholstered bosom bursting out of a tightly buttoned jacket and a great pair of legs in nothing but tights. Things seem to have reversed these days. But as Cinderella I got to wear the fairytale frocks which Barbara Hulanicki of Biba had such fun designing for me, and which were every little girl's dream, and some big girls' too. Jack Tinker, the much loved and respected theatre critic who sadly died prematurely of asthma in 1996, wrote in the *Daily Mail*: 'Her stage debut proves there is a magic aura of originality about her that can only be summed up as star-plus.' I was naturally encouraged and thrilled.

In spite of my move to the States and the Jeremiahs of the press, my career was pushing ahead. Michael's however, was not. Since *W* he had done nothing except a beer ad for American TV. It was one of a series: cowboys slaking their thirst after a hard day on the range. It was a ten-day shoot in the Nevada desert so I went with him. It was the first time I'd seen real cowboy country. Often when you go somewhere you know from photographs or the movies, the real thing can be a terrible disappointment, but not the American West. It's simply awe-inspiring, the vastness of everything, the skies, the silence. And in this case the snow.

The days were short and the nights long. As this was a beer ad, every night was party night. One night, about half-way through the shoot, Michael got drunk. Boys together, it happens.

Except that it hadn't happened before. In fact as far as I knew Michael didn't even drink. Not even a glass of wine with a meal. That night back at the hotel, he got very argumentative for no reason. It was horrible. I had no idea what was going on and just cried myself to sleep. The next day it was as if nothing had happened. An aberration. Forgive and forget. And I did. Until the next time, which was about six months later. Only then did I realise that that night in the desert was no one-off. I was living with an alcoholic.

It sounds so stupid now, but I didn't know. I didn't know because I didn't know about alcoholics. As far as I knew I'd never even met an alcoholic. I knew people who drank. People who drank a lot. But there were no big boozers in my own family. No tales told around the kitchen table of uncles who hid bottles of whisky in the coal bunker. My father's idea of a drink was a bottle of stout at Christmas when Mum had her glass of sherry. It's only when it's in a family you learn about what living with a drunkard really means. The violence, the broken nights, the physical degradation, the lies, the deceit, the pain. Leigh's father was an alcoholic and he has told me terrible stories of what it was like as a child to grow up under that black cloud.

At the time of the beer ad I'd known Michael for nearly two years and all that time — and a while before, I think, certainly on *W* — he'd been dry. It never occurred to me to wonder why he didn't drink. I had no idea. No idea what I had let myself in for. I was so much in love and so wanted it to work with Michael that I didn't ask even the most basic questions, like why did the first marriage go wrong? Or even why don't you drink? Or why do you become a different person when you do? Because if you don't know the implications, you don't ask the questions. I drank hardly at all because I didn't like it. Back to that fear of being giddy. I've been drunk once in my life, but it taught me a lesson I've never forgotten. It was at some teenage party and within the space of half an hour I had a whisky and a vodka and a glass of wine. People were just handing it to me. And I just thought, 'Oh this is fun.' I only just had time to reach the bathroom before the inevitable happened. I was so ill. It was a long time before I had another drink, though society can make it hard not to. The first time I went to Paris to a smart restaurant and ordered a Coca Cola the waiter looked down his nose and said, 'What vintage, madame?' and walked off.

On one level I was very sophisticated. I'd gone from being a schoolgirl to this famous thing, travelling around the world in great style and always with people older than me. But dealing with an alcoholic was not something I was equipped to handle. I didn't know where to begin and I had no one to talk to; I was in Los Angeles, not north London. And it's not the sort of thing you put in a letter. This was my problem and Michael's. Nobody else's.

The pattern was soon set. After two drinks he'd be jolly, four and he started being obstreperous, after that it was downhill all the way. It would begin with 'why not me', attacking producers and the studios for not casting him. For an alcoholic acting is probably the worst profession to pick. You have to have the hide of an elephant just to survive the constant undermining that is built into it. If you can't deal with the rejections, your self-confidence constantly being eroded, then don't be an actor. I've been put up for things I haven't got. All actors have. But you don't get drunk. After the producers and the studios had suffered their share of abuse, it would be my turn. How it was all my fault and how I was ruining his life. It's the classic thing with alcoholics, expressing their self-hatred and disappointment by turning on the one they love. Or the one they profess to love. But really in the end the bottle is what they love the most.

Toward the end of the run of *Cinderella* Michael came over to join me and it wasn't long before we began to talk about moving back to England. Like all alcoholics, the fault always lay somewhere else.

'It's LA. If only I could get out of that awful town.'

That was fine by me. And I'd missed my friends and family. And for all Michael's cowboy persona, he was from the east. Most east coasters hate the west coast. And Hollywood hadn't been kind to him.

Through his American agent, he was introduced to Jean Diamond, an agent in London. Only a few weeks after they'd met, she phoned: a new series about trouble-shooting in the oil industry; they needed an American. The part, the billing, the money, the timing, perfect. Within a few weeks everything had fallen into place. And Michael was so up, so happy. And so was I. Maybe the drinking was all to do with not working. Now things would be different. We bought a flat in Belsize Park.

The series was called *Oil Strike North* by Wilfred Greatorex. For British TV it was a big production, shot on location in the north of Scotland, in Peterhead. Like on *W*, he didn't drink. Then he had been on the waggon. Now he just didn't drink while he was working: on days off, that was different. As drinkers do, he found the other drinkers on the show. And they became his friends. Through them Michael discovered that great old English institution, the great old English pub. And when the Scottish filming was finished and he was back in London, so it began.

His favourite pub was on Haverstock Hill, just up the road from the flat. He wasn't working, so what else did I expect him to do but be with his buddies? And what else was he going to do with his buddies but drink? We were supposed to be doing up the flat, stripping the doors, decorating, making curtains, making a home together, but Michael often wasn't there. We'd have an arrangement to do something, or meet somebody at a certain time and I'd be waiting at home, dressed up and ready to go at the time we'd agreed, and he just wouldn't show. He'd go to the pub and start drinking and forget about or ignore anything else. He even did it to his new agent Jean Diamond. They'd arranged to have lunch and he just didn't turn up. Not exactly a confidence-building trait in a new client. Thank God Jean was such a kind understanding person.

Michael never accepted that he was an alcoholic. The fact that he could be dry for months at a time proved to him he wasn't. But then would come that one drink, and the gentle giant I'd fallen in love with would disappear. he was like Jekyll and Hyde. Somebody once told me that Robert Louis Stephenson was an alcoholic and that's where his story of Dr Jekyll and Mr Hyde came from. Writing the book was his own way of exploring the two sides to his personality. At this time Michael was never physically violent; that came years later when I finally left him.

In the meantime my new career was gradually making ground: the second series of *Twiggs* had been recorded without hitch and I had cut my first album, called (surprise, surprise) *Twiggy* for Polygram. Not pop, this time, but country, that went with my long-haired cowgirl look of fringed suede boots and jeans. The last date of the country-wide tour was at the Albert Hall. Every time I go past it I'm amazed I played it. And filled it.

It was so scary walking out on that stage. The Albert Hall is huge. Huge. And I remember somebody had to give me a shove, my knees had gone all weak. So I came out and picked up my mike and started to sing. But no sound was coming out. We'd done the sound check and everything seemed fine. In didn't know whether it was my mike or something wrong in the playback system. Then out of my playback speakers I hear this voice intoning over and over, 'Grab the other mike, Twiggs. Twiggs, grab up the other mike.' It was my sound engineer. He had worked out that his voice would come through my playback speakers. Nobody else would have heard with the orchestra going full blast. Everything seemed to be in slow motion. So I very calmly walked across the stage to my secondary mike. And carried on singing. The album did very well and went silver.

Around that time I also did my first television drama for Granada, recorded in Manchester, one of a series called *Queen Victoria's Scandals*. Michael came with me for moral support. It might not have been Shakespeare but it was pretty scary just the same. One evening I had gone straight to bed while he stayed drinking in the hotel bar. He'd already had too much to drink at dinner, but I was too tired to have a row. Next thing I knew it was one o'clock and I woke up to find Michael crashing around.

'Right, we're getting out of here. I've never been spoken to like that in my life.'

'Michael, I'm filming tomorrow.'

'I don't care. We'll find another hotel.'

Just to keep him calm I got up, packed and we left. We drove around until we found another hotel. By then it was about three in the morning and I had to get up at seven. I worked through the next day feeling like death. Luckily I was young enough for it not to show. But it was a terribly selfish thing to do when I was filming the next day. It was my first straight acting role. It was so important that I did my best.

Linda McCartney had become a really good friend. And that year she suggested we join them in Liverpool for New Year's Eve. They always went to Paul's Uncle Joe's house for New Year, she said.

'All the McCartneys will be there and all the relatives. Do come. It'll be really good fun.'

We arrived in good time and after supper Paul disappeared upstairs.

'Come up and look what I've found,' he called.

It was a box of old exercise books he'd had at school. The four of us sat on his bed laughing looking at all this old stuff. Nostalgia was in the air.

'And this is my first guitar.'

Like a proud kid he got this guitar down from the top of the wardrobe where it had been shoved and showed us how the guitar man at the shop had had to re-string it for him because it was a right-handed guitar and Paul is left handed. So sweet. No sense of showing off. Of all the people who've stayed normal Paul gets the gold star.

This trip down memory lane meant we were running late. By the time we piled into the Range Rover it must have been nearly nine o'clock, the time we were expected at Uncle Joe's. It was quite squashy, Paul driving, Linda beside him in the front; Michael, me and the kids behind; and right in the back baby James in his carry-cot. Stella and Mary would have been quite little; Heather, Linda's daughter by her first marriage, about thirteen.

Problems started as soon as we tried to cross the Mersey. The usual tunnel was closed, but Paul said he thought there was a new one. We came out the other side locked into a one-way system and Paul, having no idea where we were, was desperately looking for landmarks. Suddenly he saw his old school. 'Look,' he said pointing into the night, 'that's where me and John smoked behind the bicycle sheds.' And like a tap that's turned on, out came all these reminiscences. It was just luck that he happened to pass his old school and, because it was New Year, he was already feeling nostalgic. Next he took us to Strawberry Fields. I don't know what it's like now but then it was an open space, a wildish park thing but with railings and a gateway. Then we went down Penny Lane and past the barber's shop and he got hysterical because the barber's had gone unisex. He was on a jag and obviously loving it. And there was Linda saying, 'Come on, Paul, or we're going to be late.' She was thinking of Uncle Joe, and unlike Michael and me, had heard it all before. It was a magical night, truly truly magical. He was obviously just enjoying being back and driving around his old life.

By now we're seriously late. We're all laughing: Paul McCartney lost in Liverpool. Outside a pub we see a group of lads. Paul winds down the window. 'I'm going to have to ask the way.'

One of them staggers towards us. Paul smiles that inimitable smile.

'Hello, mate. Do you know the way to Such 'n' such street?'

What's wonderful about Paul, like Dustin Hoffman and a few other famous friends, is that they don't have this thing about 'I'm a celebrity. I can't go out.' When Dustin was in London doing *The Merchant of Venice* with Leigh, he used to walk around with us or on his own in Kensington and Chelsea. The English are quite good. Even if they did recognise him they'd probably not show it. But people who behave like stars, surrounding themselves with bodyguards and the whole Hollywood ego trip, only bring trouble on themselves. Paul is like Dustin. He's always gone out to restaurants. Yes, people recognise him, but he has decided that he's not going to let fame ruin his life. Because it can. But it's up to you. If you behave normally, then on the whole people will behave normally towards you. I don't think I've ever got out of Sainsbury's without somebody recognising me and talking to me. But so what?

Back to Liverpool and New Year's Eve. This young lad outside the pub looks at Paul, does a double take, looks again, finally twigs (excuse the pun) and backs off, first talking under his breath then shouting and gesturing to his mates, 'It's Paul McCartney, it's fucking Paul McCartney.' Inside the Range Rover we're hysterical with laughter. By this time the guy is standing in the headlights, rocking on his feet and screaming at the top of his voice and everyone seems to be pouring out into the street, so we move off, Paul driving very carefully around the drunken youth, who shows no signs of moving, with a cheery, 'Thanks mate, Happy New Year.'

By now we're in a very run down area, small factories, warehouses. No shops. No one to ask the way except one middle-aged lady walking down the street, bottles under her arm. Paul stops and opens the window.

''Scuse me love but I'm lost. I've got to get to Such 'n' such street.' She looks at him, not a flicker of recognition, and starts to give directions.

'Tell you what, I'm going that way myself,' she chirps, 'so give me a lift and I'll show you.'

'Jump in,' says Paul.

Linda slides across and this woman gets in next to her, puts her bottles down in front of her and rubs her hands.

'Bloody cold,' she says and explains that she's just finished work and is 'going home to my old man'. Then she says, 'How's the new baby then, Paul? You didn't think I knew who you were, did you? And I know who you are,' she adds, nudging Linda and laughing. Then turning around to us in the back, 'And I know who you two are and all. You're Twiggy and you're Michael, and you're Stella and Mary and Heather, and is that James in the back? Is he a good baby?'

It was hysterical. And of course Paul loved her. When we got to her street he offered to take her to her door. But she said no.

'I can walk that bit.'

As we drove off, I said to Linda, 'She'll go in now to the old man and say, 'you'll never believe who's just given me a lift home, Paul and Linda McCartney and Twiggy was in the back.' And he'll say, 'Oh yeah, how much have you been drinking?' ' I'd have loved to have been a fly on the wall.

Uncle Joe's house turns out to be straight out of Coronation Street, two up, two down and packed to the eaves with relatives, uncles and aunts and cousins. All really friendly and welcoming to two total strangers. Very Liverpudlian. As it comes up to midnight everyone makes for the door. It's what they do every year. The whole street goes out and joins hands to sing Auld Lang Syne, all the doors open, the street alive with people. Televisions down the street are turned up and we hear Big Ben strike twelve. Happy New Year. And everybody kisses everybody else like you do. I kiss Michael, then I kiss Paul, then Linda, then the kids, then Uncle Joe and the other uncles and aunts and the cousins and the friends. It goes on and on, for what seems like forever. Eventually Paul comes and explains what's happened. The word had gone round the other street that Paul was there and I was there. So they thought they may as well join in. Paul was getting all these girls from all the streets in the area and I was getting all these other fellas — an endless stream of people kissing us. And not one behaving horribly among them, for all the booze. It was so funny. A brilliant end to the most magical New Year's Eve.

And Michael? While we were toasting the New Year in champagne, Michael clinked his glass of Coke. People who wonder why I stuck it for so long don't realise that for long periods, months at a stretch, he'd clean up, and there was always this hope that this time, like he promised, it would be for ever. But what's horrible living with an alcoholic is that you live your life on a knife edge. Even if they've been dry for six weeks, you don't know when the next time's going to be. Next month? Tomorrow? Never? Looking back I don't know how I didn't crumble. But I didn't. Like Dad I was a fighter and I wasn't going to bail out. If I'd been older and wiser I'd have known this was pure rose-coloured spectacles. No one can help an alcoholic until that person decides to help themselves. But I had no experience to fall back on. No real knowledge of relationships at all, let alone something as complicated and destructive as this. If I loved him enough, I decided, he would change. Love and stability were what I could give him. So I did. On 14 June 1977, in the Royal Borough of Richmond, England, we were married.

13

Michael was born on 21 November 1931, in Ticonderoga, upstate New York on the edge of the Adirondack Mountains, a huge national park that runs up to the Canadian border, so wild and remote that parts of it are still unmapped. I had never been anywhere like it and was just knocked out. It's exquisitely beautiful, all pine forests and lakes.

Michael's real name was Whitney Armstrong but when he'd joined American Equity in the early sixties he changed it. Like in England the union won't let you have the same name as any other actor. He wanted to keep some part of his name and the Michael was pretty much chosen out of a hat.

The Armstrongs originate from the Northumbrian/Scottish borders where the clan was known as notorious cattle rustlers, border marauders and general hellraisers. It doesn't surprise me. Michael and his mother had a very tempestuous relationship. Looking back I can see they were very alike. She was very possessive. The first time he took me up to meet them she kept calling me Jo, his first wife's name. I didn't care. One more name wouldn't bother me. But Michael got very angry, insisting she was doing it on purpose. And she probably was. 'I love my mother,' he would say, 'but she drives me crazy.'

It wasn't until two years after we met that he took me to meet them. They were a normal working-class family. His father, a sweet, gentle man, had long since retired. Although then in his late seventies, he was very fit. In Ticonderoga everything is to do with wood. It's the pencil capital of America. Michael had escaped from a lifetime of making pencils through baseball. He was six foot two with the build of a natural athlete. He was a pitcher, and a very talented one, I believe, though I never saw him play. From college he was picked up by the B league of the New York Dodgers. It's hard to appreciate what it meant to an eighteen-year-old just after the war to be taken up professionally. It was huge. Both in money and status. The ones who make the major leagues become millionaires and very famous. He'd been two years with the Dodgers and had every hope of making the senior league when he injured his shoulder. He still had the scar across the shoulder blade where they had operated. He had carried on for a while. But the dream was shattered. He would never make the big time. That was when he began to drink. Goodbye baseball.

But there was another way for a handsome, all-American athlete to find fame and fortune. Michael wasn't just beefcake, as good-looking men with muscle were called in those days. He was bright, and well read. By the early sixties he had become involved with the San Francisco Globe Theatre, one of the most famous Shakespearean companies in the States, run by Bill Ball. And the theatre was always immensely important to him. His big break came in 1967 in *The Way West*, a wagon-train western starring Kirk Douglas and Robert Mitchum, based on a Pulitzer Prize-winning novel. Michael got co-star billing and played a scout who gets killed off in the first half hour. Long enough to see he had real potential. It opened the doors to TV: films and pilots for series. In 1970 came *Darling Lili*, a Blake Edwards film with Julie Andrews as a German spy. Then in 1971 *Doc*, directed by Frank Perry, a Doc Holliday/Wyatt Earp post-modernist western, with Stacy Keach and Faye Dunawaye. And finally, of course, *W*.

Los Angeles and Ticonderoga are as far apart psychologically as they are geographically. But whatever the excuse, Michael hardly ever went back to see his family, which only made it worse when he did. His guilt combined with his mother's 'ungrateful son' routine was a recipe guaranteed to bring out the worst in both of them. A terrible spiral that so many parents and children get into.

Michael and I were married in Richmond registry office and I spent my last night as a spinster at home with Mum and Dad across the Thames in Twickenham. It was a small wedding. Only about thirty people were there to hear Whitney Armstrong take Lesley Hornby as his lawful wedded wife. On Michael's side were all his actor drinking chums. Nobody came from America. We had our reception at San Lorenzo's in Wimbledon, my friends Mara and Lorenzo's other London restaurant, and for our honeymoon they very sweetly lent us their holiday villa on the Costa Smeralda in Sardinia.

Everything was falling into place. My second album *Please Get My Name Right* was getting great reviews and took me back to LA for the usual round of spectaculars to promote it.

While we were there we had dinner with David and Patsy Puttnam. The business with the four photographers was long since forgotten and we were by now good friends. It was some time since we'd seen each other and we were catching up. The one-time photographer's agent was now a film producer, in LA to finance a film about two turn-of-the-century athletes to be called *Chariots Of Fire* which was proving uphill all the way. (How the major studios must have kicked themselves when in 1981 it went on to win four Oscars, including Best Picture.) I was telling him about the new album and how I was hoping to record the next one in America. One of the people David had recently come across, he told me, was Phil Spector. Would I be interested in meeting him? Would I? Phil Spector is one of the handful of names in the history of pop who are true legends. Before him you'd get the backing track and singers on top. He originated that big deep sound, with layer upon layer. And girl groups were always his thing: the Chiffons, the Ronettes, the Shangri-Las. His first hit had been in 1957 with the Teddy Bears' 'To know, know, know, him is to love, love, him.' I was a huge fan.

There were vague rumours that he'd gone a bit weird since his divorce from Ronnie

Spector, lead singer of the Ronettes. He was now a total recluse. Nobody ever saw him. He had made a fortune and was living out in the Hollywood Hills surrounded by bodyguards. Hollywood paranoia at its most acute. But to anyone who liked that period in pop, the idea of meeting him, let along working with him was just amazing. Through David Puttnam I sent him a copy of my album. A week later David called.

'He'd love to meet you. He loved your voice but thought the production was crap.'

One of the greatest record producers in the world. Who was I to disagree?

Naturally I didn't go alone. At that time I didn't have an agent in America handling the music side of my career, so Michael came with me. Phil Spector lived in this amazing pink Spanish mansion high in the Hollywood Hills that had once belonged to a star of the silent era. Straight out of Sunset Boulevard. Massive black gates opened electronically to let us in.

As we go up the drive several brutish looking dogs are running alongside. I'm feeling very uneasy and won't get out of the car until the huge guy who opens the front door deals with the dogs. Six foot four of solid muscle, he looks like an all-American hunk, but he turns out to be English, from up north, and I begin to feel better. It's short lived. Inside everything is shuttered. Through the gloom of the entrance hall I can just make out that the whole place seems to be a shrine to Elvis. Early Gracelands. Then we go on down endless corridors into a wing and a big very comfortable drawing room. Again all the curtains and shutters are shut and there's a big log fire burning.

'Mr Spector will be down shortly,' the big guy says, and leaves us to admire the fire and flick through stacks of magazines.

So we sit and we sit and we sit. For at least half an hour, possibly more. Still nobody comes. Eventually I start giggling. It was becoming ridiculous.

'Look. He's not going to come. Let's just go.'

I nearly jumped out of my skin as this disembodied voice came over some kind of speaker system.

'I won't call you that name. I won't call you Twiggy. I won't call you that name.'

It just went on and on, punctuated by ghoulish bursts of laughter.

'Ha ha ha. I won't call you that name. I won't call you Twiggy.' On and on like some demented dubbing loop. Was it him speaking? Or was it a recording? By now I'm starting to get the willies. We've come through this maze of corridors. And who knew we were there? As this maniacal voice went on and on my imagination went into overdrive. We might never be seen again. People do disappear and Hollywood has had more than its share of horror stories.

The joke's over. I'm getting a bit tearful. Michael does his best, though later he admitted he was just as worried himself.

'Don't panic, I'm here, nothing's going to happen to you, nobody's going to hurt you.'

But we decide that when somebody comes, we'll just say we've got to go. And we'll go.

Suddenly the door opens and in walks this minuscule man in dark glasses, black leather jacket, black trousers held up with braces, cowboy boots. I start to say something, hoping to have a normal conversation. But he just repeats, 'I won't call you that.'

'Well,' I say, smiling like a royal. 'You don't have to. Call me Lesley.' (Although I actually hate being called Lesley by strangers.)

And I chattered on, just trying to lighten the situation, telling him I was a huge fan. But now he had seen Michael.

'Who are you?'

'I'm Twiggy's husband.'

He wasn't friendly.

'Why are you with her?'

'Like I say, I'm Twiggy's husband. I don't let her go anywhere on her own in this town. It's not safe.'

But now he's back staring at me.

'You've got a great voice, but I hated the album. But maybe we could work together.'

In the middle of saying this he swings around and takes his jacket off. Across his chest is a holster. And yes, that really is a gun. All these years in the States and I'd never seen one, except in the movies. I see the headlines flashing across my brain: Twiggy Found Dead In Hollywood Mansion. I think to myself, whatever you do don't cry, don't panic. We are still sitting down and I remember grabbing Michael by the knee.

Michael is tense. And totally concentrated. I know that if this guy goes for the gun he'd tackle him. Then for his final trick Spector reaches across to a cigarette box, takes out two cigarettes, lights them and puts them into his mouth. Both at once. They look like tusks. By now my knees have gone and I'm trembling like I've been swimming too long in cold water. I get to my feet. No album is worth this. Nothing is worth this. Too late. He pulled the gun out of the holster and began waving it about and rambling. And I just started running. Somehow we found our way outside. I have never been so glad to see daylight in my entire life.

Shortly after Christmas 1977 I found I was pregnant. Both of us were so happy. Ecstatic. We'd waited so long to get married, largely because of problems with Michael's divorce. And being an old-fashioned girl, there was no way I would dream of having a baby without the ceremony. I mean, what would the neighbours say? Then barely a week after I'd told the family the happy news, I had a miscarriage. It happened quite out of the blue during the night. I just woke up and realised something was wrong. I was naturally panicking but Michael stayed calm, put me in the car and took me straight round to emergency at Cedars Sinai hospital in Hollywood. Physically it wasn't that bad. I was barely two months gone. It was just like having a very heavy period. But no miscarriage is easy and emotionally it was very hard indeed. The doctor was brilliant, said it was very common and was just nature's way of getting rid of a foetus that isn't 100 per cent. And that I should take comfort at knowing that I could conceive. He was very young and had a very modern approach. 'To my way of thinking there's no need to wait, just give yourself one period and try again.'

I got pregnant straight away. And no hitches. I felt wonderful and more feminine than I had ever felt before. I adored being pregnant. My hair was half-way down my back and Twig the stick had gone for good. I even had breasts. Maternity clothes were universally horrible in those days, hiding the bump not celebrating it, which I wanted to do. So I wore all the clothes I wore normally, footless tights (what we called leggings in those days — dancers used them to keep their leg muscles warm) and long shirts. I was so excited I didn't care what anyone else thought I looked like. Though I admit that when there are a whole lot of pregnant women together, like when I went to ante-natal classes, we did all look so funny, like arthritic penguins.

I'd hoped that this new life growing inside me might give Michael the inner strength to turn his own life round, not to rely on the vagaries of work to keep him off drink. But no. The by now familiar pattern remained: months when he was fine, then a bender and a downhill spiral until the next tearful promise. One afternoon that summer my sister Shirley and her then boyfriend Trevor came round to our flat in Belsize Park. As they drove up they could hear the music bellowing out of the open windows like an open-air concert.

'Anyone else but you Lesley and I'd never have rung the bell.'

But up they came. Everyone in the flat was drunk, says Shirley, except me. I asked them to stay for a cup of tea but Trevor quite rightly said no. I felt so mortified. I don't know if that was the first time Shirley realised what was happening. But what could she do? If she'd told me to leave I wouldn't have done. I was so stubborn. And however mad it must seem, I loved him. And I was pregnant.

Another night around this time he'd been out drinking with some of his mates and when the pub chucked them out he came back to carry on drinking at the flat and kept going all night. I slept right through it. When I got up in the morning my favourite car ever, our beautiful white Mercedes 250 SEL, a two-door coupé, with the white steering wheel was missing. Michael said that one of the guys had taken the keys without his knowledge to go and get more booze, had driven it down the road, grazed a milk float and ended up wrapped around a lamppost. Most of that story was true. Except the bit about the driver. Who, of course, was Michael. The car was a write-off. And it was a collectors' item. I'd been looking for one for years and we'd only got it a few weeks before. I was not unnaturally more than a bit upset.

That summer we went back to Los Angeles to look for a house. England wasn't working. LA now had the greener grass. If you can work both places, why not? And I agreed. Without the temptations of pubs and his hard core drinking mates, I thought it might be easier for him to stay clean and be the kind, considerate man who I still loved and who loved me. The only proviso was that our baby would be born in England, because if I'd have had her in America she wouldn't have been entitled to a British passport. If you're born abroad you can have a British passport only if both parents are British. In America it's different. One American parent and the child gets an American passport wherever it's born. When they grow up they can decide for themselves. Also having her in London was nice because I'd be near Mum and Dad and my sisters. It's scary when you suddenly have a little baby. I needed all the support I could get.

While we were house-hunting in LA we rented an apartment in what is now the St James' Club, on Sunset Boulevard, a wonderful art deco building then called Sunset Towers. It wasn't long before we found the most perfect house, a lovely old Spanish property in the Hollywood Hills. White-painted, stucco, built in the twenties. Not that big, four bedrooms but wonderfully roomy and a lovely garden (I never learned to call it a yard as Americans do) with a breathtaking view over the city. You could just hear the rumbling of the traffic down on Sunset Strip. It dated from Hollywood's silent era and we fell in love with the oldness of it. High ceilings, white walls. It still had a big old kitchen, old Spanish tiles, big old china sink. American kitchens are wonderful anyway; kitchens and bathrooms are something Americans do really well. It was full of big old-fashioned cupboards. Lots of people would have ripped them out, but not me. The owner was called Peggy Burke, an older woman with grown-up children. The house was now too big for her. But for us, it was perfect.

Carly was due on 30 November 1978 and we spent the last two months of my pregnancy in the Belsize Park flat which we had put on the market. I was booked into Queen Charlotte's Maternity Hospital in Hammersmith. Carly was born one day late on 1 December. I'd gone in for a check-up the day before she was due and the consultant Colin Sims said he would like to induce me. I was ready, he said and my blood pressure was higher than he thought safe. So the next evening they did whatever they do and said to have a good night's sleep as things wouldn't really hot up till the next morning. It was a Thursday. I had a lovely room and Michael and I were just settling down to watch *Top Of The Pops* when the contractions suddenly changed from being gentle twinges to major earthquakes. I thought I was going to give birth there and then. The pain was excruciating. Nothing they'd told us at ante-natal class bore any resemblance to what I was going through.

The contractions had been coming one wave upon another, I could barely get my breath between them. 'It won't be long now,' they kept saying. But when they examined me they discovered I had barely dilated. To give birth the entrance to the womb has to have dilated to ten centimetres. I was one centimetre. Only another nine to go. They asked if I wanted anything and I said only if it wouldn't make my head fuzzy. So around midnight I was given an epidural, an anaesthetic injected into the spine which numbs the lower half of your body but leaves you feeling perfectly clearheaded. The level of anaesthetic was topped up every two hours. It was so effective I fell asleep, my tummy covered with various electrodes monitoring the baby's heart-rate and whatever else they needed. Eventually it was time to push. With an epidural you feel the pressure and you still have to do the work. It's not called labour for nothing. But I wasn't in agony. And then this little head popped out and Michael took a photo and her eyes were open, but we didn't know if it was a little girl or a little boy.

From beginning to end Michael was fantastic. Some men can't handle it. The husband of a friend of mine passed out in the delivery room. Literally keeled over. A great help. Though I'm not sure I would like to be an onlooker. It's all very well when it's happening to you — you can't see over the bump.

My wonderful darling daughter was born on 1 December 1978. And like the old rhyme, Friday's child is indeed loving and giving.

No one can describe that moment when they first hand you your baby. The moment when the dreams of a lifetime and the imagination of the last nine months come together in this scrap of warmth, this helpless little thing, this miracle, whose tiny fingers clasp one of yours with a trust that makes your heart want to break with happiness.

A few moments later the lurch in my heart was followed by a lurch in my stomach. 'Take her away,' I said, 'I'm going to be sick.' It must have been the injection they give you to expel the afterbirth but I suddenly I knew I was going to vomit and I didn't want to throw up over this little thing.

My memory of that night is all slightly blurry. A weird mixture of exhaustion and euphoria. I remember going to sleep with the midwife's words going around my head like a mantra: 'a little girl and she's perfect'. Which is all you want to hear. I stayed in Queen Charlotte's for ten days. For the first few nights they took her and put her in a separate nursery, so that I could get some sleep. There was so much to learn. The nurses used to laugh. At 6lb 5oz, she wasn't that small, but she was very long and narrow, completely dwarfed by her nappy. She was so skinny I could get my thumb and forefinger around her thigh.

I loved feeding her. Although I had an infection for a couple of days which turned my breasts into bricks I'm glad I stuck it out. Far from spoiling your figure, it's nature's way of getting you back into shape. As the baby suckles you can feel your stomach muscles being pulled in. I was so lucky to be able to feed her. Not everyone can. However women who can but don't, in my opinion are mad. Not only is it the best start for the baby but it's a wonderful feeling. Nothing could be more natural or better for mother and child. I didn't have a lot of milk so when she was six weeks old she went on to a bottle. But I could still feed her for comfort, which I did for a couple of months.

Michael came every day. He was so proud of his little girl. Completely besotted. As for names we had spent hours before she was born making lists, like you do. For a boy we'd had normal names like James, and more unusual ones, like Fletcher (from Fletcher Christian in *Mutiny on the Bounty*: Michael was a Marlon Brando fanatic). For a girl I'd liked Scarlett, not because of *Gone with the Wind*, I just thought it was a great name. Though somebody said it might be a terrible burden if she wasn't Vivien-Leigh-gorgeous when she grew up. But I needn't have worried, she is. Michael's mother didn't approve of the name at all. (Scarlet woman.) So it was Carly. I had always been a fan of Carly Simon's songs, and loved the name. Later when I met her she told me she'd been named after an aunt who was called it as a nickname for Caroline.

The media of course had their own nickname. Twiglet. One desperate snapper managed to con his way into Queen Charlotte's by pretending to be a father. He didn't get his picture. In fact he had passed me in the corridor but slopping along in my dressing gown and looking as sparkly as you do when you've just had a baby, he hadn't recognised me. The Matron was furious. Rather than just sneaking out, we decided to do a press call. That way we hoped they would leave us alone. And anyway, we were so proud. Michael and I stood on the steps of the hospital, me with this precious bundle in my arms. 'What was it like? What are you going to call her?' The usual stuff. Then one young reporter at the front made a comment that was so offensive I can't even bring myself to repeat it. I saw red. If I hadn't been holding Carly I'd have punched him.

'How dare you.'

There was a horrible silence, then another journalist, a woman, chipped in, 'What do you mean: she's gorgeous.' And the hack pack all agreed and made it very clear to this young upstart that he was out of order. He slunk away. Stupid insensitive boy. Later we used to call her Elmer Fudd — Bugs Bunny's persecutor ('I'm gonna shoot that wabbit.'). Because when she laughed, that's what she looked like. All pink gums and bald head. She was so sweet and funny.

We did have pictures taken, both before and after the great event, by Norman Parkinson, one of the great fashion photographers, and one of the most eccentric. I didn't work with him a lot but he was adorable, although he frightened me a bit when we first met; six foot two, very thin and with a huge white handlebar moustache. He always wore a little embroidered Indian hat and outrageous clothes. Parkinson was larger than life and looked and sounded like a colonel in the Indian Army at the time of the Raj.

Nothing can prepare you for the reality of life with a baby. I was so nervous and frightened. When I was pregnant I remember thinking how great it would be when the baby's born and of all the things I could do when I'd put it down to sleep: get my sewing machine out, make clothes, baby things, and cook. Forget it. The whole day, the whole twenty-four hours of it, is baby, baby, baby. A baby is not like a shoe which you can take off when you feel tired. Babies are more like your feet, you can put them up, but they're always there at the end of your legs, part of you. For ever.

Mum was already seventy so there was never a question of her helping out and I didn't want anyone I didn't know staying at our flat. So for the first couple of weeks my friend Mary Frampton came to stay.

Mary is one of my oldest and dearest friends. We had met through Terry Knight, sponsor of our ill-fated *Gotta Sing, Gotta Dance* film project. He knew the guitarist Peter Frampton and one evening when Peter was away touring, we had dinner with Terry at Mr Chow's and he brought Mary, Peter's long-time girlfriend (they had been sweethearts since they met at art school) as his 'date'. That must have been around 1968 and we've been friends ever since. We hit it off immediately. There's only six months between us in age. She's very bright, very funny, very sweet and very beautiful. In fact she modelled for a bit. I adored her from the start. We don't agree on everything: she's very different to me. Although she comes from a pukka army background she's very eccentric and fey. A natural flower child. While I'm very down to earth and grounded. Sadly the marriage with Peter broke down. By the time Carly was born she was with Hal Lindes, bass player with Dire Straits.

Those early weeks are all about adjusting, getting used to the fact that your centre of gravity has shifted. Realising that your life has changed for ever. Having Carly put everything else into perspective. The troubles with Michael were unimportant. Without Michael there would have been no Carly. Although I was very tired, I found it very joyous. I had no postnatal blues. I was really content. I can remember thinking I don't care if I ever work again, I was so besotted with her.

However the one thing I never got used to was the lack of sleep. It really threw me sideways. Wonderful though she was in every other way, Carly didn't sleep through the night until she was about three. I wasn't prepared for it. I've always been a great sleeper. The only person I've met who loves his sleep as much as I do is Leigh. I didn't think I'd ever meet someone who sleeps longer than me. We can sleep ten hours a night.

It's not only because they're crying you wake up. Sometimes it's because they're not crying. So you have to go and check they're breathing. When she woke in the night I would go in to her, pat her back and sing to her. No words. Just made up tunes. I'd wait until she went back to sleep, then creep back to bed. Unfortunately from her bedroom to the hallway there were two creaky floorboards. I'd try and step across them, but I didn't always make it. So back I'd go and try again. But no matter how tired I was

I never took her into bed with me, except in the morning for a cuddle, easy though it would have been. I'd seen it with friends. Once you start it never stops. Children need parameters they can rely on, even babies. It's how they feel secure. And you need your sleep when you can get it.

We had moved back to LA and our new family home when Carly was about two months old. To help me I had Brenda, a wonderful Scottish nanny who we had brought with us. She had answered our ad in *The Lady* magazine and I liked her instantly, so jolly and with a lovely soft Scottish accent. She stayed with us for a year. But it's a very lonely life, especially in LA where you've got to drive everywhere. No taking the pram up to Kensington Gardens for a chat and a packet of fruit gums with other nannies by the Round Pond. I've had several nannies over the years and, with one exception, they have all been wonderful.

Michael was as happy as I'd ever known him. He adored Carly, absolutely worshipped her, and he had a new channel for his ambitions. While I was being a new Mum, the new Dad was writing an original film script, *Jonah*, as a vehicle for himself. It was the coming thing. Sylvester Stallone had started this trend in 1976 with *Rocky*. Until then he was just a B-movie actor. *Jonah* was a contemporary western about a rancher who needs to raise money to build up his herd. When the bank turn him down, he takes matters into his own hands. Man against the system. Michael spent a year getting it into shape. And it was good. Very good. It wasn't just me who thought so. A couple of producers were interested, but they wanted to take it to a bankable star. Michael said no.

'I've done this for me. And I want to do it.'

I stood by him wholeheartedly. Though with hindsight, it was probably a mistake. With a big name in the lead I think it might just have happened.

When we were over in London we'd seen the McCartneys and Linda had asked if she could read it. She phoned Michael the next day. She loved the script.

'Have you seen *Electra Glide In Blue*?'

'It's one of my favourite films.'

It had been a huge cult movie in the early seventies, about a small-town motor-cycle cop in the *Easy Rider* vein. The director, James Guercio, had made his money and his name as a record producer, which is how the McCartneys knew him.

'Would you mind if I sent it to him? I think he might be interested.'

Linda had judged well. He thought it was great. And would we like to meet with him at his ranch in Colorado? Michael was elated.

Caribou was not only where Jimmy Guercio lived but he had built his recording studio there. Bands would go and record there rather than stay in the city. It was well known in the rock 'n' roll world. Chicago was his headline band. Paul McCartney recorded an album there and Elton John did *Yellow Brick Road*.

The ranch was a few miles out of Boulder, in the foothills of the Rockies. I had never been to Colorado before. It was winter and the whole place was deep in snow. We stayed in this beautiful chalet which was completely self-contained; just as well, as Carly was now coming up for her second birthday. Although she was very good, she was walking, and like all toddlers, fascinated by everything. She had a blue all-in-one padded suit. And the first time we went out in the snow and touched it, her legs went rigid. She had no idea what it was. It was so funny. I wished I'd had a video of it.

Jimmy Guercio was a sweet man. He was incredibly successful and like many successful people he had an easy, unpushy confidence. He was married to an ex-model called Lucy who had modelled a bit after me. They had two children, and one was the same age as Carly, so it was perfect. It was like a holiday. We stayed a week. Michael and Jimmy worked on the script, while Lucy and I played with the little ones. For the meetings, we'd go along as a team. I'd been involved in the script from the start. When you live with somebody you inevitably get caught up in their projects. And I so desperately wanted it to happen for him.

For a long time Jimmy was committed to doing it, and with Michael as the lead. But it just never happened. It wasn't that there was a phone call saying, 'We're going to drop your project.' Films take years to set up and the first thing he had to do was to raise the money. It didn't help that Michael wasn't bankable. It also didn't help that Michael drank. My own belief is that as he and Jimmy got closer, Michael dropped his guard and had one drink too many. And I think that's what killed it. Suddenly they see this guy who gets legless and the money people are scared. And who can blame them?

Word gets around. When it comes to alcohol, Tinseltown is so hypocritical. Ken Russell tells the story of how he had to order his favourite tipples in the commissary by code. Pepsi was vodka, Seven Up champagne, and it would arrive in the appropriate bottle. Or something like that. Ken wouldn't work without his bubbly and everybody knew it. And he wasn't the only one. The crime was being found out. Michael didn't exactly make it difficult for them. I remember one evening going to a Japanese restaurant which was arranged as a series of little cubicles; each party would have their own where you'd sit on the floor. Michael, all good intentions, had started by drinking Coke, but soon he was on to the saki. And, of course, there were producers there who we knew in one of the other little cubicles. At the beginning everyone was laughing. Nothing like a funny drunk to add to an evening's entertainment. But it ended with Michael completely out of it, running between the 'rooms' and jumping through one of those Japanese paper walls. Like most alcoholics it was self-destruction.

Once people know within the Hollywood community that you've got a problem, that's it. Why cast somebody who might be trouble? Stars have a little more leeway.

Now that Michael didn't have the pub to go to he had taken to drinking by himself. Beer with the boys had become secret vodka in his orange juice at breakfast. When people start drinking in the morning you know something is seriously wrong. I suspected he was drinking again because of how he was behaving. But he was doing it secretly so I became a snoop which I found humiliating. It's a horrible thing to have to do to another person. I'm not particularly suspicious or jealous, but when the suspicion sets in, trust goes, and it's all over really. And in the end it kills the love.

I knew where he hid his vodka and I would get up in the middle of the night and I'd pour half of the bottle down the sink and fill it up with water. In my mind I'd think it would take him longer to get drunk. It would start with breakfast and the orange juice. If vodka's been added to the glass it gets a kind of alcoholic film. When I look back I think God, why did I do it? Watering his vodka. What good was that going to do? I must have been crazy. Even now I hate the smell of vodka. People say it's odourless, but I know exactly what it smells like.

I was living on the edge. When people rang up about dinner two weeks down the line, what was I to say? I didn't know what state he'd be in; whether he'd be dry or drunk and disorderly; whether he was in love with the world or whether he hated the world. The highs and lows of an alcoholic are huge. They're either jolly and loving everything and everybody or they're down in the depths. Although there seems to be a pattern to an alcoholic's behaviour, they are also unpredictable. And from the moment we arrived anywhere, there would be that terrible subterfuge and planning how to get the car keys so that he couldn't drive home, which he always insisted on doing.

It's a devastating situation to find yourself in. That's why there are organisations to help families. By then I certainly knew about them. But when you're very well known, it's hard. Because you feel vulnerable. You feel, they're all going to know you, know there's a problem and before long the press will get hold of it and just compound the problem. So I never went.

It not only affected Michael's career, it affected mine too. Los Angeles is Network City. If you're not in, you're out. People just didn't want to have to cope with him. I know what it's like. I've been out with people who have a drink problem and it's hard work. I can see their partners nervously watching the hand reaching for yet another top-up of wine or whatever. Wondering if they've laced their glass of Chardonnay with vodka. I know what they're going through. It's so painful. So painful. But you can't say anything. It's this dreadful secret world. In the end people stopped inviting us and I don't blame them. If you've got a guy who's going to start screaming at another guest what's the point? You become social poison.

When Carly was about two I was beginning to think about working again. Until then I was perfectly happy being at home being a mother. It was what I did. I know some women who are thinking of work even before the umbilical cord is cut, but not me.

I can't remember sitting down and saying, 'I've got to work again.' But neither of us had worked in a long time and someone had to bring in the bacon. I'd come to realise that I was the breadwinner. Economics not ambition.

14

Eliza Doolittle, who Henry Higgins describes as sounding like 'a bilious pigeon', is tailor-made for a girl once described as sounding like a demented parrot. I had never seen *Pygmalion*, although I'd seen *My Fair Lady*, my first ever outing to the theatre with Mum and Dad when I was twelve. It was Patrick Garland, who had directed some wonderful things in the theatre by that time, who first suggested I should do *Pygmalion*. It was shortly after *The Boyfriend* and he was trying to get a tele-film of J. M. Barrie's *Mary Rose* off the ground with me in the title role. It didn't happen but Patrick has always been a wonderful ally and one day I hope we'll work together on something.

But in 1981 I was thirty-two and subconsciously I must have realised that if I was to play Eliza, it should be now. I'd always been a great believer in fate. If things were to happen, they would. But as you get older you realise sometimes you have to give fate a nudge.

I'd recently given my acting toes a paddle with *The Blues Brothers* film. I'd been working with Donna Summer on a possible album when a call came through to the studio from my American agent. I didn't think twice. John Belushi and Dan Ackroyd were huge. Their show, *Saturday Night Live* was America's answer to *Monty*

Python, avant garde and brave. Like Monty Python it was essentially a series of sketches, though it had a quite different format. For example it featured the hottest rock bands in town. But like Python it had become essential viewing. Going out on Saturday night was OK as long as you were home by eleven thirty to see the show. The Blues Brothers started out as a one-off sketch but the two characters, Jake and Elwood, soon became regulars.

The script was the usual mayhem and madness, a surreal road movie, studded with celebrity cameos. Which was where I came in. I had only a couple of small scenes, but I was so thrilled to be asked. ('Oh my God, Belushi and Ackroyd.') I had never met either of them but was soon thanking God that my scene was with Dan. Belushi was away with the fairies doing every drug known to the pharmaceutical industry and then some. It finally killed him when he died of some terrible drug cocktail in the Chateau Marmont in 1983. It didn't surprise me.

The Dan Ackroyd character, Elwood's, day-time job was a garage attendant. The joke was that he'd be so busy chatting up this glamorous woman in a soft top Jag (me) that he'd forget to take the nozzle out of my car and gas would be spilling out over the road, the pump running up a total of thousands of dollars. When we actually filmed it, it was bitterly cold and they put me in thermal undies and I did the scene with my bottom half wrapped up in blankets and a hotwater bottle on my lap.

It was great fun to do. *The Blues Brothers* was shot in Chicago, John Belushi's home town. (Dan is Canadian.) They had both come out of the team of improvisational comedians called Second City. By the time I got there everything was totally out of hand, mainly due to Belushi being out of it most of the time. Although everyone tried to hush it up. The original six months shooting schedule had long since been abandoned. I was a big fan and very nervous so I was very grateful when Dan suggested he pick me up to drive to the location for my day's work. A lot of comedians are revved up all the time and feel they have to make you laugh. Dan Ackroyd is not like that. He's actually quite quiet and a really sweet man. Most actors and stars I've met are really lovely. Although there are the spoiled troublesome few which Hollywood actually breeds unwittingly, or maybe wittingly. They become so huge and are treated like gods and then when they misbehave the system wonders why. Yet the system makes them. Money making machines. A vicious circle.

The Blues Brothers had come through my American agent, but I was still in touch with my English agent, Jean Diamond, who I'd met through Michael. And it was to her I suggested *Pygmalion*. She immediately took the idea to the BBC. Jean agreed with me: it was a gift. But they sat on it for a year. Unlike Cinderella, *Pygmalion* was part of England's literary heritage. Producers and casting directors are always a bit nervous of me, particularly in England. They like to categorise and I'm hard to categorise. If anything they saw me as light entertainment material. Mrs Patrick Campbell, George Bernard Shaw's muse and the finest actress of her generation, had to learn cockney to play Eliza, as had every Eliza until me. But letting the genuine article loose on the Great God Shaw was a risk too far. Finally we gave up on the Beeb and Jean tried Keith Richardson and David Cunliffe at Yorkshire TV and they jumped. From then on it was their baby. I had nothing to do with it. I was just a member of the cast.

The director was John Glenister, north London, very working class and we got on a treat. Robert Powell was cast as Professor Higgins, younger than usual but it worked really well and gave the piece a sexual frisson and made more sense of Eliza's ambivalence to him. Freddy was Shaun Scott, now best known as Detective Inspector Deakin in *The Bill* and Mona Washbourne was the housekeeper. She played the same part in *My Fair Lady*, the film. Colonel Pickering was Ronald Fraser who I knew quite well as he was a drinking buddy of Michael's. Sadly he died early in 1997.

My first dramatic play and my first classic of the stage; no singing, no dancing, the female lead. No wonder I was nervous. We rehearsed in some funny old rehearsal hall in Wimbledon, an easy drive from Mum and Dad's where Carly and I were staying. Michael stayed in LA where he was doing a pilot for a TV series. And it was good to get away. Particularly when I was working it was actually much easier if he wasn't there. Not counting the beer ad, this was the first time he'd worked as an actor since *Oil Strike North* — an agonising six years. With my ever-growing success — over and above modelling — staring him in the face, taunting him, I think his ego must have taken a terrible battering.

The last time we'd been over to England was for a music industry ceremony organised by Capital Radio, shortly after the Phil Spector experience. Elton John was to receive an award and they had booked me to do two songs from my album, including my new single, a lovely sad ballad by Roger Cook, who wrote 'Melting Pot' and 'I'd Like To Teach The World To Sing', which became the Coca Cola anthem. Polygram were thrilled. I was bloody terrified. Although it wasn't broadcast live, everybody out front would be in the business, including Paul and Linda and, of course, Elton. My run-through was fine. But by the time I went on, the band had been to the bar.

So I do my first song. It's not half as frightening as I feared. The audience feels like family. Then we're on to the title song of my new album, 'Please Get My Name Right'. Please Get My Tune Right would have been more like it. Whether the pianist wasn't watching the conductor or what I don't know. It had started all right but at the beginning of the second verse, while the pianist played one thing, the rest of them were a bar behind. I tried to sing. But I couldn't. My heart was pounding. So I just stopped and said to the audience, 'I'm sorry. I can't sing like this. Something has gone terribly wrong. It sounds Japanese. If it's all right with everyone I'm going to start again.' Everybody laughed and clapped but Linda said she'll never forget it, or the feeling of her hands getting hot with nerves when it all went haywire.

We spent the following weekend with the McCartneys. It was about three o'clock in the morning when Michael suddenly announced that we were leaving. He hadn't stopped arguing since we'd come up to bed. Carly was only tiny and fast asleep in her cot but he insisted. Anything to keep the peace. I was so embarrassed that they'd wake up and find us gone even though I left them a note to explain. They were such good friends and really trying to be nice to him though I think they were desperately worried, so concerned for me. Fighting only made it worse. So we drove off into the night: two and a half hours back to London. Madness. Only once did I refuse to play that middle-of-the-night-leaving-game. We were staying with dear friends Stewart Grimshaw and Simon Sainsbury at their weekend retreat, which was one of the gatehouses at Petworth in Sussex and was like a mini castle. This time he said he was going back to LA.

'I'm going to the airport. I never want to see you again.'

'Okay. Go.'

So he left. I can't remember what had started it. Just one of those stupid arguments. I was so fed up and I just wanted to sleep and I knew Stewart and Simon would take me back to London. And they were also concerned about me. They couldn't tell me to get out of that relationship — that had to be my own decision — but they made it clear they were always there if I needed them. And of course when I got back to London Michael hadn't gone anywhere.

By the time I got into that rehearsal room I'd read *Pygmalion* backwards and forwards till I knew the whole damn play by heart. But I was still a bag of nerves. Once you get involved and start learning, and everything's broken down, it becomes a wonderful learning experience. I knew the difficulty for me wasn't the early stuff. I just did me and leant on the Cockney — not that I was a real Cockney. But then neither was Eliza. She was from Lisson Grove, north-west London, like me.

John Glenister was a dream. I think he knew that I was probably a pale shade of green. I was dream casting for the beginning of Eliza but the second half . . . Her accent has to be cut glass. I knew I was going to need help. That's one of the good sides of my nature. I love to learn: I love going to classes, I love doing lessons. Which is great because it means you can attempt anything. I was sent to a voice coach, a lovely lady called Jenny Patrick. When we first started she really scared me. It was like going back to school. I suppose if they go into a theatre company, they've got to appear to have authority. Joan Washington who I worked with much later, another wonderful voice coach married to Richard E. Grant, was just as scary at first but we soon became good friends and would spend half the time giggling and laughing.

I had all the same problems with my vowels

that Eliza did. Like my 'I'. In upper-class English it's very short. But I tended to pronounce it as a diphthong, all slidey. Then there was the 'ow'. As in 'How'. It had to be a round sound, not the squawk you make when you shut your finger in the car door. I could do it, but it had to sound genuine, with no hint of music-hall parody. It wasn't only the accent, but my voice itself. Eliza the flower seller could sound as nasal as the *Roadrunner*, but it wouldn't work for the would-be society swan. I had to lower it. But like Eliza herself I'm a pretty good mimic. Miss Eynsford-Hill was played by Marsha Fitzalan, who's lovely and funny and is really quite posh. In fact very posh: the daughter of the Duke of Norfolk. And she had this wonderful period accent, derived from various ancient relatives. All I had to do was copy her. In the end I think I succeeded. Where my accent slips, as it did now and then, people say it only adds to the poignancy, to Eliza's vulnerability. It was genuine, if not always in the places Shaw intended.

There was only one slight sadness. *Pygmalion* was shot on video, which I hate. It can never look as good as film. I love the texture and sensuality of film. It's mainly to do with the light. My view is they should do game shows, news, documentary-type interviews, etc., on tape, but drama on film. Sadly TV companies have so much money invested in video equipment and studios, I suppose they have to use it and it's cheaper, although in my view it's a false economy in the long run. Yet they are forever trying to convince themselves and everybody else it can be as good as film. For me it never is. So they used three cameras and we did it like a play, running straight through just as if we were on stage, which was rather wonderful, because you're not constantly stopping and starting like you do when you're normally shooting on film.

After three weeks' rehearsal in London we went up to Yorkshire and shot it over a week, an act a day. The scene I loved best was the tea-party, when for the first time Eliza is introduced to people who don't know who she is. Her accent is by then top hole, but her grammar and vocabulary still lag way behind. The results are hilarious. I wore the most beautiful Edwardian dress, royal blue silk with black lace, so narrow around the ankles it was all I could do not to waddle like a Japanese Geisha. Or trip up. To give me the authentic shape and posture, I had to wear a crippling corset. Until I was pregnant with Carly I'd hardly ever worn a bra, let alone anything else. This was the first time I'd ever had a heaving bosom. The costume designer was fantastic and had given us wonderful hats. Mine was so gorgeous that John Glenister decided on a close-up. He left it till the rest of the scene was finished. The tea-party was choreographed round an Edwardian love seat — four seats joined together to form an island in the middle of Mrs Higgins' drawing room. In order to talk to the person next to you, you had to turn your head well over ninety degrees. It looked marvellous. When he set up the shot he realised he needed Pauline Jameson who played

Mrs Eynsford-Hill to come back to give me my lines off camera.

In response to a line from her, I was supposed to say to camera, 'She would have needed a hat.' Then I turn to look at her. 'Let alone a hat pin.' I didn't see Pauline come back in because I'm being powdered and they're still trying to light under the brim of the hat. Then John says 'Action'. Pauline says her line then I say half mine, and then can't believe my eyes. Instead of a glamorous old dowager in her flowerpot hat, I find I'm looking at Coco the Clown.

Of course I just exploded. Because she wasn't in shot she hadn't bothered to put her hat back on and was just wearing her curly red wig, which because the hat was so heavy had been completely plastered down on top with red curls poking out of the side. Just like Coco the Clown. I thought I was going to die, because I had the corset on and I couldn't breathe. Tears were streaming down my face. The whole crew were laughing by now. And there was me screaming 'I can't breathe, my corset, my corset.'

I was so embarrassed. By now Pauline had looked in a mirror.

'Oh my dear, I'm so sorry.'

She went and took her wig off then we tried again. I would compose myself. She would give me the line. I'd turn round and that would be that. Collapse of thin party. I'd got that visual picture of her in my head. We tried for forty-five minutes. We tried doing it with somebody else giving me the lines. But it was no good. Every time I said the line I dissolved into hysterics.

I was just like the famous out-takes with Peter Sellers doing Clouseau when sometimes they'd do a scene for a whole day. The trouble is that once you've started laughing, that's it. As I mentioned before the least silly little thing can sometimes set you off. I suppose it must be the nervous tension or something. But actors have never been able to explain it properly. And directors generally find it very annoying.

To my great relief we got some amazing reviews. Peter Fiddick of the *Guardian* said, 'This was a performance and a production to relish . . . As for Misses Andrews and Hepburn, eat your hearts out.' And if I may be immodest the *Daily Mail* said, 'Twiggy was a triumph . . . proving beyond doubt that she is an actress of great talent and with a fine sense of comic timing.' And there was more. The *Daily Telegraph* called it, 'The treat of the holiday . . . Impeccably played by the whole cast, *Pygmalion* made me want to laugh, cry and applaud in the same breath. It is possibly the best thing Yorkshire [TV] have ever done.' And get this: the *Evening Standard*: 'I was amazed at the brilliance and truthfulness of *Pygmalion* and Twiggy's performance . . . Her first entrance into Mrs Higgins' salon could not have been done better by anyone, and mention who you want.' Well — all very encouraging.

Unfortunately it went out on ITV on 28 December 1981, a direct clash with the BBC's first-ever screening on British TV of *Gone With The Wind*. And in those days VCRs were still something only very few people had. It was sold to the States as part of a parcel of programmes to a cable company, who promptly went bottom up. It still belongs to the liquidators and is sitting in a vault somewhere and has never been screened in America. Often when you look back at something you did years ago, there's that inward groan. The realisation that comes with hindsight that it could have been better, that the pleasure of the experience has spilled over into judgement. But I watched it again recently and I am very proud of it. When I think that it was the first time I'd ever done anything like it, my stomach curdles — one of the problems of having a well-known face. You can't go off and practise somewhere out of the public gaze. If I'd have joined a repertory or stock company, I couldn't have done it secretly. When I've made mistakes, and I have, they've been made in the full glare of the limelight. But I just tell myself in the end it's only a film, it's only the telly, it's only a play. You're not going to die. The worst they can do is tell you you're crap, that you'll never work again. It'll make you cry, it'll hurt you but it won't destroy you. And I just have to think of all the things I'd have missed out on, if I'd have been too frightened to try.

My courage was about to be put to the test.

Michael's TV pilot, like the majority of TV pilots in America, had not been picked up and his script deal with Jimmy Guercio had finally come to nothing. So we decided to up sticks and move back to London. There was nothing now to keep Michael in LA and after all my good notices for *Pygmalion* I was optimistic that something would come of it. Over Christmas I'd done *Captain Beaky's Musical Christmas* at the Apollo Theatre in London's West End, Jeremy Lloyd's sequence of poems about animals, with Eleanor Bron, Keith Michell and Jeremy himself. And they seemed to like it. I was thrilled — and not a little embarrassed — to read Jack Tinker's review in the *Mail*: 'Twiggy is quite simply the loveliest thing on the London stage and she has that affectionate quality which gives her songs and stories the magic that made Gracie Fields and Stanley Holloway masters of the art of the comic monologue.' Francis King reviewing for the *Sunday Telegraph* wrote: 'As in the case of Vivien Leigh the perfection of Twiggy's features has for too long retarded recognition of her emergent talents as an actress of style and subtlety. Someone should now write her a musical of her own.' Just the boost my confidence needed — and the recording of the show won us another silver disc.

Carly was by now rising four and Michael and I agreed that we wanted her schooled in England. Los Angeles wasn't a city for young children. There were parks, but you couldn't walk in them for fear of being mugged. Just too many freaky people, not to mention the drugs. And much as I loved the house, no one could say we'd been happy there. So we put it on the market, shipped our furniture back to Mum and Dad's and rented a flat near Hampstead Heath.

We arrived back in England in August 1981. In October I got a call from Tommy Tune. Over the past ten years since *The Boyfriend*, Tommy had gone from strength to strength and had broken just about every record on Broadway. In Hollywood the six foot six dancer from Wichita Falls, Texas was pretty much uncastable but Broadway adored him. It was where he had started, in the chorus line of *Baker Street*. In 1973 he'd won a Tony for Best Featured Actor in a Musical: *Seesaw*. In 1980 he won the Tony for Best Choreography: *A Day In Hollywood, A Night in the Ukraine*. When he called me he'd just finished *Nine*, which he'd directed and which went on to win him another Tony for Best Direction of a Musical. The show itself won five Tonys. To date Tommy Tune has won nine Tonys: the only person in theatrical history to win in all four categories and the only person to win the same two awards two years in a row. In 1981 when I got his call he was as hot as you get short of spontaneous combustion.

It was a few years since he had been on stage himself — even on Broadway being six foot six has its drawbacks — and he'd concentrated on choreography and direction. He'd never given up on our plan to do something together and the time and energy we had invested in *Gotta Sing, Gotta Dance*, exactly ten years before was about to pay dividends. How would I like to star with him on Broadway in a remake of the Gershwin musical *Funny Face*? Not the Astaire/Hepburn film but the original 1927 Broadway show with Fred and his sister Adele.

'Don't be silly,' I said, 'I can't do that.'

'There's no such thing as can't.'

He said he'd send me the script.

When it arrived, the champagne lost its fizz. I even wondered if I'd been sent the right envelope. It was weird and certainly didn't read like a period musical, except one seen through the eyes of Salvador Dali perhaps. The director was the young avant garde theatre director Peter Sellars (not to be confused with the late actor). The script was by his friend Timothy Mayer, a Yale academic, best known for his 'reinterpretation of the classics'.

Thanks to Ken Russell and Phillip Jenkinson I'd seen just about every film musical ever made. But I'd never come across anything like this. I called Tommy.

'Look, perhaps I'm thick, but this is unbelievable.'

He told me not to worry. That it was still only a draft and by the time we were into rehearsal everything would be ironed out.

The script just did not work, and to be honest I found it hard to understand. Frankly, in my opinion, the script was pretty awful. The back-drop was the race to fly the Atlantic (which Lindbergh won in 1927). It took in gun-running in Mexico; white slavery in Morocco, Freud, Trotsky, Lenin; a phoney black bishop; stock market gamblers; a Russian spy disguised as a mechanic and as heroine, Edythe Herbert, the first woman to swim the English Channel. Tommy's character (a pilot): 'I buried eighteen friends in the Sierra Madres. Lousy real estate and I didn't have a shovel. But I used the butt end of a carbine and I dug me eighteen beaner graves' — all this cut with good ol' Gershwin standards like 'S'Wonderful', 'Funny Face', 'My One and Only', and 'How Long Has This Been Going On'. Which after about ten minutes is what the audience would have been thinking. What Ira Gershwin thought about it I don't like to imagine. But he was still alive and actually wrote new lyrics for us. As for what I thought, to quote a classic line from the script: 'Shove this for a giggle.'

But I did believe in Tommy. And I trusted him. He must know what he was doing. And I knew that Peter Sellars, this new, very hot, exciting, mad, young genius director was his choice. On paper it made sense. Tommy hadn't been on stage in years and he wanted to concentrate on his performance and the choreography. He didn't want to direct.

When Tommy called a year later in the late summer of 1982 to tell me that *My One and Only*, as it was now called (having strayed so far from the original) had been given the green light, I was pretty amazed. I certainly hadn't been counting on it. So after little more than a year in England, it was major pack-up time and back to the States. Two months' rehearsal in New York, six weeks in Boston, then opening on Broadway at the St James Theatre on 24 March 1983. Whether we'd be there for two days or two years depended on Frank Rich, the *New York Times* critic known as the Butcher of Broadway. If he gave us the thumbs down, we wouldn't last a week.

I'd always loved New York, though I hadn't

been back for years. The show's major backers were Robert and Jimmy Nederlander, a famous theatrical dynasty that goes back generations. As well as owning eleven Broadway theatres, the Nederlanders at that time owned the Adelphi and the Aldwych theatres in London. Jimmy let us stay in his amazing apartment in the Sherry Netherlands hotel until we found somewhere to rent. It overlooks Central Park on the east side across from the Plaza on the corner of Fifth avenue.

I was straight into rehearsals so it was Michael who found us the apartment on Broadway and 81st. It was a nice old building, old fashioned, with four big rooms and a kitchen with a good play area for Carly. There was no lift but we were only on the second floor. Alone of Manhattan's great avenues, Broadway doesn't follow the grid system, but swings diagonally north-west. The Upper West Side is probably my favourite part of Manhattan, with wonderful pre-war buildings, now very fashionable but then a bit rundown, funky and arty.

The first day of rehearsals I was excited but terrified. Since *The Boyfriend* and that indelible year spent dancing with Tommy, I'd only done some dancing on my TV shows and that was about it. We'd start at nine then I'd go off with Karen Tamburrelli, one of the lead dancers, and I would spend most of my day with her. She was wonderful. She would learn a routine from Tommy just like that, and then spend whatever time was needed teaching it to me, 'learning my feet' as I always called it. Karen was quite voluptuous, and her Italian mum used to be so worried about how thin I was and was forever sending pasta round to fatten me up.

Peter, Tim and Tommy were still putting the show together. Tommy choreographed on the hoof, inspired by the music. All I said to him was, 'Don't give me too many pirouettes or I'll fall over.'

Tommy built our duets around me. He's such an amazing dancer and could so easily have overshadowed me, but he very generously gave me the spotlight. He reserved his virtuoso bits for the number he did with Honi Coles, a famous old black tap dancer from Vaudeville days. Although Tommy was by then forty-four, ten years older than me, he was still in great shape. But the prize for fitness married to pure artistry has to go to Honi. Their double act in the second half brought the house down every night. I used to go and watch it in the wings every performance. I didn't believe pairs of feet could do that. It wasn't big things but things close to the floor. And the rhythm. His part was built around him. Honi was seventy-three.

The songs weren't a problem because Gershwin was very much my style and I knew I was going to be miked. Most musicals are miked now, so you don't have to have the lung power of Ethel Merman. They spent days getting the amplification right, to get an authentic period sound. Nothing brash. After all we were singing over an orchestra, not fighting to be heard over a big rock band. All I prayed was that my voice would hold up. Apart from *Cinderella*, I'd never done a continuous run and *Cinderella* was only for two months. But in fact my voice seemed to muscle up and got stronger and stronger.

Just to be working again was pure joy. At home things with Michael were really bad. Made worse by the fact that I was happy — as long as I wasn't with him. Christmas in New York, then off to the Colonial Theater, Boston, and another two weeks' rehearsal before previews began. We all knew the show wasn't working. Great chunks would be thrown out in rehearsal. Sometimes I'd say something quietly to Tommy and he'd try to reassure me.

'I know it's not right, but that's why we're trying out.'

But it was really nothing to do with me. I was employed as an actress. And I had my own worries; life at home and the sheer panic of 'learning my feet' and trying to find the courage to go out there and do it.

One morning soon after we arrived in Boston Tommy gave me the news.

'Don't panic and don't get upset, but Peter and the team have gone.'

Peter Sellars was only twenty-five but already had forty productions under his belt, most of them at Harvard. He was known for doing things differently. He once staged *Anthony and Cleopatra* in a Harvard swimming pool. Just before his departure he won a $144,000 five-year grant from an arts foundation 'for exceptionally talented individuals'. Bernard Carragher, the producer who had originally introduced Peter Sellars to Tommy, later admitted that the *wunderkind*, as everyone called him, had conceived the whole thing as 'neo-Brechtian', which would contrast 'the lightness of the musical numbers with the impending doom of the Depression'. On a personal level I got on well with Peter, but some people didn't. It's easy to look back and see what went wrong. (The script was totally inappropriate for a start.) But with Peter's amazing reputation and Tommy's amazing track record, everyone thought between the two of them they would turn out brilliant work. But the first post-modernist Broadway musical had turned out to be the first post-modernist flop. In the end they took the only decision they could. And without a backward glance Tommy and his co-choreographer Thommie Walsh set about creating the show I had always envisaged: a new look at a lovely old-fashioned musical. In the meantime the show must go on. We had dates, people booked. We had to open. The hardest part was having to be twinkly for all the publicity. We did have a show, great dancing and great songs, but it was a mish-mash. Tommy immediately started cutting away some of the problem areas. But it needed more than pruning, however radical.

My One and Only opened in Boston to terrible reviews. The *Boston Globe* had it pretty well taped: 'After eight previews, endless revisions, midnight editing, startling re-arrangements, not to mention firings and hirings, the show is nothing but a shambles.' I was accused of sounding like 'a throaty scandals headliner'.

The show was 'an infinite disorder within emptiness' and 'an amalgam of hubbub and hysteria'. Tommy wouldn't let me read it. With notices like that on Broadway, of course, we were dead meat. They go for the jugular. If we even got there. And he felt responsible to the Nederlanders and all the other backers. I mean, we're talking millions of dollars. He needed another hand, another eye: 'Somebody I can really trust.'

The first person called in was Peter Stone, the famous librettist. He won an Oscar in 1964 for *Father Goose* starring starring Cary Grant and Leslie Caron. He wrote *Charade* with Cary Grant and Audrey Hepburn and the film of *Sweet Charity* starring Shirley Maclaine. He had just done a successful stage version of the Tracy/Hepburn screen classic *Woman of the Year* for Lauren Bacall. The next name on Tommy's want list was his old friend Mike Nichols.

Strangely Mike Nichols was almost exactly the same age as my husband Michael; they were born just two weeks apart. There all similarities ended. Mike Nichols was born in Berlin of Russian-Jewish extraction and arrived in New York in 1939, an émigré from Nazi Germany. He was very bright and started acting at the University of Chicago. He studied in New York with Lee Strasburg, then went back to Chicago where he formed an improvisational comedy group with Elaine May, Alan Arkin and Shelley Berman that later evolved into Second City, where Dan Ackroyd and John Belushi started. In

1957 the legendary partnership of Mike Nichols and Elaine May began. When they split, Mike turned from performance to direction and in 1963 did Neil Simon's *Barefoot in the Park*. Then came films. *Who's Afraid of Virginia Woolf* with Richard Burton and Elizabeth Taylor was nominated for eight Oscars (all four actors). It won five. Then *The Graduate* for which he won the Best Director Oscar and which was the start of Dustin Hoffman's film career, and *Catch 22*. Later would come *Working Girl* and *Postcards from the Edge*, and most recently *The Birdcage*. Not that he ever abandoned the theatre. Straight after *My One and Only* opened he directed Tom Stoppard's *The Real Thing* with Jeremy Irons. In the nineties he directed Ariel Dorfmann's *Death and the Maiden* and Samuel Beckett's *Waiting for Godot*, starring Steve Martin and Robin Williams, in 1996 he was performing brilliantly as an actor at the National Theatre in London. In short, Mike Nichols is something of a genius.

'I need someone as clever as Mike to say if we've got anything, and what we have to do.' It's called doctoring a show. When Tommy sent out his cry for help Mike had just finished shooting *Silkwood* with Meryl Streep and was in the middle of cutting it. But he came anyway. Not that I knew anything about it at the time. Tommy only told me about what happened afterwards. 'You've got to be completely honest,' he told them. 'I need to know if we've got anything.' What they said was that the show didn't work, but that the two of us together was magical. The songs were wonderful and the dancing was wonderful. And that's what Tommy needed to hear. There was a diamond at the heart. He just had to chip away at the setting. Peter Stone stayed and took charge. Mike flitted back and forth as best he could.

To complete the new team of surgeons, Tommy drafted in Tony Walton, who had designed *The Boyfriend*. All three of us had stayed in touch over the years and it was very reassuring for me to have him on board. Tony, even more than Tommy, has been a constant point throughout my professional and private life. The final pair of hands belonged to Jules Fisher, a lighting whiz. None of them, except Peter, were credited in the final show for contractual reasons.

Because of the budget we had to keep most of the sets, costumes and the little bi-plane. Tony Walton didn't have much scope in terms of cash but what paint and imagination could do, he did. He's another genius. The original *My One and Only* had been no cheapskate production. My wig was a case in point. Ken Russell was right to have made me cut my hair, but on stage you really can't see, and a wig is so much more practical. Until the finale, when it hung straight down my back in a long braid under the top hat, my hair stayed tightly pin-curled under the wig. Most wigs are not that well made and you end up looking like you've got a dead cat on your head. But this one was amazing and cost a fortune, $1,500 apiece. I had two.

Six songs were dropped and six were added.

Even the name of the little plane was changed from Funny Face to Lone Star. Sadly whole characters disappeared, including a barbershop quintet who sang wonderful *a cappella*. Unfortunately when something like this happens there are always innocent casualties.

The producers had done a deal with the Gershwin estate and we had the whole of the Gershwin catalogue to chose from. Ira Gershwin, the brother who wrote the lyrics, is one of the greatest songwriters of all time. The audacity of his rhymes ('embraceable' twinned with 'silk-and-laceable') and his mix of humour and poignancy are unbeaten by anyone else, from 'Fascinating Rhythm' to 'Summertime' from *Porgy and Bess*. In 1931 he was the first lyricist to be awarded a Pulitzer Prize. His brother George Gershwin died in 1939 of a brain tumour but nearly half a century later Ira was still alive, though sadly not well enough to receive visitors, so I never met him. The new numbers were chosen because they fitted the storyline. And we had quite a choice: during his life Ira Gershwin wrote the lyrics to seven hundred songs.

The new plot was kept very simple. Peter Stone had worked a miracle. Out went Freud and Trotsky, in came love and romance. We'd get pages every day. Cuts. New dialogue. We'd be rehearsing new stuff during the day while still doing the old script at night. Sometimes we'd do new stuff right away. I remember going on the stage in Boston with new dialogue written on my hand. Some we could incorporate immediately, some you couldn't, like Tommy's big opening number which had to go. Everyone agreed it needed a big company number as an opener. We were into full-time re-rehearsal while still doing a show every night.

It's amazing I didn't have a nervous breakdown. Back home things were going from bad to worse. Because Michael wasn't working, we hadn't brought a nanny with us. I thought he would be able to deal with taking responsibility for Carly and we'd never imagined I'd be working fifteen hours a day. I had managed to get her into a local playgroup and we were surviving. Till a message arrived at the stage door: 'Would you please ask your husband not to pick up your daughter from school when he's drunk.'

It was my worst nightmare. I had to have someone I trusted. An agency nanny who neither Carly nor I knew from Adam just wouldn't do. So I picked up the phone and called Peggy Burke, who we'd bought our LA house from. Over the past four years we had become very close. To Carly she was like her American grandmother. She dropped everything and caught the first flight out.

A Boston winter is not like an English winter. Heavy snow several feet deep, more blizzard than Christmas card. One night there were only eight people in the theatre, but that was an exception. Even with the scathing reviews they turned up, pre-booked because they wanted to see Tommy Tune, King of Broadway, live. Plus the novelty value of me. Lots of people came just to see if I could do it.

The next thing we learnt was that somebody in the organisation had 'lost' a million dollars. Tommy had to ask everyone if they would work for deferred wages. And God bless them, they did. There was an amazing camaraderie among the cast:

'We're going to fight for this because this is our show and we're not going to get beaten.'

If I can get through this, I thought, I could get through anything.

15

On 26 february 1983 I got home late, drained and exhausted. The show had been pretty traumatic. It was the last night of the Boston run. After the curtain Tommy had made the apologetic speech that he always did now.

'There are parts of this show you don't understand, and we don't understand them either.'

He thanked Boston for its patience, brought out the long suffering stage hands for a bow and then asked the audience a favour.

'Please say a prayer for us.'

We'd had the usual long notes and then Tommy and I had had something to eat so it was well past midnight when I got in. the apartment we had rented was in fact half a brownstone town house. Carly and Peggy were downstairs asleep. Michael was upstairs out of his head.

The story of the end of me and Michael can't be told without Peggy Burke. To call her my guardian angel is not an exaggeration. When we bought our house from her, that should have been that. Thank God it wasn't. Peggy had introduced us to our next-door neighbour Milo Anderson, who was then in his eighties. Milo had been a costume designer in the golden days of Hollywood and in 1948 had won an Oscar for *Johnny Belinda*, the film that got

Jane Wyman an Oscar. I adored him and so did Peggy and she continued to visit him and that's when she began to drop in on us. Years before she'd been a dancer and a showgirl and she was still blonde, beautiful and glamorous. She had been married to the actor Paul Burke, star of *The Naked City*, and had three grown-up children and several grandchildren.

Milo lived in the old style of Hollywood in his wonderful run-down house filled with extraordinary things, most of which probably found their way there from film sets. He was full of stories about people he'd met and the film stars he'd dressed. I've always been very into clothes and used to sit with him for hours just talking.

When he died Peggy took care of everything. He had no one else. Though there were lots of friends. We used to love his soirées. Many of his other guests were from his era. We rarely went to other Hollywood parties as we were not really party people.

Peggy's son was an alcoholic and so she completely understood what I was going through. She was almost like a therapist. When Michael was in a state (i.e. drunk) I would ring her. She had the patience of a saint. She'd sit for hours and hours calming him down, trying to persuade him to get help. But the only way that an alcoholic can start to deal with the problem is first to actually admit they have a problem. Michael's problem was that he enjoyed getting very drunk. He happily admitted it. He liked the process.

Michael loved and respected Peggy. When he was sober he would listen. But when he was hitting the bottle you couldn't talk to him about anything. That last night in Boston Michael was as drunk as he got without blacking out. The tirade started as soon as I walked in: about the show and how Tommy was more important to me than him.

'Look. I've just got to go to bed. I'm exhausted.'

He was so angry he punched the wall and it went right through the plasterboard. Not just a dent. Right through a gap between the joists. The noise woke Peggy up. She came in, saw what had happened, then called the police. I was in tears. Frightened and distressed from seeing him like that. Four big cops came and took him away. 'Just to dry out,' they said.

He was in a terrible state. And so was I.

The next day, I talked to Peggy for hours. Those weeks in Boston I had felt guilty. There I was, doing what I loved, while he was utterly demoralised and probably bored to tears. What was he to do but drink? This time Peggy would hear none of it.

'You can't go on like this. It has to stop.'

Of course she was right. And I finally knew it. It was like something clicked in me. He had broken his promise so many times about cleaning up. Why not admit it. Michael was never going to clean up. Did I want to live this life? And more importantly did Carly? What about when she went to school. Would she bring friends home to a drunken father? There were mornings when he couldn't remember anything about the night before. This time his fist hit the wall. Next time?

But Michael was right about Tommy and the show. It may sound selfish but *My One and Only* was my salvation, my sanity. I loved what I was doing. I was working with a company of very talented people and I suddenly realised yet again there was a whole other world out there. And Tommy was worried sick about the way Michael was behaving. During breaks in rehearsals we'd have a cup of tea and he'd say over and over again, 'You can't go on like this, it'll destroy you.' And this was someone who loved me and didn't demand anything from me, except professionally.

Tommy agreed with Peggy that Carly and I should go back to New York on our own. So I left Michael his airline ticket, the keys to the apartment and a note saying I'd call him in New York and we left. By the time he'd been discharged from three nights in the cells we were gone. It was 1 March 1983.

The relief was enormous. In New York we checked into a hotel until Peggy found us somewhere to rent. As a result when Michael got back to New York, he didn't know where we were. He went off his head. He called my sisters in England saying that he would fight for custody of Carly. That I was a no-good mother. When we went into the theatre, he'd turn up at the stage door, drunk, insisting on seeing me. Predictable maybe, but still distressing.

The Nederlanders banned him from the

theatre and gave me a bodyguard, a huge black guy who Carly and I called Big George. Soon after that Michael went on a binge and ended up in hospital. He had collapsed on the street and somebody took him in. Peggy went to see him. I couldn't. I just couldn't.

Meanwhile Peggy found us a three-bedrom apartment off 41st and 2nd. A sweet little place called Tudor City which most unusually for Manhattan is a cul-de-sac. To get to the next avenue you had to walk down an alleyway. It had a little park with swings. Perfect for Carly and rare in New York. Peggy's next job was to find a nanny. She had her own life in LA to get back to.

I was pushing myself to the limit. Half the changes we'd made for the Boston patch job were thrown out. By the time we opened on Broadway there was practically nothing left. Panic crept in between the cracks in my confidence.

I told Tommy, 'You can change my songs, you can change my frocks, you can change my dialogue, but you can't change my dances.'

They'd taken me so long to learn and now they were etched on my brain as well as on the soles of my feet.

Peter Stone was like a teddy bear; deep growly voice, glasses and permanent smile. He's one of the funniest men I have ever met and he did wonders with the script. Much of the storyline had to be kept because of the costumes and props like the little aeroplane. I was an English swimming star, *à la* Esther Williams; Tommy was an aviator, and when he sees my picture in a newspaper, it's love at first sight.

Most of my songs didn't change, but I got one added, making it six songs from *Funny Face* and eleven from other Gershwin scores. In the new script, after boy meets girl, there's the traditional misunderstanding when girl thinks she's lost him. What I wanted was 'But Not For Me', one of my favourite songs. In the end they went for 'Nice Work If You Can Get It', because the lyrics worked perfectly for the new storyline. All I had to do was slow down the tempo. And at the end I ran off sobbing.

The work was exhausting but exhilarating. The worst that could happen, I thought, is that it won't work, that it will be absolutely awful, and we'll get slammed by the critics; but there's no school or college in the world where I can learn what I'm about to learn now through the experience of working with Mike Nichols and Tommy Tune on Broadway.

The St James Theatre was on West 44th Street. It was a big old theatre built in 1927, which I love. It was the home of some great musicals, including *Oklahoma*, which opened in 1943 and ran for five years. Then came *The King and I*, *The Pyjama Game* and in 1964 *Hello Dolly*, which ran for seven years. Carol Channing was the first Dolly, but she was followed by other legendary musical stars: Ginger Rogers, Pearl Bailey, Betty Grable and Ethel Merman. The show before us had been *Barnum*. What I hadn't realised before was that on Broadway itself there are not that many theatres. They're on the side streets, like West 46th, West 47th, and of course 42nd Street. Over the last few years the whole area around Times Square had got very seedy. In the eighties it became like London's Soho in the bad old days, porn shops and porn cinemas, prostitutes and drug dealers, with the grand old cinemas all boarded up. So depressing and dangerous. Not before time, with the encouragement of the new mayor, organisations like Disney are now beginning to move in to reclaim and re-condition the theatres, Broadway's great heritage.

After Boston the money people were very nervous. Rumours were rife that it wasn't going to happen. When it became known that Mike Nichols was coming in, everything changed. Peter, Tommy and Mike were a dream team. But the bottom line was that we needed another million dollars to open. Opening night had been postponed till 16 April but new backers had to be found, or it would be postponed for ever. Then one morning Tommy announced that he'd arranged a performance for the heads of Paramount. It turned out that this still huge Hollywood studio had a theatre division.

It was the scariest day of my life. They wanted to see the first act of the new show. I can still see the chairs lined up against the huge wall of mirrors in the rehearsal room. And there they sat in their business suits and ties. Then, at the other end of the room, there's us in our leotards and leg warmers and hairbands with just a pianist and smiles to hide our nerves. At least the acoustics are good. Our voices soar.

But they don't clap or laugh. Not a smile cracks their lips.

We knew they were the studio heads. The big boys. But in fact they were bigger than any of us realised. Michael Eisner now runs Disney, and is one of the most powerful film executives in the world: Barry Diller who left Paramount to run Twentieth Century Fox is now involved with TV shopping channels. Jeffrey Katzenburg went to Disney with Michael Eisner and some time later left Disney to join Steven Spielberg and David Geffen to form Dreamworks.

We keep on rehearsing. We're all saying we're going to open but without the extra million we know we can't.

'If Paramount don't come through we'll go somewhere else.'

We were like kids in the playground. But although no one would admit it, we all knew Paramount was the end of the road.

It was about a week later when Tommy came in and just said, 'We've got it.' After the whoops it was back to work. The Broadway opening was now pushed back to 1 May, the deadline for the Tony Award nominations. We had three weeks.

We worked like dogs. Three days before opening night I came down with tonsillitis and Tommy did something to his hip. But we had to open. We were ready to open. They sent me off to the throat doctor and I got pumped with dreadful things. Tommy insisted I miss the matinée the day before. What I really needed was rest. The one thing I couldn't have.

On opening night my voice might have been a bit throaty and Tommy's kicks waist high rather than above his shoulders, but it didn't matter. It's the moment you stand there and think, 'Oh my God. What am I doing here? I should have gone and got a job in Woolworths.' I can only remember two things: my first entrance — coming down the steps of a train in a flurry of feathers — and the final applause. Everything between is a blurr.

Then I'm running downstairs to Tommy's dressing room so utterly high. I just want to hug him and say 'we did it, we did it'. I have taken my tail coat off and my hat but I still have my tap shoes on and I've just reached the bottom of the stairs when this tall woman is picking me up and hugging me. 'You were wonderful. You were wonderful.' It was Lauren Bacall. The whirlwind of success had begun.

First stop was Sardi's restaurant for the ritual champagne. Everyone does it on a Broadway first night. It's bad luck not to. An actor friend tells the story that after the first night of the play *Loot* in the sixties the reviews were so dire that within seconds of the papers arriving, glasses were whipped out of their hands and they closed the bar. The cast were on the plane out the next day. Success on Broadway is like nowhere else. You're either in or you're out. I didn't need the champagne, I was high on adrenaline. The curtain calls had been amazing and even I didn't imagine they were just being polite. And everyone was smiling, the Nederlander brothers most of all. Next stop Central Park and the big party at the Tavern On The Green. Everyone was there, including the two people I'd put at the top of my guest list, Lawrence Olivier and Joan Plowright. Ever since I saw him in *Wuthering Heights* at one of our film shows, and then when I was taken by my friend Stuart Grimshaw to see him as Shylock in *The Merchant of Venice* on stage, Olivier had been one of my gods. It turned out he'd even acted in the same theatre on Broadway, in the early sixties with Anthony Quinn in *Becket*. And now here he was telling little me I was wonderful. And I felt wonderful. The next morning he sent me the most amazing letter I've ever had. It is one of my most treasured possessions. It reads:

> My Lovely Twiglet
> What a sweet joy it was to meet last night, having adored you from afar.
> I am so deep in admiration for your talent, which seems to gain strides every year — every hour.
> Joan and I do congratulate you from our very warmest hearts and wish you more and more success at the same rate.
> Ever and ever
> Larry

Long after I'd forgotten there were such things as reviews, there came this 'WHOOP' from the table where the producers were sitting. 'What's that?' I asked Tommy. And he said it must be the *New York Times* review. Everyone else can love you, but if their critic Frank Rich doesn't, forget it. Then somebody brought the paper over and Tommy read it and passed it to me. '*My One And Only* levitates with some of the most inspired choreography Broadway has seen in several seasons, all set to the celestial music of George Gershwin and danced to kill by a company glittering in Art Deco swank.'

He finished by saying, 'The only musical of the season that sends us home on air', which considering the other musicals on Broadway then included *A Chorus Line, Cats, Dreamgirls, Nine, On Your Toes, Little Shop of Horrors* and *Showboat* wasn't bad.

Clive Barnes of the *New York Post* was so nice to me it was almost embarrassing: 'Twiggy was a revelation. She is delicious, she is sexy . . . you can almost hear her count when she tap dances but the woman's a genuine star.' And so we knew from that night we were okay. There would be no shortage of quotes to put outside the theatre. 'A Triumph', 'A Hit', 'A Revelation', 'Heart-stopping', 'Explosive', 'Sensational', 'Betwitching', 'Suberb'. This one would run and run. We played to full houses every night for eighteen months.

When I think how I stepped out on to that Broadway stage, it makes my blood run cold. But it's how I've always been. That initial 'Blimey, that's a good idea' always carries me through the first stages. The fear doesn't hit until I'm committed. If I'd have sat back and thought about it, I would never have done it. Doing *My One and Only* was like diving head first into shark-infested waters. But I wouldn't have missed it for the world.

A week after we opened Michael was arrested outside our flat. I had asked him to leave us alone and he wouldn't. He was drunk. He was angry because by now the press knew that we had separated and were trying to make out there was something between me and Tommy. And Michael couldn't stand that. Not that he believed for one moment that there was any romance. Far from it. He didn't approve of Tommy's world. In a story that ran in the *Daily Mail* he was quoted as saying: 'Does anybody really think that I'm going to let my child go into the atmosphere that surrounds a certain member of my wife's cast?' And about our marriage he said, 'We have just had a rough patch, that's all.'

What was I to do? Go public about Michael and his drinking? That's not my style. The producers were quite happy for stories about me and Tommy to run. An off-stage romance between the stars was always good publicity. And of course I was photographed by paparazzi having dinner with Tommy. It wasn't exactly difficult because we had dinner together nearly every night after the show.

I was so happy in my new extended theatre family and they all rallied around me. I was having the best time in eight years. I was in a hugely successful show, the toast of the town. For the first time in years I didn't have to worry about me or Carly. The more time I spent with other people, the more I realised the nightmare I'd been living. But when you're living it you just can't see it. And if I commit to somebody or something, then it's a commitment. Project or person, if I believe in something I fight and fight and fight.

Peggy had gone back to LA. The new nanny seemed fine and, anyway, five days out of seven I could spend with my lovely little girl. Michael went into some kind of re-hab and when he came out later that summer, he finally did what I had been begging him to do for years, and joined the Alcoholics Anonymous programme. It was like a weight had been lifted from my shoulders.

One Sunday evening I went with him to a meeting. He'd asked me to go, he wanted to show me what his life was now. He had become very involved and had made a couple of really good friends, both recovering alcoholics. It was held in a Church Hall and there must have been about fifty people, men and women, boys and girls. All ages. All colours. It was one of the most moving things I have ever experienced. Newcomers were asked to introduce themselves and tell us their story if they felt able to. They said their first name only. It's all first names only. Even the man who started AA is known as Bill W. The 'testimonies' always began the same way. 'My name is such and such and I am an alcoholic.' Beth was only about twenty and so beautiful. She told us she was an alcoholic and drug user. And told this terrible story. How she started drinking at school, social drinking. How she'd met some guy and fell in love and he got her into cocaine. And how she was drunk or stoned every hour of every waking day. How for the past three years she couldn't tell you what she had been doing from 6.00 p.m. till 6.00 a.m. Please God she stayed with it and never went down that road to hell again.

Towards the end of July my sister Vivien came out from England. She and her sons Ben and Adam stayed the whole of the summer holidays. Michael asked if he could see her, and of course I agreed. Viv was really shocked by how he looked. The handsome man I'd fallen in love with was long gone. Haggard and thin, the muscles from his legs all wasted. His clothes hung on him. His hands shook. His eyes were bloodshot and he had bloodhound-sized bags under them. He was still addicted. Before, it was alcohol; now it was coffee and aspirin for the pain in his back. Too much. Too often. He desperately wanted us to get back together again. And my answer was always the same. It's early days and I'm working so hard. Let's wait and see. If he sorted himself out then it might work out. And I think I half believed it. It wasn't as if there was anyone else waiting in the wings. But in my heart I knew I could never go back. Did I still love him? No. I cared for him. I was worried for him. I pitied him. And you can't love somebody you pity in that way. All the sleepless nights. All the arguments. They just chip away. He had killed whatever we did have.

By the autumn, once I was convinced he was dry, I agreed to Michael taking Carly out. He was her father and he absolutely adored her. It was right that they should spend time together.

Sober he would never put her in harm's way. He had given up swearing blind he would never drink again. He stuck by the AA philosophy of 'one day at a time'. I was still very wary. I wouldn't let him come up to the flat. I couldn't risk him getting too comfortable. I would meet him with Carly in a neighbourhood coffee bar, then he'd bring her back to the apartment around six thirty when it was time for bed and the nanny would be waiting in the lobby.

November 30, 1983 was a Wednesday. I had a matinée and I had arranged to meet Michael between shows. It was the day before Carly's fifth birthday. She had come to the matinée with me which she often did. She used to love it in the girls' communal dressing room, because the sequins off their dresses fell on the floor and she used to collect them. She was like their mascot and they were wonderful with her. There would always be somebody down there. If not the dancers, then a dresser. It was like a family.

Because it was her birthday the next day, Michael was going to take Carly ice-skating at the Rockefeller Center where every winter they have a skating rink. Then they would have some supper and he would take her home and Peggy would come down and collect her.

Peggy had once more had to dust off her halo. A week or so before I'd been off for a couple of nights with flu. The first evening I staggered out of bed to get a glass of water and, as I went into the sitting room I saw the nanny and the woman who did the cooking and cleaning sitting watching TV.

'Where's Carly?'

'Oh, she's in the bath.'

My heart went in my mouth. You never, ever leave a young child alone in the bath. I always made that rule quite clear with new nannies. I just ran. The bathroom door wasn't even open. And there she was. In a bath with far too much water. Carly was fine and singing away, thank God, but I shudder to think what could have happened. That stupid girl was packed and out that night.

Which was why Peggy was there that night. She'd flown up immediately. We had found another girl, who'd been working for an American family on Long Island, and Peggy was only staying until the new nanny was broken in.

Michael and I met as arranged. I remember saying 'I'll see you tomorrow' as I waved them both goodbye. We were going to have a party for Carly's birthday in the little play school with all her friends. I don't know whether they went skating or whether they just watched. But afterwards he took her to MacDonalds, her favourite. They'd finished their meal and were just playing with a toy car when Michael had a massive heart attack. Apparently the staff were amazing. They called the paramedics and got Carly out of the way, out back. But there was nothing anyone could do. He died in the restaurant. Apparently he wouldn't have suffered. It was instantaneous.

Which left this little five-year-old mite on her own in downtown Manhattan. I had never told her our address. There never seemed the need. But when the police asked her where she lived, she'd heard me say it so often every time we stepped into a cab or a limo, she just said what I said. And unlike most Manhattan addresses, it wasn't difficult.

'Do you know your name, little girl?'

'Yes, I'm Carly.'

'And do you know where you live?'

'Yes, Two Tudor City.'

I don't think she knew exactly what had happened. I had to break it to her over a few days. But she knew her daddy hadn't been well. All she could talk about was the ride from MacDonalds to the apartment in a police car with the blue light on and the siren going. When they got there the doorman recognised Carly and immediately buzzed up. And luckily Peggy was there.

As soon as she had settled Carly, Peggy telephoned the producer and asked him to tell me what had happened. They didn't. It was by then about seven thirty. The show went up at eight. If one of the stars was off they had to offer ticket holders their money back. They professed they didn't want to upset me.

The first I knew, I came off stage after the final curtain and Peggy was in my dressing room. The first thing she said was, 'Don't worry, Carly's all right.' Because she knew how I'd be thinking. Then came the crunch.

'I don't know how to tell you this. Michael is dead.'

And then she told me what she knew. I was struck by an unfathomable tangle of every emotion. But all my thoughts were for Carly, appalled at what she'd witnessed. Obviously one of the first things I asked Peggy was, 'When did it happen?' When she told me at six o'clock, I was furious. How could they have let me sing and dance the night away? It was too late to do anything for Michael, but I should have been with my daughter. Luckily she was in Peggy's wonderful hands. But they didn't know that. I felt great anger, huge sadness but also relief. Relief that Carly was all right and safe.

We decided to go ahead with her birthday party. She was five and had looked forward to it so much. I phoned the school and explained what had happened and they were great. Not everyone was as sympathetic. The next morning we came down into the street and a photographer, a woman, started snapping away. I had dark glasses on — it had been a tough night — but I was with Carly and being jolly for her, it was her birthday. And I said to this woman. 'Please don't do this. This is not on. Please don't.'

I asked her to give me the camera and when she showed no sign of stopping, I knocked it out of her hand and pulled out the film. I had never done anything like that before. 'How can you do this? You're a woman, you should know better.'

'It's news,' she said.

A week later I flew up to Ticonderoga for the funeral. Peggy Burke and Stewart Grimshaw came with me. That's when you know who your friends are. I hadn't asked Stewart to fly out. When I called to tell him what had happened he just said he was taking the next plane out. I took one day off from the show. Ticonderoga is six hours from New York by car and a difficult place to get to, so the Nederlanders hired a private plane for us. It was only small and because it was snowing I was a bit worried. However, I remember that the flight across the snow-covered landscape was very beautiful. Everything had been taken care of by my saintly friend Peggy. I was very lucky. I was being protected on all sides. My big concern was Carly. We left her with Sarah, her lovely new nanny. I think it was the right decision.

The funeral was the last time I saw Michael's mum and dad. For years I sent them a Christmas card and photographs of Carly, but I never had any reply. One of Michael's oldest friends, H. G. Burleigh, did keep in touch. They had been at school together. H. G., as he was always called, had stayed in Ticonderoga and had become headmaster of a local school. A few years later he wrote to tell me that Michael's mum had died. Michael also had a brother and I used to write to him too. But again, I never got anything back. Carly has never been up there. Perhaps one day she will. When she's older and she wants to. It is a very beautiful place.

The post mortem confirmed that Michael had died of a cardiac arrest. I didn't ask details. I knew what killed him. It was the drink. Years and years and years of abuse finally took its toll. He was fifty-two.

16

Summer in New York is hot and humid with temperatures regularly in the nineties. Unbearable in the city, lovely on the beach. So every weekend from Memorial Day (26 May) to Labor Day (2 September) almost everyone in the city hightails it out to the coast. The first summer of *My One and Only* I rented a beach house on Fire Island, on the south side of Long Island not far from where Tommy had a house.

Although the ocean side is much more glamorous, with amazing beaches and miles and miles of white sand pounded flat by great Atlantic breakers, I actually prefer the north side, known as the bay side, where the sea is completely calm, which meant Carly could go in and out without any real danger. So the second summer of the Broadway run, I swapped sides and rented a beach house at Northsea, directly north of Southampton. It looks a bit like the south coast of England did before it was spoiled and there are lots of families with small children because the sea is so much safer than the other side.

It was really pretty, like a little Shaker house, all wood and painted white. Like most of the other beach houses, it was only one storey, with a galleried room upstairs in the big roof space. Everything was bare wood, stripped floorboards and beams and a fireplace downstairs for when it got cold at night. You just opened the French doors and you were on the beach. Outside was the deck and an eating-out area under the acacia trees and a little path leading down to the sea less than twenty yards away. It was a dream for Carly at that age. I could kick myself now for not having bought it. It was actually for sale.

During that summer of 1984, Carly spent nearly half of every week there. Because Sarah her nanny couldn't drive, they would usually go down with Carlotta Floria, the secretary of one of the show's new producers, who had become a very good friend and remains so today. They would leave on Friday evening and I would join them on Sunday after the matinée. It would only take me two hours in the car, so I could be there by seven. Our working week was Tuesday evening through Sunday matinée, leaving Sunday night and Monday free. The theatre week on Broadway is different to London. I was in shock when I heard we had to work on Christmas Day. But it's always a huge sell-out day for musicals. Being a holiday it's a great opportunity for a family day out. It was the same on the Sunday matinée.

It was a great summer. And God how I needed it. Everyone knew where we were so people would just drop in. It was open house. Some were more regular visitors than others, like Carlotta, and Bruce McGill, who played the baddy, my boyfriend/manager in the show, who was wonderful with Carly and had become a good friend. By then the cast were like one huge family, with our own jokes that nobody else would understand. Humour is incredibly important backstage in a long-running show. It diffuses tensions like nothing else. Our favourite catchphrase was 'It's not the quiche, Harry'. It was my dresser's story. Between matinée and evening shows you would always try and get something to eat. Sitting on her own in a packed restaurant early one Saturday evening, she had noticed this middle-aged couple in the corner. Suddenly the restaurant goes quiet, as sometimes happens for no reason, and this woman's voice rings out in a strong New York accent: 'It's not the quiche, Harry, it's the whole seven years.' Poor Harry.

Everyone had to eat and you never knew who you might see at lunch. Once I found myself sitting next to Richard Burton and Elizabeth Taylor who were doing Noel Coward's *Private Lives* literally across the street. We said 'hello' even though we'd never met. America is so informal and it's catching, even for dyed-in-the-wool Brits like me. For the rest of the meal I tried to concentrate on my food, but with two legends sitting at the next table it was very difficult. That year the Brits were out in force on Broadway. My friend Jeremy Irons was doing Tom Stoppard's *The Real Thing* and it was one of the big hits of the season. The director was of course Mike Nichols who came up with the idea of doing *Pygmalion* on Broadway with Jeremy and me. It was a great idea; we were both coming out of hit shows. Mike had seen a tape of my Eliza in the TV *Pygmalion* and he loved it. To play Eliza again on stage straight after *My One and Only* would have been fantastic, and Jeremy would have made the perfect Higgins. But it wasn't to be. The rights were not available.

That summer the sun always seemed to be shining. On the gentle shores of Long Island's bay side, Carly learnt to swim. I remember the day we actually got the arm bands off. Me being the paranoid mother, I was really, really careful. Just because you are an actor you don't stop having a family life. When you're in town doing a play you naturally link up with people who have kids and she had plenty of little friends to play with. Not to mention her cousins.

Viv and her kids, Ben and Adam, spent the whole of the school holidays with us. The next time Ben found himself in America was in 1996 having won a golf scholarship to Navarro College, Texas. It's so lovely to see his photograph splashed on the front of all the sports pages — 'Navarro's talented Ben Smith' — winning tournaments left, right and centre. He is really exceptionally talented and golf is his life. We are all so proud of him.

Big sister Shirley came as well and Tracey, her daughter, dropped in for a while. It was a real family summer. Just one great sadness. I had so hoped Mum and Dad would come. We'd tried everything. But Mum couldn't be shifted. She wouldn't fly and she wouldn't come by sea and Dad wouldn't leave her. I know he'd have loved *My One and Only*. It nearly broke my heart that he never saw it. Shirley came about six times and from what I gather watched every performance with tears streaming down her face. But of course I wasn't with her: I was out there doing it. But then Shirley has always been like that. Very emotional. She even cried when we took the Staten Island ferry for a close look at the Statue of Liberty.

'I never imagined that I'd ever be here,' she howled.

* * *

The show had been playing to packed houses. We were the toast ('and caviar') of New York: 'A triumph of swank, savvy and style. A wonder of theatrical invention.' 'The two Ts tapping and vamping their way into one's heart.' 'Twiggy and Tommy Tune are the most delicious team since Ginger Rogers and Fred Astaire.' And as for Tommy and Honi's brilliant dance, Frank Rich had it right. 'A jolt of lightning occurs when the dapper and immortal Charles 'Honi' Coles teaches the towering Mr Tune a lesson abut wooing. This show-stopper by two master hoofers is a rare reminder of how less can be more in a big musical.'

Things sometimes went wrong on stage, of course; they always do. And on a musical, if they can, they will. Our first accident happened in Boston. At one point the script had us marooned on a desert island. It had been Tommy's dream to tap dance in water — a bit like Gene Kelly in *Singing in the Rain* — and this was the perfect opportunity. We were barefoot and did tap steps, but instead of 'tap tap', they went 'slosh slosh', water going everywhere. It was more for effect than the sound and it always brought the house down; clapping, cheering, they loved it. It was joyful to do. But even though it looked spontaneous and fun it was still hard work. The tank was about four inches deep, not more than four feet across and about twenty feet wide. It was sunk into the stage and covered by a flush-fitting lid when not in use. It was lined with rubber to stop us slipping. Or that was the plan. However, three days into previews I went flying, flat on my back, legs in the air. I was all right. Tommy helped me up and we carried on, if rather gingerly. When they drained the tank that night, it was obvious what had happened. Whoever designed it hadn't reckoned on the force of nature. After only a few days, the rubber was covered in a layer of algae, which is incredibly slippery. Before we opened on Broadway the design team spent weeks trying to come up with the right combination of rubber and cleaning chemicals to make it safe. In the end it was lined with ribbed rubber which had to be scrubbed every night with gritty cleansing powder, rinsed, then left open to get completely dry before being filled for the next performance. And it seemed to work, although I never jumped in with quite the same gay abandon again.

Then there was the time I disappeared. Tony Walton had made this wonderful moon chair for my second scene, a huge padded disc with a sickle moon seat curving round the edge, on which I lie back and look glamorous. I'm in my boudoir, wearing a devoree negligee and I sing a lovely song called 'Boy Wanted'. Tommy meanwhile is in his aeroplane hangar on the other side of the stage reading a newspaper report about me. He sings a song, 'Soon', about meeting the girl in the paper and falling in love, then I join him with the wonderful 'Boy Wanted'. Very, very cleverly the two numbers then become a duet, dovetailed together by our talented musical director Jack Lee.

Anyway, this moon chair was on runners and after a quick change in the wings I would climb on, pose on the narrow 'seat' and the stage hands would slide me out onto the stage. The chair was very top heavy as it was made of metal, and to stop it tipping over they put weights on the bottom as a counter-balance. We had done it hundreds of times. But on this night as the guys are pushing me out, I knew something was wrong. So did they, but it was too late. Before I could do anything I began to tip forward. Seconds later I was nowhere to be seen, completely engulfed by this huge moon that had fallen on top of me. Thank God I had the presence of mind to curl up. If I'd had my arms and legs out they'd surely have been broken.

When I didn't start singing Tommy turned and all he could see was this huge moon thing with the hem of my pink velvet costume sticking out. He nearly had a heart attack; he thought I was dead. He later told me it looked just like I'd been eaten by a giant clam. They brought the curtain in really fast. Everyone was in a real panic. When they got me out, they gave me a double brandy. I was in shock, but physically okay, though there was no way I could go back on that night, I was so out of it. So they stopped the show and gave everyone their money back. It was the only night the show closed down.

Looking back the whole thing seems very funny. It wasn't at the time. It was terrifying. I went to hospital to be checked out but luckily there was no harm done. It turned out the guy who usually did the weights was off and they had a sub in and no one had remembered to tell him to put the weights in the chair. But when something like that happens you get wary about everything. From that day on I always asked, 'Are the weights in?' Theatres can be incredibly dangerous places. One hears horrendous stories of injuries incurred on stage.

But the worst accident I had during *My One and Only* was not on stage at all but back at the apartment. That Monday morning I had tripped on a cushion lying on the floor and turned my ankle. It happened regularly. My ankle's been weak since I caught my foot in a trampoline at school when I was eleven. I knew what I had to do, click it back in and pack it with ice. But it always makes me feel sick and still freaks me out when it happens. By Tuesday morning it was still really stiff. I called Tommy and said, 'Look, I can act, I can sing but I just can't dance.' And he said, 'I've got a great idea.'

That night he went on at the top of the show and talked straight to the audience. 'I'm afraid over the weekend Twiggy had a bit of an accident. But it's all right. She can sing, she can act, but she can't do the dancing. Because she's twisted her ankle. You'll see the bandage. So we want you to use your imagination.'

Tommy was brilliant. He had the audience in the palm of his hand. 'When we get to the dances Twiggy will hopefully magically disappear and another young lady, her understudy, Niki Harris, will appear in her place.'

And that's what happened. Niki was our dance captain, and she was brilliant. She was what's called the 'swing', which means if any of the girls were off, she'd go on. She knew everybody's steps, boys as well as girls, and it was her job to teach anybody coming in to the show to take over a part. That night was such a great show and when we came out for the curtain, Niki and I came down stage together and she got a great reception. I could walk quite normally, but I couldn't have danced. We carried on our double act for four more performances until my ankle was strong enough and I took over that Friday night.

Niki had taken over from me once before. At one point I was dancing backwards, feet together, two at a time, jump sliding on my heels, when the heel of one shoe got caught where the 'lid' of the tank was proud from the stage, where it had warped from water being spilt. With one foot trapped and the rest of me still in momentum, the inevitable happened. I fell backwards like a skittle.

There was nothing I could do to break my fall. Niki took over straight away. But apart from the shock, my ankle was better by the next day.

Not so Carly. It was a matinée and she'd been watching the show up in the circle with Peggy. She was distraught. It wasn't long after Michael had died and to see her mum keel over was just too distressing. She never came to see the show again.

The trapped heel accident had happened at the end of the first half of the show, during the dance I used to call my 'mountain'. Tommy and I are in a cinema, watching stills of ourselves as silent movie stars in romantic poses. Then we go into the song 'He Loves and She Loves'. And we do the love dance. At the end I am absolutely smitten. I am also very glad that the dance is over and I haven't died. Eight minutes of solid tap. Apparently it looked wonderful; I wore a very finely pleated knee-length skirt under a long twenties knitted sweater, so when I danced the skirt would kick out. Not that I ever saw myself. A film was made of the show, but it was for archive purposes only and is stored in the Lincoln Center for the Performing Arts. I've never seen it. But it might be quite fun to do so now.

When the producers heard Tommy and I had been invited to appear on the Royal Variety Performance in London in front of the Queen and Prince Philip they were beside themselves. It was fantastic publicity and made all the New York newspapers. Americans are mad about British royalty. And it really was a great honour and I was thrilled to do it. Starring on Broadway is the pinnacle but to be able to do even a part of it in your own home town means a lot.

It was a tight schedule. Straight after the Sunday matinée Tommy and I were bundled into a limo and caught Concorde for London around seven. As soon as we touched down on Monday morning, we went straight into rehearsals at the Theatre Royal, Drury Lane. The plan was that we would do the performance that night, sleep in London then Concorde it back to New York ready for Tuesday night's show. Niki Harris and Tommy's understudy Jeff Calhoun were standing by just in case we didn't make it in time for our eight o'clock curtain.

We were doing the water dance. The plans for the set and the tank had been sent over several weeks before. At some point in the afternoon they told us that somebody very special was going to be doing our introduction. But they wouldn't tell us who. The whole show that year was devoted to dance. And the celebrity host was Gene Kelly, special enough for anyone. So at the beginning of the number the head curtain was in, we were in position on our bright yellow triangular modernist island and we heard Gene Kelly say:

'Now, ladies and gentlemen, to introduce our next guests we have a very special person. Sir Laurence Olivier.'

Tommy and I looked at each other completely amazed. Then from the front of the stage curtain came that unmistakable voice.

'If you grew up in Neasden and you went up to somebody and said 'How do I get to Broadway?', they'd probably say you can't get there from here. But the young lady you're about to see did actually do that, and here she is with her co-star from the hit show *My One and Only*, the hottest thing on four legs, Twiggy and Tommy Tune.'

Tommy and I were just open-eyed and open-mouthed. Both thinking, 'OH MY GOD.' We really wanted to just jump off our island and hug him. It was one of the most thrilling moments ever. Not only that it was him, my hero, but everyone knew he had recently been very ill, so we were truly flattered and moved. Being in a big hit like *My One and Only* gives you acceptance as a performer. But to have the greatest actor of the twentieth century coming out for you is the ultimate stamp of approval and, let's face it, a slap in the face for all those 'jumped-up-model' barbs I'd faced all my career.

I was beginning to find my emotional feet again. Being in a hit Broadway show is pretty good therapy for what I'd been through. Everyone came to see it. The great excitement every night was finding out if there was someone famous out front. The girls would be tapping away in their opening number and I'd be in the wings waiting for my entrance and as they came off they'd say, 'Row six, tenth seat along.' You could see faces. Believe it or not the person that the cast got the biggest kick out of being there was Benny Hill. But I didn't find it quite as exotic as they did, although I was a big fan. One night after the show there was a knock on the door and there was Donald Sutherland on his knees. 'Will you marry me? I've asked my wife and she says it's fine by her.'

Placido Domingo came twice. The second time he brought his family and they all came backstage. Of course I was thrilled to meet him but horror-struck when I realised he'd been out there listening to me. One of the greatest voices in the world, I think my throat would have seized up if I'd known beforehand. A few months later when I was flown down to Florida on my day off to appear in Bob Hope's annual birthday special — thrilling enough in its own right — one of the other guests was Placido Domingo and when he saw me, he came up and immediately started serenading me with 'My One and Only', complete with adorable Spanish accent. It was unforgettable. I've met him several times since, and he always sings me a few bars of 'My One and Only'. He's such a sweet man, full of old-world charm.

Ginger Rogers was of course a huge thrill. When I heard she was out front, I was so nervous. All I thought was 'God, I hope she's not watching my feet.' For one of the all time greats to come backstage and sing my praises, after all that she and Fred had meant to me, was like a dream. Ruby Keeler, another great dancer and the star of *42nd Street*, came twice and wrote me a sweet letter.

When the knock came, you never knew who it might be. One night I opened my dressing-room door and there stood the most handsome man, in his high seventies, with silver hair and a tan, impeccably dressed in a pin-striped, beautifully cut suit (Savile Row, no question), white shirt, pink handkerchief and a pink tie. It was Douglas Fairbanks Jnr, such a gentleman and still gorgeous. One time it was Liza Minelli, another night it was Lillian Gish, one of the great stars of the silent era. Meeting these old-time movie stars was always strangely moving and touching. And I was also extremely touched when I was chosen to be Miss Ziegfeld. Once a year veterans of the Ziegfeld Follies, showgirls of the thirties, have a big get-together — although there must be fewer and fewer of them now — and they choose a young performer to crown as an honorary Ziegfeld girl. Previous recipients include Barbra Streisand and Liza Minnelli. It was great fun, all these wonderful, glamorous old ladies, well into their eighties then. I still have my tiara inscribed Miss Ziegfeld 1983.

Jack Nicholson, who I'd met before with Angelica Huston, his then girlfriend, sent me a dozen roses, and two cases of champagne to the cast. But not all men were so gallant, as we regularly discovered on Saturday nights when women brought their husbands, men who would never go to the theatre unless they were dragged. Duty theatre. As these were out-of-towners, they would eat beforehand and of course have a couple of drinks. The results were audible. You could almost hear them snoring from the wings.

One Saturday Niki came off stage with the news that there's a guy sound asleep in the front row. It's half-way through the first act. Tommy decides he's going to get him. So he goes right down stage and taps as loudly as he can. And he's got huge feet. Suddenly the guy jerks awake and Tommy comes off mightily pleased. But later in the second half, after the interval, at the end of his dance Tommy notices the snoring man's seat is empty at the end. The quickest way back for Tommy's next entrance is into the street, through the lobby, and back through the pass door to stage left. Also he gets a bit of fresh air. So he's half-way round — in his top hat and tails he's well over seven foot — rushing through the lobby when he sees this man smoking, the same one that had been asleep. He takes one look at Tommy, guiltily stubs out his cigarette, holds his hands up in the air and says, 'It's okay. I'm going back, I'm going back. I just had to have a cigarette. But I'm really enjoying it,' and disappears back into the auditorium.

Tommy was convinced the guy thought he'd come off stage to look for him. At the end he was clapping and standing as if his life depended on it. We were all on the floor. How we got through the show without collapsing into hysterics I don't know.

The time I did lose it on the stage was just before Halloween. Everyone was talking about what they were going to wear. In the States it's not only kids that do their trick or treating. Halloween is a big thing; in Greenwich Village it's almost like carnival with everyone parading in the streets, especially in the gay area. The idea was to drive down there after the show, and we were planning our costumes. It was the buzz for weeks before the night. I had decided to go as a black cat. Tommy didn't know what he wanted to be.

So we were waiting in the wings about to go on for the water dance when I suddenly have an idea.

'I'm going to go as a cat. Why don't you go as a mouse?' I say, and we start to laugh at the idea.

Then it's time to run on and the curtain goes up. And he starts singing the first verse of 'S'Wonderful' to me and I completely lose it. All I could see in my mind when I looked at my romantic lead was a very tall mouse, with ears, whiskers, sticky-out teeth and tail. My shoulders were going up and down and tears were streaming down my face and my tummy hurt so much from keeping the sound in. I was supposed to take over and sing the second verse to him. But you can't sing when you're laughing. It's one of the laws of nature. So Tommy did the only thing he could and sang the whole song on his own. What a pro. Once we had slid off the island and into the water, it was okay. We were laughing anyway, so we got the song out. But my stomach muscles ached for a day afterwards.

But come Halloween, cat and mouse it had to be. Tommy had some grey tights and I got some grey material and made him a funny hat with ears and did his make-up. It was a wonderful night. It was like being at a kids' party. We had so much fun. So many happy memories among the sad ones.

My One and Only was nominated for nine

Tonys and won five. I was nominated for Best Actress in a Musical. The show won Best Musical, Tommy went on to win Best Actor in a Musical and Best Choreography, and Honi Coles won Best Supporting Actor. When his name came up I just screamed. It's the big Broadway night, like the Oscars and because it's all filmed the doors are locked so you can't go out and leave any empty seats. That would look bad on camera. So everyone is told to make sure they've been to the loo beforehand. I lost out to Natalia Makarova, the Brilliant Russian ballerina who defected to the West in the early seventies and was making her Broadway debut in the Rogers and Hart musical *On Your Toes*. Obviously I was disappointed not to get it. But we had always been the two front runners and the blow was softened because she is such an incredible talent.

My One and Only ends with a top hat and tails number. As Tommy said, we just had to, as a tribute to Fred Astaire and all that talent and tradition which had gone before. It was a huge tap dance, with the whole company moving down the stage, that builds and builds and builds to an amazing crescendo till we're on top of the footlights punching the air, and the tension in the audience is finally released with a huge roar. And I would turn to Tommy and shout, 'GOAL.' Which is just what it sounded like. And as Tommy and I and the full company tapped and sang to 'Kicking The Clouds Away', it echoed everything I felt. During this extraordinary life-changing time, *My*

One and Only had certainly done that.

When we opened, Francine LeFrak, one of the original producers, had given me a heart-shaped needlepoint cushion with 'Look Up And Smile' embroidered on it, which was what she was constantly telling me when we were previewing in Boston. Now, a year after Michael's traumatic death and after eighteen months of sheer magic, with my beautiful Carly at my side, I was beginning to see I could.

Being surrounded and nurtured by such wonderful people had a lot to do with it. When the show came to an end, it was almost like a divorce. And for quite some time I felt very unsettled, adrift from the anchor of the routine that had ruled my life. I would find myself looking at my watch and it was always eight o'clock. Curtain up. When you do a show everything is geared to that evening performance. And I missed it. There's nothing more wonderful for your confidence than being cheered every night. It's a terrible trap. But it doesn't last. It's important that your priority is your family, your kids. Leigh always says, quite rightly, 'There's no point in being adored by millions of strangers if you're not loved and respected by your family and children.' I've been amazed by how many people I've met who have made the wrong decision and fallen into that trap.

What is so sad was that the most wonderfully fulfilling time of my career as an actress was the most horrendous time of my life as a person. Had Michael not drunk, he could have shared this wonderful life. The great tragedy is that he threw it away down a bottle.

I have this dream. I am in the wings about to go on stage and I don't know the song and I don't know the words and I'm trying to tell them that I don't know. But nobody will listen. It's the most terrible feeling. In the dream I never get so far as to find myself on the stage. It's never happened in life. I always thought that if ever it happened I would crumple up and scream and cry. But in real life you don't. Something takes over and you just go on and do it.

17

The last night of *My One and Only* was 31 October 1984. We had a combined last night and Halloween party. This time Tommy went as a skeleton and I went as Vampira. Then bye bye Broadway. For the first time in two years — unless you count one night in Drury Lane — I was going home. Not that I really had a home, except with Mum and Dad in Twickenham. So that's where we went. But Carly and I plus nanny was stretching it a bit for two older people well into their seventies so I only planned to stay until I decided what I was going to do. After two years of *My One and Only* I felt very disconnected, which I suppose I was, cut off from the people in the show who had become almost like family.

Within a week of getting back, my friend Mary Frampton called. Her husband Hal was recording a new abum in Montserrat in the Caribbean with his band Dire Straits. She and Alexi, their three-year-old son, were going. Why didn't we come too? Sarah, Carly's nanny, had come back with us to England. Carly adored her, so all three of us flew out for two weeks in the sun. I had been to the Caribbean before. My first trip had been back in 1970; then the January after Michael died Peggy, Carly and I had flown down to St Thomas for a week, which we timed so that my sister Viv could come too. Unfortunately Shirley couldn't make it because she was at work. But for me it was more recuperation than holiday.

We arrived in Montserrat tired and jet lagged, and we all three went straight to bed although it was only about eight. Carly and Sarah's room was next door to mine. We were staying on a holiday estate of little bungalows and each room had sliding doors that opened out on to our own swimming pool. Suddenly I woke up. I must have heard something but just remember sitting bolt upright in bed and seeing this hand coming through the narrow gap in the open window, feeling for the handle of the sliding patio doors. I shrieked, 'Go away'.

And the hand disappeared.

Sarah came running but whoever it was had long gone. It was only about ten o'clock but I know the first night is often when hotel guests get burgled, before you've had time to put your valuables in the safety deposit box. Bags may not even have been unpacked. Sarah fetched Mary and she phoned Hal at the recording studio and he organised for one of the security guards at the studio to come round and spend the night in the sitting room. The next day someone at the studio offered to lend me their Alsatian. I said yes please. He was gorgeous and seemed quite happy to be with us and we all made a huge fuss of him. And most importantly we felt safe.

A bad beginning to an otherwise really nice holiday. Hal was in the studio till the small hours, so most of the time it was just Mary, me and our little ones. It was so long since I had felt so completely unstressed. And Montserrat was very spectacular with a volcano and black sand. We would walk two hours up a ravine to an amazing waterfall. But all I really wanted was rest, rest and more rest.

I'd left for Montserrat knowing I had work to come back to in England, on *The Doctor and the Devils*, a film based on the real life story of the Victorian 'body snatchers', Burke and Hare, who provided all-too-fresh corpses for the celebrated anatomist Dr Robert Knox to demonstrate on to his students and anyone else who wanted to attend his lectures. The only legal way he could get bodies was from the hangman. All very macabre. Ronald Harwood, who wrote the play *The Dresser*, had adapted the script from an original screenplay by Dylan Thomas, the only one the extraordinary Welsh poet ever did. The director was Freddie Francis, one of the all time great cinematographers. I had lunch with him at Shepperton Studios, the ritual which often passes for an audition.

Christmas was in Twickenham, the family together for the first time in years. Then Carly, Sarah and I moved into Stewart Grimshaw's house in Chelsea as an interim measure. Although we didn't know it then, Dad was in the early stages of Alzheimer's and it wasn't easy for him having us around all the time. Especially with a young child.

The Doctor and the Devils starred Timothy Dalton (later to be James Bond) as the doctor and Jonathan Pryce and Stephen Rea as the

Burke and Hare characters. Nicola McAuliffe and I played prostitutes. Stephen Rea had just started his screen career with Neil Jordan's *Angel* and later went on to score such a big success in *The Crying Game*, but then he was still primarily a stage actor, one of the founding members of Field Day, the theatre company committed to new Irish writing. Jonathan Pryce was also at the beginning of his film career. He had done *Brazil*, and *Something Wicked This Way Comes*, but was best known to theatre-goers; one of the Royal Shakespeare Company's rising stars. Most of my scenes were with Jonathan.

During the last few months of *My One and Only*, the whole company had discovered Trivial Pursuit, which was then the big new thing in the States. Being a board game fanatic I was soon hooked. For a long-running show it was perfect. It was also perfect for a film because there's always so much sitting around. Hurry up and wait. And in 1985 Trivial Pursuit hadn't yet come out in England. I had a dressing room with a sitting room and that's where we played. As soon as we weren't wanted on set we'd be back there playing: me, Jonathan, Nicola, Stephen and Julian Sands who played the young doctor. We all got on like a house on fire and had this running game. For the first couple of days I always won because of course I'd been playing it for months. But before too long Jonathan was beating me. That's how Jonathan and I became friends, through endless games of Trivial Pursuit. Little did I realise at this time that he was to play an important role in the drama of my real life — but that came later.

Over the next couple of years I seemed to specialise in Victorian songbirds. A year after *The Doctor and the Devils*, came a television two-hour special, *The Little Matchgirl* with Roger Daltrey, where I played a music hall singer. Like me, Roger had made his screen debut in a film directed by Ken Russell, in Pete Townsend's rock opera *Tommy*. Roger was a great rock star as a member of The Who, but it didn't surprise me that he was trying to explore more acting roles because Ken has this ability to get you to jettison any pre-conceived ideas of who you are and what you can do. We worked well together — he proved to be a very talented, dedicated and natural actor.

In *Young Charlie Chaplin* in 1987 I both sang, drank and went mad as Charlie Chaplin's poor benighted mother. The six-part series made for Thames Television took Chaplin up to the age of fifteen when he goes off to America. It was a huge challenge artistically. Hannah Chaplin started off as a music hall artiste but ended up in a lunatic asylum. There's no evidence that she was ever a great beauty and her end was as unglamorous as they come, and the script by Colin Shindler didn't pull its punches. Ian McShane played Charlie's father, who also worked the halls, a drunken sot who actually died of alcoholism and treated Hannah and the children appallingly. We shot the madhouse scenes in an old asylum near

Virginia Water in Surrey, a bizarre building to find out in the middle of the countryside, and I found filming there pretty harrowing knowing the terrible tragedies that had gone on under that very roof.

Hannah Chaplin was a great part. When you've made your name as a look, as a face, it's great to get offered roles that aren't based on that, and in spite of a couple of songs this was an acting part. I spent most of the time looking haggard under a grey wig, broken and disillusioned. In America it was put out on PBS (Public Broadcasting Service) in two parts mid-evening. We had wonderful reviews both for me and the piece; it was nominated for an Emmy.

Doing a six-part series is hard work. Television is always a much tighter schedule than feature films. Filming involves long hours but a lot of that is just sitting around waiting while cameras and lighting are changed for new set ups. You might get through two or three pages of the shooting script a day on a film. In television it's more like eight or ten because you don't have the luxury of doing take after take. For me that works fine. Directors often say that my best takes are in the first few.

In March 1985, immediately after *The Doctor and the Devils*, I flew straight to Jamaica to shoot *Club Paradise* with Robin Williams. Along with my lovely friend Billy Connolly, Robin is the funniest person I have ever met. Although they are clearly very different, they both have this quirky perspective on life and people, and a way of telling rambling stories rather than jokes. *Club Paradise* was all set to be a huge hit. Robin plays a fire-fighter from Chicago who decides to chuck it all in, cash in his pension and open a low-rent Club Med in the Caribbean. Needless to say it's disastrous. The place hasn't even got running water. I play a dizzy blonde he's trying to impress, but end up staying to help him out.

Everyone thought it would be huge. All the markers were there: Robin Williams, wacky and wonderful; director Harold Ramis who did *Ghostbusters*, and a very talented cast including Peter O'Toole, Rick Moranis, Joanna Cassidy and the great reggae star Jimmy Cliff who played Robin's partner in the ill-judged venture. But it never really took off, although we had great fun making it and watching Robin at work was an extraordinary experience in itself. At the end of every scene, after Harold was satisfied he'd got what he wanted in the can, we had 'Robin's take', when he would use the basic framework of the scene as a springboard for his manic genius. You never knew what he might do. Talk rubbish language or go off on some weird tangent of his own. Though how many of these ended up in the final movie I'm not sure. And I got to do my first love scene. Although that's putting it a bit strong. Naturally with Robin it was hysterically funny. Robin was truly delightful to work with and we became good friends.

* * *

While I was in Jamaica I made up my mind that for the time being I would base myself in London. Carly was now six and a half and needed a proper school. Once I was back I called up everyone I knew with children. One name kept cropping up: Thomas's School in Kensington. We were both interviewed, first me, then Carly. She would start in September.

I rented a little furnished house at the Hyde Park end of Gloucester Road in Kensington as all my furniture was either gone or in storage and I didn't know how long I would stay. The lease was six months. I needed time to think about my long-term future. Although I had my family in England and some very good friends, I felt my life lay in New York. All my mates were there and I missed the buzz of Manhattan, and careerwise it would be better to be back there because *My One and Only* had still not faded from people's memories. We had been such a huge hit.

Over the years I've often been asked about bringing *My One and Only* to London. But I've always said no. I do think every project has its time and place and the only reason to re-do something is do it better. And I don't think we could. And Tommy wouldn't want to perform in it any more — much of the magic of the show was the two of us together, and if you take that element away, you've lost a lot. Most people have the memory of it being wonderful, and I think one should leave it at that. I'd rather do another musical. And I will. But it takes time to find a project that's right and get it on.

Three months in Jamaica had left me feeling relaxed and healthy. For the first time in my adult life I was enjoying being single. I'd ricocheted from Justin to Michael and then into *My One and Only* and Tommy who was like my other half. Now it was just me and Carly. At first I was a bit frightened about being on my own but that was more to do with companionship than anything else. I'd dated one or two people since Michael died, but nothing of any significance. Six months on and I thought, this isn't so bad. I can do what I want, go where I want, see who I want.

I was lucky. The trap, when you have been with somebody all your life, is thinking 'Oh my God, I can't survive on my own'. It's much harder on women who can't make ends meet. But I was financially secure and that makes a huge difference. Personally I think it's good for a woman to have a career. Not that I'm putting down women who decide to have babies and stay at home. That's a choice too. But if she can, a woman should try to have interests or a career to fall back on. If things go wrong you can support yourself and when the children grow up it's important to have somewhere satisfying and fulfilling to channel your energies.

With the acting career bubbling along nicely, it was time to think about a new album.

In 1977, straight after my second album, Polygram had sent me to Nashville. I remember it was my first time on Concorde. Working with all these real country musicians was an amazing experience. We did some good tracks but the record company fell out with the producer, there was some big legal hassle and it was never released. Nonetheless I wouldn't have missed it for anything and Nashville even made me an honorary colonel. I have my legal certificate, proclaiming Colonel Twiggy (what a hoot).

As *My One and Only* was drawing to a close I had started working on a few ideas in New York. Hal Lindes and Frank Carillo, one of Mary and Hal's oldest friends, had written some songs for me. So after the show I'd meet up with them and lay down some tracks. At one session Carly Simon did back-up. The boys nearly died when I told them she was coming. I had met her towards the beginning of *My One and Only*. I remember being amazed at how tall she was, about five foot eleven. Anyway, we were having lunch and I was telling her about what I was doing and she said 'Oh, can I come along and sing back-up?'

'You must be joking.'

'I'm serious. I'd love to.'

So along she came. Hal and Frank were like two little schoolboys, trying to be really cool, but so excited.

Now back in London I was working with Charlie Skarbeck and Tim Smit, producer/songwriters who had approached me with the idea of recording some of their new songs. They'd just had a huge European hit called 'Midnight Blue'. And we did release a couple of singles, good songs, but unfortunately they didn't break the charts. The problem with England is the Radio One playlist. If you can't get on it, it's almost impossible to get a hit record. I remember when I was doing *Matchgirl* with Roger Daltrey him bemoaning the same, which amazed me. You can hardly get more famous in the rock world than Roger Daltrey of The Who and even he couldn't make the playlist with the single he'd just put out. There are hundreds of records that never get heard. A rather sad, limiting state of affairs, down to the vagaries of the producer's decision, I suppose.

One evening in July Mary, Hal, Stewart and I had been to see Lauren Bacall in Tennessee Williams' play *Sweet Bird of Youth* and we were at one of my favourite restaurants, the Caprice, having dinner. Like The Ivy and Joe Allen's, the Caprice is a favourite haunt of film and theatre people. I saw Jonathan Pryce sitting at another table with a group of people. We said hello. I hadn't seen him since *The Doctor and the Devils* some months earlier. He introduced me to his wife, Kate Fahy. Then another man stood up. We said 'hello, how are you?' at exactly the same time, laughed and he mentioned we had met ten years ago. I didn't need to be reminded. His name was Leigh Lawson. Nothing trivial about this pursuit, Jonathan. Fate had decided to take charge of the dice.

Back in 1975 when Michael and I were living in Belsize Park and I had been doing my second *Twiggs* series, for the BBC, we had been to a John Denver concert at the Hammersmith Odeon. At the reception after the concert at a club called The Elephant on the River we found ourselves sharing a table with Leigh and his then lady Hayley Mills. They were charming and the four of us chatted away. Michael guessed that Hayley was pregnant and, being American and very direct, asked her if she was. We were sworn to secrecy.

Ten years on, I knew he wasn't with Hayley any more: the split had been in the papers a couple of years before. I'd always thought him a very good and interesting actor. I'd seen him as Alec D'Urberville in Roman Polanski's film *Tess*, of course, but also much earlier in Zeffirelli's 1972 film about Francis of Assisi, *Brother Sun, Sister Moon*. In 1983 he'd made a great hit with a British television series called *Travelling Man*, which I'd missed at the time because I was on Broadway. By chance they were re-running it late at night and I was watching it. Leigh was wonderful.

Meanwhile back at the Caprice when I returned to my table, Mary was all agog.

'Who was that with Jonathan? He's absolutely gorgeous.'

I told her.

'Is he with anybody?'

I told her that I didn't know, but said what I thought, that somebody so gorgeous was unlikely to be unattached. But I was wrong. Leigh was on his own. Jonathan was at that time doing *The Seagull* and that night Leigh had accompanied Jonathan's wife Kate to see the show. I remembered reading a huge article on Leigh in a magazine about a week before about his life and how he had said he didn't plan on having another serious relationship for at least ten years, if ever. His split with Hayley had been very painful.

About three days later, I got a phone call from Robert and Babs Powell. After two years in New York I was catching up with all my old mates. Robert and I had been friends since *Pygmalion*. Babs used to be a dancer with Pan's People, the regular stars of *Top of the Pops*. Babs said they were going to dinner with Richard Johnson and his wife at La Famiglia, an Italian restaurant in World's End, Chelsea and would I like to join them. When I got to the restaurant Babs and Robert told me the Johnsons had cancelled last-minute and they'd invited another old friend, Mike King. When he arrived he had Leigh with him. I vaguely thought that somebody was matchmaking.

But it was pure coincidence. Robert and Babs had known Leigh for years. When Richard Johnson pulled out — quite genuine — Babs had called Mike, an old friend of theirs and, as it happens, an old friend of Leigh's, to make up the numbers. Mike had been one of the King Brothers, a really popular pre-Beatles singing trio. When Babs called Mike, Leigh happened to be sitting with him in the kitchen. They were about to pop over to the pub. Mike says, 'I'm with Leigh.' Bob says: 'Great. Bring him with you.'

So we were all at the restaurant and it was a really, really nice evening. I tell Leigh how I've been watching *Travelling Man* and we talk about our kids, like you do. Just chatting; with just the merest hint of flirtation; but Leigh didn't ask for my phone number or anything. He hadn't even asked where I lived. And I was a bit disappointed if the truth be told. I thought he was lovely and we'd been getting on so well.

Two days later and I was driving along in my lovely new navy blue Jaguar XJS sportscar which was my present to myself after *My One and Only*. I had been to see Carly's new school, although it was only a short distance away from where we were living in Gloucester Road. And walking along the pavement reading a newspaper I see this guy. Something drew my eye to him. It was Leigh. I stopped the car.

'What are you doing here?' I said.

'What do you mean? I live here.'

I couldn't believe it. His flat was dead opposite Thomas's School. And just down the road from us. I said the only thing a good neighbour could say — and all that I could think of.

'Do you want a cup of tea?'

So he got in the car, and that was it really.

I made a pot of tea and found some biscuits. Carly and Sarah were out somewhere. He eventually asked me what I was doing for dinner the following night. Nothing, I said, adding that it was my nanny's night off. 'But you're more than welcome to come here.'

Which is exactly what he did. Our first date was an Indian takeaway.

So we started seeing each other regularly. We took things slowly. We had both been through the mill and thoroughly scalded. So we were very careful. Also I was nervous.

'Number one, he's an actor; number two he's

drop dead gorgeous.'

I'd come across a couple of guys like that since being on my own, dreadful womanisers and just not reliable. And I really didn't want to go down that track. In fact I thought he was too good to be true. I was frightened of falling in too deep too soon and getting hurt. But he did make my heart flutter. He still makes my heart flutter.

The first couple of weeks, our relationship was very gentle and careful. We went to restaurants, we went to the movies, we went to the theatre, which I loved because he was so knowledgeable. The nice thing was we got on really well and he really made me laugh. And Leigh is truly funny. But he's also very kind and romantic.

He'd always bring me flowers. Pink roses and pink champagne. Pink became our colour. The day we saw the cottage we later bought in Oxfordshire, it was covered with pink roses. And when we got the house in LA, although it was winter there was one pink rose out in the back yard.

In America I'd been asked out a few times but there hadn't been anyone serious. When you go through what I'd been through with Michael, you're very raw. It's fear. When I met Leigh I was just coming to terms with being on my own and I was fine. I was still a bit worried because he was an actor. But Leigh isn't like most actors and I'm not like most actresses. Neither of us are particularly moody or egotistical and ambition doesn't eat away at us. As we're both successful in our fields, neither of us feels threatened by the other. Leigh actually works more than I do.

He never stops, with one project after another in films, TV and his greatest love, theatre.

That was one of the things that sank Michael and me. Fortunately or unfortunately I am famous all over the world. You say the name and everyone knows it. Lots of men would find that very difficult. But Leigh is used to strong independent women and admires and is not threatened by them. He grew up with a wonderful mother who had to be strong and cope with an alcoholic husband and because of Hayley he knew what it was like to live with somebody very famous. He understood the pressures of that kind of life. Usually women in our field, like her, like me, are quite strong. You have to be. You learn to be. Leigh and I both have strong personalities and opinions but you can be strong together.

Introducing the kids turned out to be very easy. Every weekend and holidays Leigh saw his son Ace, who was eight, and Ace's half-brother Crispian, who was eleven. Within a week of the famous cup of tea, Leigh asked if we'd like to go with him and his boys for a jaunt on a boat on the River Thames that some friends of his were organising.

It was a great day out. As well as Leigh, Ace and Crispian there was Peter Firth and his little boy Rory. Peter and Leigh were buddies from way back, from *Brother Sun, Sister Moon*. Then there was Sebastian Graham Jones, who directed *Travelling Man*, his son Luke and Sebastian's girlfriend Susan Fleetwood, a wonderful actress, who tragically died of cancer far too young in

1995. We all met up somewhere near Henley. Leigh and I would have gone together but between us we had three children and neither of our cars could fit five. I had the Jag which would take two kids at a pinch and Leigh had a Mercedes sports, which could barely do that. It turned out we had both bought our cars as treats or rewards to ourselves. His was after the film *Golden Rendezvous* with Richard Harris, shot in South Africa, a nightmare experience to make.

It was a great day out. Our children met without there being any kind of pressure and Leigh was lovely with Carly. Having been a stepfather for so many years with Crispian, he knew the pitfalls and how important it was to be sensitive to the situation.

Getting involved with someone when you have kids and they don't can be difficult. They don't really understand. Meeting each other's children so early in our relationship meant we talked about them. And people's attitudes towards kids are very telling. Right from the beginning he introduced me to Ace as Lesley, not Twiggy. He explained that whereas Carly could yell 'Mum' across a supermarket and no one would think anything of it, if Ace started yelling 'Twiggy' everyone would turn and stare. Ace still calls me Lesley, and apart from my sisters and my Mum, he's one of the very few who does. To everyone else I'm Twiggs or Twiggy.

About three or four weeks into our stepping out we bumped into Ringo Starr and his wife Barbara Bach at the launch party of an exhibition by photographer Terry O'Neill. We'd been snapped a few times, 'seen together' by the tabloid press. 'Hmmmm,' said Ringo in rich Liverpudlian accent, 'You're becoming a couple.' It was the first time anyone had ever said it. And we looked at each other and laughed, realising indeed that we were.

A few weeks after this I began to realise I didn't want to go back to New York. I was falling in love, though I was still a bit cautious of it all going wrong. My friends adored him. And no wonder. Leigh is a really good man. And as the song says, a good man is hard to find. We were so lucky to meet when we did. We always say someone was watching over us from above. For all those out there who think they're never going to meet anybody, at whatever time in your life, you never know when and you never know how. It happens when you least expect it.

18

The owner of the Gloucester Road house wanted it back at the end of my six-month lease, so I decided to look for somewhere to buy. Carly was very happy in her new school so it had to be in the Kensington and Chelsea area. I wanted somewhere oldish — anyway not new — probably a Victorian mansion flat, somewhere with big rooms and high ceilings.

As soon as I walked into that huge sitting room with French windows onto the balcony that overlooked the trees in the lovely garden square, I knew I'd found what I'd been looking for and I made an offer the same day. The owner was Margaret Thatcher's press secretary Michael Allison and it was several years before journalists realised he'd moved. I was always getting calls whenever there was a political crisis or scandal. I never let on it was me answering the phone.

Leigh was also in the process of buying a very similar flat and we'd joked about 'two nights at your place and two nights at mine'. But while the sale of my flat was being completed, Leigh's fell through: the vendors couldn't move out, a break in the chain.

'Maybe this is fate that your flat has fallen through at this time,' I said. 'It seems a bit silly having two flats. Why don't we join forces?'

It could have been terribly embarrassing, but that's me. To my intense relief and delight he said he thought it was a good idea. By the time we moved in together we had known each other for about six months. During the day we played house getting the flat together; at night he was at the National Theatre playing a very demanding role in Peter Shaffer's new play *Yonadab*, an Old Testament story, with Alan Bates and Patrick Stewart, directed by Peter Hall.

The stage was in Leigh's blood. His dad had been a song 'n' dance man, half of a duo known as Lawson and Young, and he had met Leigh's mother when she managed the Windmill Theatre in London in the 1930s when it was a variety theatre. It later had a motto, 'we never closed', because through all the wartime bombing the show went on. His great aunt had been the famous music hall star Marie Lloyd. During the Blitz the Lawsons were bombed out of London and moved to Coventry. Bombed out of Coventry they moved to Atherstone in Warwickshire, just north of Stratford where Leigh was born, and if you listen carefully you can still hear the Warwickshire lilt in Leigh's voice.

In the days when Leigh was at the Royal Academy of Dramatic Art, they were inclined to knock regional accents out of young actors. And because of Leigh's rich cultured voice everybody thinks he must be quite posh. In fact he's very no-nonsense working class, which is one reason he's so normal. When they moved to Warwickshire his father gave up show business, went to work in a factory and started drinking heavily. Things didn't really work out, so his family were poorer than mine. We've both got two older sisters who get on well together. We're so lucky. We have lovely Christmases because both our families enjoy each other's company. A lot of laughter can be heard in the Lawson household on these occasions. Both families are a bit noisy.

Like me, Leigh remembers a special teacher at his school: an art teacher. But the reason he joined the drama group (and I've heard this from a lot of actors) was because that's where all the pretty girls were. In 1994 Vincent, an old friend of Leigh's from that time, came down to London to see him starring in the West End with Julie Christie and Harriet Walter in Harold Pinter's *Old Times* directed by the amazing Lindy Davies. In Leigh's dressing room after the show, Vincent said, 'Your job's so glamorous. All the famous people you must meet.' And Leigh said, 'Well that's what you may think, but it's not really that glamorous.' Just then there was a knock at the door. Leigh answered it and Lindy said, 'There's someone who wants to meet you.' Standing there were Barbra Streisand and Jon Voight, Barbra Streisand looking amazing in a white suit and huge picture hat. Vincent's face was a sight to behold. Streisand was so flattering about Leigh in the play, she stayed chatting for about half an hour. For Vincent it was amazing. He adored Streisand, and Leigh said that of all the people in the world, he was so glad it was his old friend Vincent who was in his dressing room that night when there was a bit of glamour about.

In the 1960s Leigh moved to London and began a two-year evening drama course at Mountview Drama School in Crouch End where he had a wonderful mentor, the principal, Peter Coxhead. One day Peter stopped Leigh in the corridor and said, 'I think you should try for RADA.' Leigh nearly fainted. To him Peter Coxhead was God. For the first time in his life he thought there might be a chance he could become an actor. Once you've got somebody you respect and admire telling you that you're good, it gives you huge confidence. When he auditioned and was offered a place at RADA, he was walking on air. His mother quite understandably was a bit concerned, and suggested it might be wiser to get a small business rather than risk the ups and downs of a life in the theatre. But acting was Leigh's passion and nothing would dissuade him.

In those days he was Allan Leigh Lawson, but because there was another actor called Alan Lawson he had to use his second name, Leigh. After RADA came leading roles in repertory at the Belgrade Theatre, Coventry, one of the best repertory theatres in the country. In 1970 his agent sent him to meet Franco Zeffirelli, who cast him as Bernardo, a leading role in *Brother Sun, Sister Moon* the story of St Francis of Assisi. Since when — film, television and theatre — Leigh has virtually never stopped working. Not surprising. He is the most wonderful actor with an extraordinary range, from character actor to romantic lead.

It was in 1985, around the time I met Leigh,

that I began to think about *Betty* again. In 1982, just after *Pygmalion* when I was still living in LA and thinking about coming back to England, I had had a call from a producer called Barry Hanson. I didn't know Barry personally but I knew his reputation as a highly respected, independent producer who had done *The Naked Civil Servant* for television with John Hurt as Quentin Crisp and *The Long Good Friday*, that brilliant film which launched the career of Bob Hoskins, an old friend of Leigh's and now, I am happy to say, of mine.

Barry told me he'd just bought the rights to a book called *Betty* by Allen Saddler.

'I think it would make a great television series. Read it. If you like it I think we should try and put it together.'

Betty is the story of a good-time girl, a hostess turned night club singer turned femme fatale, with her eye on the main chance. It's much more fun to play a bad lady than a goody girl. But I usually never get the opportunity. The main part of the action is set in the twenties but the story is told in flashback through the eyes of the young guy who becomes obsessed by her and whom she ends up destroying. Barry described it as a cross between *Double Indemnity* and *Cabaret*.

I loved it. Barry and I got on right away. He's a real Yorkshireman and, like me, believes in saying what he thinks. All he had to do now was persuade one of the networks to back it. In the meantime, along came *My One and Only*. From time to time during my eighteen months on Broadway Barry and I would speak, but the last thing I heard he had had no luck. It was two years and the option had dropped.

Now that I was back in England and picking up the threads of my English career, I gave the book to Leigh and he agreed it was fantastic and made for television. If Barry's not going to do anything with it, I thought, maybe I can get it going. So I rang the publishers and took out an option for two years. All pretty scary. I'd never done anything like it before. Or even thought about it.

It was becoming much more common for actors to get their own productions going, like my friend Susan George, who I had known from LA when we were both living there, when Carly was small. After Michael died Susan and her husband Simon McCorkindale proved really good friends and before I met Leigh, took me under their wing, making sure I wasn't on my own. She and Simon have their own production company and have produced quite a few films. And as the old saying goes, 'if you want something done, do it yourself'.

It wasn't that I was desperate to be a producer, I just wanted to get it made. But it needed somebody in the driving seat as committed as I was. Barry Hanson was the obvious candidate. So I called him.

'The publishers told me that somebody had bought the option. They wouldn't say who,' he said. 'But I guessed it was you.'

I told him I just didn't want anyone else to get hold of it. The reason he had called the publishers was that the week before he had been pitching another idea to Nick Elliot, London Weekend Television's head of drama, but he hadn't liked it.

Then Nick said, 'Have you got anything else up your sleeve?' Off the top of my head I told them about *Betty*. He said 'Sounds wonderful. I'd like to develop it.' '

So Barry and I became co-producers, set up a company. First we needed a screenwriter and Barry brought in Barrie Keefe who had done such a brilliant job on *The Long Good Friday*. The scripts were sensational. Barrie had written the most fantastic six-hour musical psycho-thriller, an original. And London Weekend went for it in a big way. *Betty* would be their big showcase drama for autumn 1988, no expense spared. They had such confidence in it, they agreed to put up all the money. This was unusual. Normally the network puts up half and the originating producers go outside for the rest. This was going to have huge implications later, but at the time we had no bad premonitions. On the contrary, we were delighted. It meant not having to go through the business of pre-selling *Betty* abroad. Now it really was the green light.

The crucial question of whether it was to be shot on film or video was decided by LWT's big boss himself, Greg Dyke, Controller of Programming. When he saw the script he said, 'This is sensational. I take it we're doing it on film?'

Not a fan of video for drama, I was over the moon.

So we went into pre-production. In terms of casting there were three key roles: Betty, her young lover Jimmy who narrates the story from contemporary old age, and the night-club owner. Jimmy has to be young and very street but very vulnerable. He's been a boxer. We started with a handful of names but the one we wanted was Sean Bean, a complete unknown in those days. For him it was a huge break and a great role: his part was bigger than mine and also he tells the story. But for me Betty was the part of a lifetime. Because beneath her glamorous exterior, there's no heart of gold. She's a two-timing, self-serving bitch who will stop at nothing to get what she wants. As the night-club owner we cast Christopher Lee, a difficult role that needed just the right mix of dash and steel. He was thrilled. It was a great part for him.

Our main set was the night club. The period had been shifted slightly to the end of the twenties/early thirties and the club was the ultimate in opulence, including a dance floor which opens to reveal a swimming pool. It was being built at Shepperton Studios, where our company was now based. And it cost serious money. £350,000 to be precise. For the music we used period songs but Manfred Mann, a friend of Barrie Keefe's was doing the arranging. Our original director was Jim Goddard but when he had to drop out Barry brought in a new young Scottish director called Sandy Johnson. I had never heard of him, but I trusted Barry's opinion. If you work with people you think are brilliant, you trust them. And Barry *was* brilliant and always finding great new talent.

It was 12 January 1988, five weeks before we were due to start shooting, and I was in the middle of a costume fitting; a wonderful thirties silver lamé dress, I remember. Then the phone rang. It was Barry Hanson. 'Now don't get upset,' he said. 'But I think we've got a bit of a problem.'

The 'bit of a problem' had begun when Barry went to a meeting at the Musicians Union (the trades union that negotiates contracts for their members) to agree terms and conditions. It's a rubber stamp job. Or should be. The production company before Barry were in there five minutes. The MU are a very strong union and I'd come across them before on TV shows. In those days if you were a group you could mime to your records. But as a vocalist without your own band you had to sing live. And there would often be an MU official in the studio to check that people were playing by the rules, rules that were often broken because it's ridiculous to expect something recorded in half an hour in a TV studio to achieve the sound it took days to get right in a recording studio.

In essence the deal being offered to the musicians (who had already negotiated their individual fees) was the same as the actors were getting, the standard BFTPA (British Film and Television Producers Association) agreement: a one-off fee which covered all rights. But there was another form of agreement used by television companies — ITVA (Independent Television Association). This gave performers much less money up front, but it included provision for royalties later on, if and when the show was repeated and sold abroad. And it was this form of contract that the MU said that it wanted for *Betty*.

If it had just been the MU we could have got round it. Manfred Mann had already been paid and I had already recorded most of my songs. For the ones that remained, much as I would have preferred to do the music in England, if push came to shove we'd go abroad. The next day all such hopes were dashed. The MU had been joined by the actors' union, Equity. As *Betty* was wholly financed by London Weekend, they said, calling it an independent production was just a ruse to get actors to work at a cut-price rate. *Betty* was not really an independent production at all, they claimed. It was an in-house production and as such should fall within the ITVA deal. And that unless London Weekend agreed to re-negotiate the contracts Equity would call all their members out.

I just couldn't believe what was happening. A major TV drama, employing seventy-two actors, the very people Equity was supposed to be supporting, was being threatened with closure. And why? Far from being a cut-price rate our actors were being offered 317 per cent more up front than they would under a TV contract.

London Weekend were equally incensed and felt, quite rightly, that Stan Hibbert of the MU and Peter Plouviez of Equity had left it till the eleventh hour to raise this issue because they calculated that London Weekend were in so deep, they would have to jump to Equity's tune. Everyone in the business knew *Betty* was being made: it was LWT's production of the year. If the BFTPA agreement was so terrible, why wait till four weeks before shooting before crying foul? London Weekend had been prepared to fully finance *Betty* simply because it was so brilliant. Pre-selling to overseas buyers — which inevitably would have meant America — would have saddled *Betty* with American casting. This was a very British story, a wonderful showcase for British technicians, British actors and British musicians, British talent unfettered with any outside interference. And God knows, we've all seen enough co-productions which have been completely ruined by stupid casting imposed from outside.

Betty was expensive to mount. It was budgeted at £4.5 million. Of course LWT were going to have to sell it abroad. They could only justify £2 million from their own budget. Earlier on, who knows, something could have been arranged. But it was too late now for them to re-structure the financing. Understandably it stuck in Greg Dyke's craw that Equity and the MU had clearly just waited till they thought they had them by the short and curlies. In the *Daily Mail* he said, 'We refuse to be held to ransom.'

And what of the people whose jobs were actually threatened? The actors and musicians? What did they want? Without exception they wanted *Betty* to get done. And in an industry where eighty per cent of actors are unemployed it's no wonder. They were more than happy with their film contracts. It was dreadful. Actors would call up the office in a terrible state. I remember one dancer sobbing down the phone because it was the first part she'd been offered in years. Then I had another actor in tears because he had installed a new kitchen that he now didn't have the money to pay for. We were inundated with letters and calls of support. Everyone saying, 'It's not us, it's the union.' Everyone asking, 'Is there anything we can do?' And not only from actors. All the musicians we had worked with said that if necessary they would record the music in Paris. And for actors and dancers, projects like *Betty* are so rare. No member of Equity wanted to pull the plug.

We had a full crew, over two hundred people. What about them? Both NATKE and the most powerful film union of them all, the ACTT, which covered all the big boys, the directors, the cameramen, petitioned Equity to reconsider because it affected them too. Suddenly, a few weeks before commencement of principal photography, they find they're out of a job. At that late stage it's very hard to find anything else. They tried to get the arbitration service, ACAS, and the TUC involved, along the lines of 'You've got to do something about these guys, because us guys want to work.' It was a living nightmare. But it seemed nothing would budge Mr Plouviez.

Naturally as soon as it began to go wrong the press got involved and they were amazing. From *The Times* to the *Guardian*, politics was irrelevant. Everyone recognised the injustice of what was happening. But still Plouviez wouldn't budge.

London Weekend tried to talk to him. No dice. Barry Hanson tried to talk to him. Ditto. Then the penny dropped.

'You will have to go in and talk to Plouviez,' reasoned Barry. 'He can refuse to see me, I'm a producer, but you're an actor. You, Sean, Christopher, he'll have to see all of you.'

And of course he was right. We were all members of Equity. In those days you had to be. Equity was what was called a closed shop. I'd had a run-in with Peter Plouviez before over *The Boyfriend*. Getting your 'card' as it was called was hard even for actors trained at drama school; for outsiders like me, forget it. Obviously the idea of Twiggy the model starring in *The Boyfriend* really got up his nose. The first we heard what was happening was when Robert Stephens telephoned me from his dressing room at the Old Vic. He told me he had just sent one of Plouviez's lackeys packing after being asked to sign some kind of petition to get me blacked and that we should be warned. Ken Russell went ballistic: he would make *The Boyfriend* with Twiggy, he said, or he would not make it at all. Threatened by Ken at his maddest Plouviez capitulated. I got my card and the film was made.

It hadn't been Ken's last encounter with Plouviez. In 1977, while shooting *Valentino* with Nureyev on location in Spain, an actor playing a twenties film director collapsed with vertigo when he had to climb up to a high camera position. There was no time to re-cast; they needed somebody else immediately. So Ken donned twenties director costume, climbed up to the prop camera, and did the take. When Plouviez heard what had happened back in England, he went mad. Threatened to black the film. Till Ken remembered that he was still a member of Equity himself from his ballet-dancing days. Faces were saved and war was averted.

Now it was my turn to try and find a way out of the *Betty* mess. I called Equity and asked to see Plouviez. By this time I didn't care about Equity. What were they going to do? Black me? Kill me? Every day, time was ticking away all that money. We could only hang on so long. But I still hadn't given up hope; I couldn't believe that something so good could go down. But I was completely desperate. I had nurtured Betty from conception to birth. I didn't understand what was happening at all. Because frankly it was irrelevant. I was an actress and I had negotiated my deal just like everyone else, through my agent.

I tell the secretary that I need to see him. 'I'm sorry but Mr Plouviez is tied up.'

'This is Twiggy. I have to see him.'

'I'm sorry. But there's nothing I can do.'

'Then just tell Mr Plouviez that if he doesn't agree to see Sean Bean, Christopher Lee and myself this afternoon, we will be outside with all the national press when he leaves the office at five o'clock and he can talk to us on the steps of Equity.'

I didn't like behaving like that but I really didn't have a choice. Came the call. Peter Plouviez would see us that afternoon.

Christopher, Sean and I meet ahead of time to work out our plan of action. Sean is murderous. This is his launch pad. The big break. Christopher will be our spokesman. He's so bright and articulate and he's a 'chap' who having been an officer in the British Army still has that built-in authority. Christopher explains that if we go in guns firing, it leaves us with nowhere to run. We decide to go in calmly, talk logically, and try to find some kind of face-saver for Plouviez, which we reckoned was the stage the game had reached.

By this time it seemed to us Plouviez had boxed himself into a corner. He and Stan Hibbert thought they had LWT by the throat. But if the Unions had chosen their battleground, so had LWT. Poor *Betty* wasn't a show any longer. It was a test case. The Government had recently enacted a bill to force twenty-five per cent of TV productions to be made by independent companies. Both the ITVA and BFTPA agreements were up for renewal and re-negotiation in April. However you looked at it we were a pawn in somebody else's war. Innocent victims caught in the crossfire.

So we arrived at Equity's offices in Harley Street. And we were really nice and really polite. I was nervous. This wasn't where I belonged. All I ever wanted to do was put my frocks on and perform. So we sat down and the first thing Plouviez said was would you like a drink?

'No thank you,' I said. 'It's a bit early for me, I'll have a cup of tea'.

'Well, I'm going to have a vodka,' he said. 'It's probably something to do with my politics.'

I can see him now, dressed in a black leather jacket and black trousers, pouring this drink, the drink I hate most in the world.

Then Christopher began.

'Look, we want to make this. There's going to be a lot of your members out of work. We understand your end of it. But what can we do? What do you want from London Weekend?'

Christopher was brilliant. He put our case so eloquently, with no ambiguities. Back to Plouviez.

'My job is to protect my members. It's all very well for people like you,' he says (looking at me). 'But I have to protect the little dancer and the little actor.'

'Well, Peter,' I said, 'it may interest you to know that I've just had the little dancer on the phone in tears saying this is the first job she's had in two and a half years.'

Then he took down a book from the shelf behind him and started quoting from it. Article blank, paragraph blank. Double Dutch to me. And totally irrelevant.

Our quest from that meeting with Plouviez was to set up a meeting between Equity and London Weekend. And Christopher never lost sight of that:

'We are here to ask you, will you sit down with

London Weekend and try and work it out? We are members of Equity and we want to work.'

By the end of the meeting Plouviez said he would arrange a meeting with Greg Dyke of LWT. Whatever else happened it wasn't down to us any more.

And so they began to talk to try and thrash out some kind of compromise. I never went to these meetings. Barry did. I was too distraught. I could see it all just slipping away. I remember waking up day after day in a state of complete panic and nervous tension. Weeping and weeping. For the first few days after it all started, I thought, don't be stupid. Of course it will sort itself out. But by the second week, I knew that if we didn't get things sorted, it would slip away. It's unbelievably difficult to get a drama project launched and to the stage of production we had arrived at.

The clock was ticking. Barry Hanson was the only person who seemed prepared to compromise. In order to satisfy Equity's demands that *Betty* was being produced by an independent company he raised another £750,000 in under two weeks. But Equity weren't impressed. They came up with some kind of compromise between the two deals. But everyone agreed it was unworkable. And Greg Dyke quite rightly was adamant: *Betty* would go ahead under the terms of the original BFTPA contract or not at all. So that was it. The plug was pulled. On 12 February dismissal letters (called 'Chinese handbills' in the industry) were sent out.

Everyone was aghast. But we fought on. The

Lee brothers who owned Shepperton Studios offered their support and money and said they would keep the set for as long as they could. Christopher wrote to Norman Fowler, then Employment Secretary in Margaret Thatcher's government, enclosing a dossier documenting it all, stressing that we were being denied the right to work. He even managed to collar Mrs Thatcher herself at some do.

'I got her in a corner and I told her the whole story,' he recounted. 'I wasn't frightened of the bloody Germans in the war and I'm not frightened of bloody Plouviez.' God Bless Christopher Lee.

But by the time the matter was raised in Parliament at the end of March and Mrs Thatcher had denounced the film and television unions as 'the last bastion of restrictive practices', it was too late for us. The men with the sledgehammers had moved in and the set had been destroyed.

What happened to us will never happen again. On 28 March 1988 Tyne Tees became the first TV company to sign a deal which did away with union practices. It was on the same day that *Betty's* sabotage was referred to in Parliament. The *Times* confirmed what I had believed all along: 'Ministers interpreted the union move as a test case with shop stewards trying to impose old-style restrictive practices on the flourishing independent sector.' The fiasco over *Betty* led directly to a government inquiry set up by the Home Office into restrictive practices in the film and television industries. I'm not by any means politically or personally opposed to unions — they have been very necessary. But there was a period when it did all seem to get out of hand.

Because of what happened on *Betty*, everything changed. Equity is no longer a closed shop. Anyone can work as an actor. But it's small comfort. London Weekend lost a lot of money. Hundreds of performers and technicians lost three months' work. Barrie Keefe, who wrote those wonderful scripts, never got paid. And he says it's the best thing he's ever written. I have no doubt that it affected my career adversely. And it still upsets me.

Peter Plouviez is the only person in my life I have ever hated. Ultimately, what good did he achieve? If he had any power to help his members before *Betty*, he had less after. He shot himself in the foot, but somehow managed to limp through a few more years at Equity before retiring.

On 26 March 1988, World Theatre Day, I was to present an award at a ceremony at the Garrick Club. My wounds were still very raw. I had hardly been out. I didn't want to see anybody. But as I was climbing up on the podium to give the award I saw Plouviez at the back of the room. I wanted to die. Leigh knew something had gone wrong: I went completely white. I couldn't believe that he had the gall to stand there. I had specifically asked whether Plouviez had been invited. And he hadn't. He had come on somebody else's invitation. He knew I would be there. I was the guest of honour. Leigh told me to stay calm and just blank him. So of course I rose above it and after giving the award made my exit as I couldn't bear being in the same room as this man who I considered to be a destructive useless worm.

But, like the trouper she was, *Betty* refused to lie down. Two years later in December 1989 I was in New York where Leigh was doing *The Merchant of Venice* on Broadway with Dustin Hoffman. I got a call from Barry Hanson who in the meantime had been made Head of Drama at BBC Pebble Mill in Birmingham. Although he had a pretty free hand, we still had to submit a proposal and script, but *Betty* was once again on the cards. He said that he felt enough time had passed and the dust had settled. It got the green light. But unlike London Weekend they couldn't afford to put up all the money.

We needed £2 million. So Barry found this guy who said he could raise the money. He was quite young and looked like a city gent. I had lunch with him once with Barry and he certainly seemed confident. But when it came to the crunch he couldn't deliver. It's like a house of cards, if one of them goes, then it all falls down. Poor jinxed *Betty*.

This time Barrie Keefe had honed down the script into four hours rather than six. We'd gone into early pre-production; costume fittings, all new music. Same cast, same songs, but this time Richard Hartley was doing the music. The tracks had been laid but I hadn't done the vocals. This time round it was recorded with full orchestra. And this time I was singing live with a live orchestra, which I had never done before in a studio setting. It was all a bit scary. My songs included 'Love Me or Leave Me', 'Love is the Sweetest Thing' and 'We're in the Money'. All picked to tie in with what was happening in the plot.

This time we went back to our original director, Jim Goddard. All the deals were done, everything was in place. Except for the money. Although it was promised right down to the wire, the money man never delivered. The first time around we had people like the Lee brothers saying, 'How can we help?' We didn't need money then. This time we did. But it was too late. Again it was traumatic. But not as traumatic as the first time.

Over the years we've all tried. Tried and tried and tried. Every so often I get a call from Jim or Barry or Barrie or Sean or Christopher: 'Just to let you know I'm talking to so-and-so.' The problem is having got so close twice, TV people are nervous. I had a meeting with Nick Elliot recently about something else. And I always punch it in.

'Have you thought about *Betty*?'

'It's wonderful, I know it is, but with what was hanging over it, I just don't think I'm ready to do it yet.'

I haven't given up. Barry Hanson and I still own the rights, but it doesn't drive my life like it did for about two years.

'How's *Betty*?' people ask.

'She's not dead, just sleeping,' I reply.

What gives me deep hope is that Barrie Keefe

told me that whenever he finishes a script and it's going to go into production, which *Betty* was, he puts the script in a certain part of his office. And he didn't do that with *Betty*. She stayed on his desk. And she's still sitting there, waiting to be done.

On 17 March 1988 the son of Allen Saddler, the author of *Betty* wrote to me: 'Your involvement meant a lot to my old man . . . I had a feeling in my bones when he first wrote the book that it had to make a TV or film story. You had the perception and imagination to see it . . . I am no prophet. I can't see into the future. But still I have the feeling that *Betty* is not dead. If there is anything more you can do carry on, be strong, and don't take no for an answer.'

19

In early 1987, while *Betty* was still in the early stages of pre-production, Leigh was offered an American mini series called *Queenie*, based on the life of Merle Oberon. I had met her in 1971, when she was well over sixty, but she was still glowing with star quality. But like many great Hollywood legends, Merle Oberon had a past, a dark secret that was only discovered on her death in 1979. Unbelievably, the pale consumptive heroine of *Wuthering Heights*, one of my all-time favourite weepies, was a quarter Asian Indian. Her real name was Estelle Merle O'Brien Thompson. She was born in India but told people she'd been born in Tasmania. She was working as an extra in London when she was discovered by Alexander Korda in 1933 (they married in 1939) who cast her as Ann Boleyn opposite Charles Laughton in *The Private Life of Henry VIII*. And that brought her to the attention of Hollywood. It was a fascinating story. Her own skin was very fair, but her mother, whose father had been English but whose own mother was completely Indian, was much darker so she travelled with her film star daughter and was introduced as her maid because Merle didn't want anyone to know. She thought the prejudice in those days would affect her career. Probably true.

The series was called *Queenie* because that's

what her family always called her. Leigh played her half-Indian uncle, a none-too-pleasant saxophone player, the brother of her mother, player by Claire Bloom. The early scenes were shot on location in India and I joined him towards the end of shooting so we could then spend three weeks exploring Rajastan. It was produced by Bob Sertner and Frank von Zerneck (the Hollywood king of the mini series and TV movies). Frank and his gorgeous wife Julie and daughter Danielle became and have remained our very good friends.

I'd never been to India but Leigh had, in 1974, on a film called *Ghost Story*. He'd fallen in love with India and really wanted me to experience it too.

Leigh arranged for someone to pick me up from Delhi airport but it was a six-hour drive to Jaipur where they were filming. The car was a pale green Morris 1000, very old but gleaming like a jewel in the Indian sun and the driver spoke wonderful Peter Sellers' Indian-English. We drove off into the flat scrubby landscape, me clinging for dear life onto the seat in front as we careered along the pot-holed road, narrowly missing people, elephants and camels. I had expected the landscape to be far more exotic. But it was just very, very flat for hour after hour after hour, with just the odd elephant to remind you where you were, plus hazardous trucks that rattled along decorated like carnival floats. And of course the cows, which are sacred in India, sitting in the middle of the road. It's hysterical. You have to drive around them. Eventually my driver turned right towards an outcrop of hills. And as we dropped down behind the hill, it was like entering a film set. I thought this can't be real. It was so breathtakingly amazing. The landscape had completely changed. In front of me was this ancient fort clinging to a hillside, above a lake that reflected its terraces. It was like a mirage. It's called the Amber Palace and was built in 1592, and was the ancient capital of Rajastan. Six miles on we turn another bend and this old walled city appears. They call it the pink city. Jaipur itself. As we drove through the ramparts there were monkeys playing all around and once inside, hundreds of bicycles and beautiful ladies dressed in the most colourful saris I've ever seen, shocking pinks and purples and lime greens. Their beauty astounded me.

We were staying at the Rambagh Palace former home of the Maharajas of Jaipur, now turned into a hotel. It was amazingly luxurious and I found it hard to cope with the poverty that was, literally, outside the gates, where there was a whole cardboard city of beggars. I found that very difficult and never really came to terms with it. That and the strange smells from the drains and gutters. Cow dung is used for fuel for cooking and heating by the poor — the smell can quite literally turn your stomach.

I'd always said I'd love an emerald ring and India is famous for its beautiful stones. So Madeleine, the wife of Larry Pierce, the director, took us to a jeweller she'd found deep in the old city and he proudly showed us the things he was making for Tiffany's and Van Cleef and Arples.

But they just weren't my style. Mia Sara (who was playing the young Queenie, and who later married Jason Connery) and Sarah Miles who was also in the film were looking at ancient Indian jewellery that would have been worn by Maharanis — headdresses: unwearable but gorgeous — and I had spotted a whole load of shoe boxes full of old jewellery. And that's where I found the ring. It's hard to date it. But it was probably made for somebody in the last days of the Raj, in the 1930s. The owner couldn't quite believe I preferred it to the new ones and tried to talk us out of it. But I knew it was for me.

And lo and behold, it ended up on my engagement finger.

Filming over, we organised a car and set out on our travels. The Taj Mahal was extraordinary, perfect, everything we dreamed it would be. But seeing these incredible palaces and forts day after day became too much after a while and it was also becoming unbearably hot. Leigh had been working really hard and what he needed was a rest. I had read an article about Goa, the former Portuguese colony on the south-west coast of India and it sounded like paradise. So we agreed to go there. Enough of old buildings — on to the beach. So we spent ten days by the sea going for long walks along the sand and eating wonderful food at our hotel; chargrilled lobster and fresh fish to die for. It was such a relief to be able to trust the food. Leigh had drummed it into me that I couldn't be too careful in India, so I'd been living on bananas, oranges and boiled eggs, because they were all sealed. But in Goa it was much less of a threat.

Leigh and I had always said we'd love to do something professionally together. And in 1988 it happened, but completely unplanned. Where I've been very, very lucky is that I've been blessed by having worked with exceptionally talented people. First there was Ken Russell. Then I had Tommy. Then I had Mike Nichols. A roll call of the greats. Now I was being offered a film with John Schlesinger.

Like Mike Nichols, John Schlesinger is an actor turned director who works in both the theatre and cinema. And like Ken Russell he started off making documentaries for television, including Ken's own cradle *Monitor*. But his background was very different to Ken's. He is quite posh and went to Oxford which was where he started acting. The first film John made for the cinema was *Terminus*, now very famous, about twenty-four hours in the life of Waterloo railway station. After that it was success after success. His first feature film was *A Kind of Loving* with Alan Bates, then hard on its heels *Billy Liar* with Tom Courtney. But the first film I ever saw of John's was *Darling* with Julie Christie in 1965, then came *Far from the Madding Crowd*, with Julie Christie and Terence Stamp and *Sunday Bloody Sunday*. And for *Midnight Cowboy* with Dustin Hoffman and Jon Voight he won Oscars both for Best Film and Best Director.

When he wasn't making films, John was either directing theatre or opera. Another genius. The film I had been offered was *Madame Sousatzka* and he had written the screenplay with Ruth Prawer Jhabvala, who has done so many brilliant Merchant/Ivory screenplays. It had been adapted from a novel by Bernice Rubens, who won the Booker prize in 1970 for *The Elected Member*, and was about the relationship between an émigré Russian pianist and her pupil, Marek. The original novel centred around the Jewish community, but now, although Shirley was still Russian (American Russian) her protégé was a young Asian Indian boy. The producer, previously a literary agent, was Robin Dalton who is Australian, very clever, eccentric and absolutely lovely. And she told me later that casting me came to her in a dream. 'I told John, I've got this brilliant idea for Jenny.' And he agreed. I had known John socially for years.

The part of Jenny was of a struggling pop singer, a bit of a goodtime girl. I loved the script but I gulped when I saw there were two major nude scenes. I have never done a nude scene. And I just can't. It doesn't offend me in other people. But I'm the only person on a Spanish beach with their top on.

And I also feel that once you have had a child what you do on screen is terribly important. Imagine if I were to appear naked in a film in some raunchy rampant sex thing: it could be so embarrassing for Carly.

So I rang John and said, look, I'd love to do it, but I can't take my clothes off. I'm always very up front and believe in getting things off my chest. No pun intended. He said, 'It's not a problem.' I ended up doing the scene wearing a long T-shirt with pants underneath.

The film had taken years to get off the ground. Jeanne Moreau was originally cast as Madame Sousatzka but by the time the money was raised, she was doing something else. Getting a film together is like doing a jigsaw with only half the pieces available at any one time. But when I heard it was Shirley Maclaine, I was thrilled. The cast was altogether pretty amazing, with Dame Peggy Ashcroft playing the landlady. Yet again I had landed on my feet and was working with the best. There was only one gap. They hadn't cast my boyfriend; a sleazy agent, middle-aged, short, bald and portly: Jenny was the type of girl who wasn't too choosy about the company she kept if it would help her career.

John had apparently interviewed dozens of actors. No joy. Two weeks from shooting, Robin Dalton brought Leigh's name up. And of course John knew Leigh. He was hardly middle-aged; and as for short, portly and bald: no.

'You're not finding the man the way he's written,' Robin argued, 'so let's go another way.'

So we get a phone call. Leigh has read the script already — we always read each other's scripts — and he knows he's not right for it. But Robin Dalton says, 'Come round to see John.'

And Leigh said of course. But as he set off he was very much in two minds.

'I'm not sure this a good idea.' I knew what he meant. I've been sent scripts that are quite wrong. The worst was an American sitcom where the part I was up for was written for a big fat black lady, and it was all written in black lady dialogue. It was hysterical. I said no thank you. They ended up casting a big fat black lady.

John's house was less than half a mile away, so Leigh walked there. John used the downstairs as an office and when Leigh got there it was full of ladies in saris, as John was busy casting aunties. (Marek's mother was played by Shabana Azmi, who is exquisite, the Sophia Loren of India.) So Leigh went in, they chatted a bit and Leigh repeated the thing about not feeling that it's right for him and then John got called to the outer office. Leigh, thinking the whole thing is hopeless, leaves and walks home.

Just then the phone rang. It was John.

'Is Leigh there? I had to go out and when I came back he'd gone. I went out to the street to look for him, but he'd disappeared. I need to talk to him because I want to offer him the part.'

When Leigh came in he was so down.

'What's the matter?' I said.

'Oh, it was terrible. Totally useless. I'll never work for John now. It was a bad idea.'

Which just shows how wrong you can get. I haven't auditioned much. Generally people either know me or they don't. The downside of being Twiggy is that people have a preconceived idea of what I'm like, though it's surprising how often people tell me how different I am from what they imagined.

Doing *Sousatzka* was great fun. It was great

wearing all the tarty costumes, tight skirts, back-combed hair, pink lipsick. We shot some of it in a big house in Notting Hill, just round the corner from where Ken and Shirley used to live. It was bitterly cold, but at least Leigh and I got to share a dressing room. Shirley Maclaine gave a fantastic performance; she was so brave taking on the part of a woman much older than herself. She wasn't interested in looking glamorous, only in what was right for the part.

About a year before we worked on *Madame Sousatzka*, Leigh and I had been to a screening. It was quite glitzy and at the reception that followed I found myself talking to Princess Michael of Kent. When Leigh came over I took my leave to give them an opportunity to talk on their own. Princess Michael is a very beautiful and charming lady and she and Leigh hadn't been chatting for long before she said: 'Have you asked Twiggy to marry you yet?' Leigh was very taken aback but had to admit that, no, he hadn't.

'Well you should. She's ready,' said Her Royal Highness.

And she was right. When he said to me, do you think it might be quite nice to get married, it was everything I ever dreamed of, though I don't remember him getting down on his knees or anything. The romantic bit would come later. I suppose it must have been soon after we bought the ring in Jaipur. It hadn't been intended as an engagement ring, but that's what it became.

Before going ahead we decided to discuss it with the kids. We always said, 'If they don't want us to get married, then we won't.' We didn't want it to upset them, especially Ace. I think it was more difficult for him. Carly's father wasn't alive. But for Ace it was different and we wanted to get his feelings on the subject.

The chance came when I was doing *Charlie Chaplin*. The kids had come down to visit the location and we were all in my little caravan. Leigh began.

'Lesley and I were thinking that sometime next year, we might get married. How would you feel about that?'

Carly's first words were, 'Great, then Ace will be my real brother.' And Ace said, 'I think that would be really nice.' And they went out of the caravan, ten and twelve, and they were holding hands and we watched them skip up the road. Needless to say we were over the moon.

Leigh has an extraordinary way with children. He understands so perfectly the boundaries they need and we have friends who always ask his advice. He is certainly no pushover. He believes in being honest and kind but very clear with them. And children respond to that. He believes it's worth being disliked sometimes for a few hours to be loved for thirty years. You've got to think long term with children. Not enough parents do that. And it works, for his real son, his stepson and for Carly. They all absolutely adore him and he's the first one they go to to seek advice. Ace and Carly talk to him about everything and anything. Some things Carly doesn't talk to about with me because she doesn't want to upset me. Also Leigh is very wise, and what he says comes from love.

I still didn't know when, how or where we were going to do it. But from that moment on Leigh began planning the wedding in secret. I wasn't allowed to ask questions. It was really killing me as I am the nosiest person on earth. Such a busybody. He was always on the phone, then when I came in the room, ringing off. He later told me that first he had tried Gretna Green but was told there was a three-month waiting list. So much for eloping.

Then he thought of the QE2 because the captain can marry you. The trouble is that you're on a ship full of people you don't know. And you can't get off. If they found out it could be a nightmare. Not that I knew anything about these plans at the time. All I knew was that at some time it would happen and that it would be very low key: we'd both been married before and we wanted this to be private and personal. Probably deep down our families would have liked a more conventional wedding. But they're great and they all understood. Unless you do a really big one, you end up offending people because you just can't invite everybody.

It was when the production company contacted us about the American promotional tour for *Madame Sousatzka* in September 1988 that Leigh hit upon the answer. He told me to make sure I took with me something special to wear.

'Is it to do with getting married?'

'Don't ask any questions, but take something special.'

So I kind of guessed. I bought a little white suit. Even if it's in some posh building, I thought, at least I'll look smart with my picture hat on. I did try on a few long dresses but in the end decided against it; I didn't want to be overdressed if it wasn't that formal. And if it wasn't a wedding at all I'd be really embarrassed.

We flew out to New York on my thirty-ninth birthday, 19 September, and the first I knew that I was about to get married was when I opened Leigh's birthday card on the plane. He may never make Poet Laureate, but he had written the most beautiful and funny poem any fair lady could hope to receive from her knight in armour. The whole poem was like clues to a treasure hunt. Though I was surprised to see he planned to get married at S.A.G.

'We're not getting married at the Screen Actors Guild, are we?'

'No, you daft thing. Sag Harbor on Long Island. I just couldn't think of anything to rhyme with Harbor.'

By now tears were streaming down my face, it was so romantic.

Sag Harbor is a very beautiful old whaling village on the bay side of Long Island, where our dearest friends Tony and Jen Walton have a house. It's like going back in time. Sag Harbor is a real village; grey painted clapboard, and looks like Peyton Place with a main street and a little cinema and a theatre run by Emma Walton, Tony's daughter from his first marriage to Julie Andrews. Tony and Jen have been together for twenty-five years, but only decided to get married a couple of years ago. Leigh and I sent them a telegram saying, 'It worries us when you rush into things like this.' Sadly Jen was back in Guernsey for a family wedding so it would just be Tony as witness, the judge, Leigh and me.

He'd originally planned it for 21 September, two days after my birthday, but then realised it was Yom Kippur, the Day of Atonement. Not the best day for a wedding. So it was put back till 23 September.

The night before the wedding at Sag Harbor, staying at Tony and Jen's beautiful house, Leigh began acting very oddly. For instance, he seemed determined to have dinner in one particular restaurant. I didn't want to.

'We ate there last night,' I said.

'But I've booked.'

I couldn't understand why he was being so keen on this particular place. He's usually so easygoing.

'So just tell them we're not coming,' I said. 'They won't mind.'

I remember being quite stubborn.

'Let's try that place across the street,' I continued. 'I passed it today and it looked really nice.'

But he was so insistent that in the end I went where he wanted. If it was that important to him . . .

The next morning, we were getting ready and it was around eleven. I was so excited. We put a call in to the kids who were in England. We had thought long and hard about bringing them over but logistically it was very difficult: Ace was at boarding school and term had already started and it could have been an emotionally difficult thing for them to deal with. And we had the whole publicity thing for *Madame Sousatzka* to go straight on to do in America. But we did know they were both fine about it. Then about eleven, the doorbell rang, and Leigh said, you'd better get that. 'It might be the photographer, or the flowers, or the judge come a bit early.'

So I went down and opened the door. And standing there was my guardian angel, Peggy. For a moment I didn't understand. Peggy was in California. Then I burst into tears. And we hugged and she came in. Then the doorbell rang again, I opened it again and this time it was Leigh's best mate Peter Firth. More hugs. Then another ring: Carlotta Florio, my dear friend from *My One and Only*. When Mary and Hal arrived I just lost it. Tears of happiness. And my then manager Neville Shulman. They had come all the way from London. Leigh says at this point he got a bit nervous and thought I was going to have a heart attack or go into severe shock.

So, in the company of some of our dearest friends, we were married in the garden of Tony Walton's house in Sag Harbor under a beautiful weeping willow tree. The branches reached down to the grass and Leigh had cut an arbour under which we were to be wed. He's so romantic. A few years later that tree was struck by lightning and Tony and Jen called us to tell us our willow was dead. Obviously we were very upset: it was our wedding tree. But the following spring we were overjoyed to hear that it had survived and young shoots were appearing. Now it's almost back to its former glory.

Tony and Jen's house is our favourite house in the world, real Norman Rockwell. It was the most perfect wedding. The business with the restaurant the night before finally made sense. All our friends had been staying in the hotel where we were to have the wedding breakfast but they needed somewhere to eat that night. So Leigh had told them they could take their pick of restaurants but just not to go to the one we were going to. Sag Harbor is very small.

I had hoped to have Carmen Schiavone, a photographer I had worked with in the sixties, to come and take the pictures. But unfortunately he wasn't in the best of health. So Carlotta found this other photographer and swore him to secrecy. The deal was that he could sell the pictures afterwards but only after we'd gone off on our honeymoon. He must have made a tidy sum. We owed a huge amount of thanks to Carlotta who had done most of the organising with Leigh brilliantly and with her usual love and concern.

Leigh had arranged that we spent our honeymoon on Mustique in the Caribbean. It was how all honeymoons should be. Two people in paradise. Heaven on earth. Then back to New York and the usual chat show round for *Madame Sousatzka*. As we'd just got married we did them together. Inevitably the first question was always 'And how did you two meet?' Completely straight-faced, Leigh replied,

'Jesus brought us together.' And you could see in the interviewers' eyes definite signs of panic, that I'd married this religious nut, until they realised it was a wind up, as he continued 'in the form of Robert Powell, who played Jesus in Zeffirelli's TV series *Jesus of Nazareth*,' although who knows, maybe other forces were at work too.

There's a fashion now for some hosts of chat shows to try and play the game of one-upmanship over their guests and even try to humiliate or make fun of them and I have never understood the point, not to mention why people willingly put themselves through such embarrassment. It only happened once to me but once was enough.

It must have been around 1970. We'd had a call at the office in Charlotte Mews from *The Frost Show* which was always hitting the headlines. It went out live, late at night, and there were regular dust-ups, even punch-ups. I immediately said, 'No'. I'd seen the show and I knew what the format was — after the preliminary chat, the audience would get to ask the questions — and I thought 'Why should I go on there and get mauled?'

Anyway *The Frost Show* called and called. And I didn't call back. Then one day I got home to Twickenham and found Mum in a terrible state.

'You've got to call David Frost. He's rung every half an hour. He says you've got to call him.'

I was furious that he'd had the nerve to call

me at home and upset Mum — and she was really upset, David Frost was a very well-known celebrity — so I did call him back, and gave him a piece of my mind.

'Don't ever call me at home again. My Mum suffers from her nerves and she's been in a terrible state.'

Of course now he had me on the phone he pushed on.

'Why won't you do my show?'

'I'm a model. Not a performer. An audience would scare me. And you must admit it, David, good as it is, your show is about confrontation, arguments and even fights.'

David Frost turns on his undoubted charm.

'What if I promise that it's a straight interview with me and I won't bring the audience in on the questions. Will you do it then? I'll give you my word.'

And I fell for it.

You're always slightly nervous on live television; you want to make sure you don't say something really stupid. Also I was still quite young and inexperienced. Anyway, David begins with the usual 'How did it start?' questions: the modelling, the people I'd met.

I remember being vaguely aware of something not quite right about the audience, but they're in the dark and with all those lights and concentrating on David's questions, it was nothing more than a slight sense of unease.

Then he throws me a couple of slightly dodgy questions, nothing nasty, just something he'd dug up about me having kicked Jean Shrimpton off the number one spot as top model, which was completely ridiculous. Then he turns to the audience: 'I wonder what men think about thin girls?' And I glared at him. He'd given me his word and I'd trusted him. I was so young and gullible. And as the lights got stronger I realised what I'd been vaguely aware of: they have booked a complete audience of fat people. And then he called on one of them in the front row, a very large lady I recognised. She was a radio journalist at the time. She had obviously been to the studio make-up and hair department in preparation for the show. It was a set-up. She stood up and said, 'I know if you took your clothes off and I took mine off who all the men in the audience would like to go to bed with.' It opened the door to a flurry of equally abusive questions. I was being ridiculed for the way I looked. I expained I didn't try to be thin, I just was. I was in an impossible position: I wasn't about to attack fat people for being fat. Why would I? I was mortified. My knees went weak and I felt sick. All I can remember thinking was 'Don't cry. Don't cry.' That awful prickly feeling when you feel the tears coming.

What David Frost wanted was an argument. He wanted me to let loose at her. I didn't give him the satisfaction.

'I am a professional model,' I said. 'To be a professional model you have to be slim. And that's just the way it is.'

Fortunately this was ITV, and the commercial break came. It was horrible. I held it together until I got backstage but then I burst into tears.

I was hysterical. The whole thing was going to be a 'Have A Go At Twiggy' Show. David came after me, trying to get me to go back on. But wild horses wouldn't have dragged me. By then my eyelashes were probably down on my cheeks. And I left. What they did for the second half I don't know. On a live show like that they had standby guests in case something happened. I was really distressed. He'd given me his word.

A month or so later I bumped into him at a screening of a wonderful documentary George Harrison had backed called *The Queen*, about New York drag artistes. He saw me and came over and my back was immediately up.

'I know you hate me,' he said. 'But I thought you might be interested to know that I got more complaint letters from the show I did with you than from anything I have ever done. All saying what a horrible thing to do to Twiggy. They were all on your side and they all hated me.'

Then I said, 'But you lied to me, David.' And he said, 'Yeah, but it was a great show.' All has been forgiven and Sir David, as he now is, and I are friends when we meet.

Most people do these shows to plug their latest film, book or whatever and to gather the momentum of fame. But fame is a two-edged sword. My name, because it's such a silly name, has become part of the language, part of the culture of the period. My problem was to be accepted in the world that I had chosen to be in: theatre, films, singing and dancing. It wasn't a problem in the States, where they love success and accept changes in direction as perfectly normal. They love fame too. The more successful you are, the more famous you are, the more they love you.

20

One of the reasons there are so many broken marriages in our business is that if you spend too long apart, even the best relationship is put under the most terrible strain. Leigh and I had always agreed that whichever way our careers went we would try and stay together. When Leigh was offered *The Merchant of Venice* to be directed by Peter Hall, we were both thrilled. It would open in London's West End then go on to Broadway. Leigh had known Peter from his time at the National Theatre and had been directed by him in *Yonadab* in 1985–6. Leigh was cast as Antonio, the Merchant, with Dustin Hoffman as Shylock and Geraldine James as Portia.

No sooner was *Merchant* up and running than I got offered a film in Australia. It's always the way: you spend months longing to do a movie, then you get offered three at the same time. I love a lot of Australian films and I was really disappointed to have to say no. I tried to see if they could delay it, but it was no good. Europe we might have managed. You can flit back and forth. But Australia? No weekend breaks to Australia. It would have meant six to eight months apart. It was a sad decision, because I would have loved to have done it. But, as I always tell myself, you can always get another movie, TV or stage show but you can't get another Leigh. He did the same for me when *Princesses* happened two years later.

So much of our business is down to chance and luck. *Princesses* came about because Joan Sittenfeld, head of casting at Universal who had cast Leigh in several projects had been to see him in *Merchant* on Broadway. When she came backstage to say hello, I was there. A year later a producer called Barry Kemp came to her with *Princesses* — a sitcom with three girls sharing a New York apartment. Barry was hot. He had a hugely successful comedy show called *Coach*, about a football coach, which gave him terrific clout. He had a commitment deal with an actress called Julie Haggerty from *Airplane* (the ditzy stewardess), and this was an idea he had thought up with her in mind. But he needed two other women, one of whom was English. Joan said to him, 'You've got to use Twiggs.'

As luck would have it Leigh and I were in New York, house-hunting north of the city on the coast. During the Broadway run of *Merchant* we had thought about buying a place in Manhattan. Friends had suggested we try further out and because the idea of having a New York base still appealed we were looking around the Larchmont, Rye area and had found a beautiful old ship's captain's house overlooking a bird sanctuary in Mamaroneck when we got the call from my New York agent Lisa Loosemore. We flew out to Los Angeles the next day.

A hit sitcom is a bottomless crock of gold to a network and about forty pilots are done every year. Only a tiny handful get picked up, and of those only a few make the big time. In England scripts for a series are written in advance but it doesn't happen like that in States. The writing team — who are usually producers as well as writers — write only the pilot to begin with, and don't write any more episodes until the pilot is picked up, and then only one episode at a time. So that everyone knows where they are all the sitcom pilots for the year are shot in March and April. The last date they have to be handed in is 1 May and you're told if you're going to be picked up by mid-May.

Actors can only do one pilot a year because to do a pilot you have to sign a five-year contract. If it does get picked up, you're committed. Some English actors are very wary of doing them if most of their work and family are based in England. But it was a wonderful chance for me and I took it with Leigh and the children's full support.

TV used to be seen as a proving ground, but now everything has changed. The lead in a sitcom is what every actor, or more often actress wants, particularly if she has small children. Both because of the money and the parent-friendly lifestyle, it now attracts major names, like Candice Bergen, Faye Dunaway, Burt Reynolds and Gene Wilder. And who can blame them when someone like Ted Danson on *Cheers* might end up earning $400,000 an episode. With twenty-two episodes a year, year after successful year, you can see the attraction. On a half-hour sitcom (in reality barely over twenty minutes of film) the working week is Monday to Friday and you get every fourth week off (it's called hiatus). Shooting is from August through March, which gives you four months off every summer for other projects. Hour-long shows like *The X-Files* or *Murder She Wrote* are different, with a very heavy shooting schedule and an early start to shoot an hour show in nine days. Then one day off and back on the treadmill. Leigh has done several pilots for hour-long series in America and played the leading role in three of his own series in Britain: *Travelling Man, Kinsey* and *Stick With Me, Kid*. They are exhausting, draining schedules always, and take over your life.

The premise of *Princesses* was very simple: three women from very different backgrounds sharing a flat in Manhattan. Fran Drescher was the wise-cracking New York Jewish Princess; Julie Haggerty was the sweet-as-apple-pie, All-American Princess and I was the English Princess. And that's when I began to get cold feet. In the States you only have to speak with an English accent and everyone thinks you're posh.

Barry Kemp, the big honcho, turned out to be really nice and we hit it off immediately. Even before Leigh and I left for London, I heard I'd been offered the part. But over the next few weeks I got more and more twitchy, wearing a hole in the carpet in the flat just walking up and down. Twiggy as a real aristo princess just isn't on. The script arrived and only confirmed my fears. Number one, I was totally miscast. Number two, it's one joke, then it's over. Number three, the way it was written there were definite Princess Di digs and I didn't want any of that. I really like and admire her.

Shooting was scheduled for March. Luckily it was over the Easter holidays so both Carly and Ace could come with us. And the timing was perfect for Leigh who had spent all spring playing *Kinsey*, his hit series for Granada Television about a maverick Midlands solicitor, produced by our friend from *Betty*, Barry Hanson.

We had both decided that I had to discuss my feelings and worries with the producers and I went into that first read-through as nervous as I've ever been in my life, to the point that I was about to say to Barry Kemp, 'Look, I think you had better recast me.' During the first day's rehearsal I could see the way they were going with my character, trying to get me to do this funny voice. Fran and Julie were playing themselves; I was the only person 'acting', a completely alien character for me. So I said my piece. But if I was to survive I had to have another alternative ready. And I did. They didn't even look flustered, bless 'em. Twenty-four hours later we had another script.

Instead of making her a real royal I suggested that we made her a royal by marriage. I thought it should be some foreign prince. But they had this thing about him being English. So that night Leigh came up with a great idea.

'There's this place off the south coast of England called the Scilly Isles, pronounced 'silly',' I told them at our next meeting. 'So she could be the Princess of Scilly.' Of course they went for it. A name like that is a comedy writer's dream. And few in America would have heard of the Scilly Isles.

It was the first sitcom either Julie or I had done and we had both come to the first rehearsal word perfect, much to everyone else's amusement. Sitcoms in America don't work like that. Every day there are changes and new lines. When the actors go home at six the writers are working till the small hours re-writing. They have a terribly exhausting job. Lots of writers on sitcoms have nervous breakdowns. But because scripts are not written ahead of time, it means they can adjust very quickly or pursue a good new idea, and if they get somebody in playing a secondary role who works really well, they can bring them up. Or take them down if they don't like them.

So we did the pilot. There was a lot at stake and they had spent serious money. It looked amazing: we all wanted to move in to our set to live. We did it like a mini play, in front of a live audience, including Leigh and the kids who'd had a great time doing all the touristy things, like the Universal tour and Disneyland.

The feedback was great and we returned to London, putting our lives on hold until mid-May. Six weeks. For all the talking up, which Americans always do, we knew the ratio of pickups. In some ways I was more worried we would be picked up. A hit series changes your life. And there was another sadness to bring me down to earth. After two years of stubborn fighting, my Dad died of cancer. One of my great regrets is that because of his dementia Leigh never really knew him as he was. Except once when we visited him and a great glimmer of the old Norman came through. I'm glad about that at least. I adored my Dad, and although his death was expected it was heartbreaking.

The night we heard about *Princesses* we had been to a charity film premiere. Di was the Royal and we were very excited because neither of us had seen her before. She wore a beautiful shocking pink and lavender dress and looked amazing. As she went past she gave one of her little looks to Leigh and mouthed 'Hello' and Leigh went bright pink. It was so sweet. A few years later we met her properly, at the opening of Richard Avedon's retrospective at the National Portrait Gallery in the autumn of 1995. A beautiful portrait Richard had done of me in the sixties was the first one you saw on entering the exhibition. It was a huge blow up, eight foot high. Diana went out of her way to be so nice and friendly to Leigh and Ace who were with me. She didn't have to. Officials were trying to hustle her on, but she took no notice of them. She was really lovely and genuinely friendly. She won our hearts.

We didn't get back home that night until about 2.00 a.m. Crispian, who happened to be staying, had taken the message.

'A man called Barry Kemp keeps calling you. He says will you call him as soon as you get in. He said to tell you you've been picked up.'

I called Barry, just to make sure Crispian

had got the message right. He had. We'd been picked up for eight episodes, starting 1 August. You go into a spin. We cracked open a bottle of champagne and prepared to change our lives.

The the day after Ace and Carly broke up from school at the end of that summer term, we were on the flight to LA. We rented a lovely house from John Irvin, the film director, in the lower Hollywood Hills. Neither Leigh nor I are Hollywood Hill lovers. We find it too cut off. You're miles from the shops and restaurants and it can be scary at night, especially in that town. To get anywhere you've got to drive down a canyon. We started house-hunting immediately and soon found just what we wanted in Hancock Park, the beautiful flat part of old Hollywood; huge old mansions, immaculate gardens and streets and a walk to the village, a little pocket of LA that looks like all those Frank Capra movies. In fact it's probably where most of them were shot. Hancock Park was built around the turn of the century and could be any posh suburb of old-fashioned America. It's in a kind of time warp, with a little village park with shops, and lots of families lived there. Perfect for us.

As luck would have it Carly was just the right age to change school systems. In the States she was just at the beginning of High School. The only problem was getting her in. You were supposed to apply in February. Our favourite and Carly's was Marlborough High, an all-girls school in Hancock Park, that had been there since the turn of the century. Although it's freer than a similar school in England, pupils wear uniform and it's comparatively structured; as close to an English school as you get in LA, and just a walk from our new house.

She did the test and passed with flying colours, but there was just no space. The fire regulations are very strict and their numbers were right up. I couldn't believe it. The headmistress was very kind: 'Ten days before term starts we always get someone who cancels. Don't panic, Mrs Lawson.'

Of course I did. The trouble was I didn't really know anyone who could help. Then my agent put me in touch with the actress Sharon Gless of *Cagney and Lacey* fame who it turned out was an old Marlborough girl, and she wrote a letter to the board of governors on my behalf, which was extremely kind. We hadn't even met then. When we did she turned out to be a gorgeous woman in every way. About a week before the autumn term was due to start the phone went to tell us that Carly was in.

'We've talked to the fire chief and told them that she's only a very little girl, and that we're very keen to have her, so they've said we could.'

How much it was that, how much Sharon's letter or me just driving them mad with my calls I will never know. A combination of everything probably. I always believe if you want something that much, you've really got to go for it, leave no stone unturned. Marlborough was a great success and Carly was very happy there. For two years she grew and blossomed.

It was Leigh's determination that we should

live in LA for a time that had persuaded me even to try for the pilot of *Princesses.* My memories of Tinseltown were not that happy. After *Tess*, he had had lots of offers of work in Hollywood, but he and Hayley didn't want to move out there. And he didn't want to be away from her and the children. I can understand. The children were only small. So Leigh just felt it was something he wanted to experience. His joke was that I was going out to work and he was going to lie by the pool drinking marguerita. Of course as soon as we got there offers started coming in for him too.

Not long after we had arrived in Los Angeles I had a call from Robin Williams' wife, Marsha. She was planning a big party for Robin's fortieth birthday and was contacting all his friends ahead of time, asking them to write or make something special for the occasion. I dug out a photograph of him, taken when we did *Club Paradise*, and wrote a nice message underneath. The things people sent, Marsha then put together into a beautiful, huge, leather-bound album which she presented to Robin on the day of his birthday. It was a wonderful tribute, full of inscriptions, photographs, drawings and even paintings.

For the party itself we flew up to San Francisco with Carly and Ace. Robin and Marsha live an hour or so away up in the mountains above the Nappa Valley and the next morning, several mini-buses arrived at the hotel where we and other guests were staying to take us up to the ranch, through a landscape dominated by vineyards. It's got to be one of the best parties we've ever been to. It lasted two days. On the second day, because it was just such beautiful weather, it was all out of doors. The kids went swimming and Robin took those who felt like it on a walk into the hills. It went on all afternoon and well into the evening, one band was succeeded by another. The guest list was pretty amazing, so many famous faces including: Glenn Close, Woody Harrelson, Billy Crystal and Joan Baez, one of my great heroes. She and I even had a bop together on the dance floor.

Another great party-giver was Roddy McDowell. Roddy started his Hollywood career as a child star, and I first met him after *The Boyfriend*, at a party given by a mutual friend and film buff; Roddy is mad about old films and sometimes gives wonderful parties including a film show. Roddy's parties are legendary. He luckily often asks us and if we can we always go. His guests are always a wonderful mix. Anthony Quinn, Joan Plowright, Shirley Maclaine, Helen Mirren, Anthony Hopkins, Tracey Ullman and her husband Alan McEwen, George Axelrod and Vincent Price who spent nearly the whole of one evening talking to Carly. She must have been about twelve and had seen him in all those Hammer horror films. She was thrilled. One Christmas Elizabeth Taylor was there. She really is stunning, with the most beautiful violet eyes, friendly and relaxed at Roddy's. She had a fluffy white dog with her, so we sat and chatted about animals. Roddy has a wonderful screening room and he would get original prints of great cinema classics. I remember once watching *Captain Blood* with Errol Flynn. And I never miss a trip to Roddy's downstairs loo, because it is filled with his amazing collection of old autographed photographs, which he started collecting when he was a little English child star. He seems to have everyone you could possibly think of. It must be unique. He has left his collection to the Smithsonian Institution. As well as acting Roddy is a wonderful photographer and has done a number of books of portraits, where he takes the pictures and another celebrity comments on the subject. A clever format. He did me for his most recent book and he got my old friend Tony Walton to do the words.

We moved into the new house in September. It was big, but not enormous, and had been built in 1910 and had a lovely garden with a swimming pool. In Peggy's old house, where I had lived with Michael, we didn't have one and I always regretted it, although with little ones a pool can be dangerous. Our two were much older now and during the summer months rarely strayed from the pool and the garden. We remodelled the house back to its original state and converted the garage in the back garden to a summer-house and built a big deck onto the back of the house. During the time we were there we had some great parties. LA is a very social place, and we had lots of British ex-pat friends as well as American friends.

Princesses started production on 1 August. It was a very happy show. Barry couldn't believe he'd got three women who really got on. The schedule was always the same: start midday on Monday for the read-through, then rough blocking in the afternoon. Tuesday, Wednesday, Thursday, in at 10.00 a.m. for rehearsals, home at 6.00 p.m. The big day is Friday, Recording Day. In our case, on film, not video. In at midday. Make-up and hair, and keep in your rollers for camera blocking in the afternoon. We used four cameras simultaneously. In the evening, the show; live in front of an invited audience of about three hundred. It's like a mini play in a small theatre; you just keep going. I was frightened to death at the beginning because there was so much to learn and the changes kept coming thick and fast: new lines, or even entire scenes every day. Sometimes even on recording day, between camera rehearsal in the afternoon and recording at night. It wasn't just the directors and writers that were making the changes. The network bosses, or the suits as they are called, were in there too. The final show was often totally different from the script that you had read on the Monday. Strenuous as it was, I found it a fascinating process. Situation comedy is an art, or at least a style in itself, a whole other way of working and terrifying when you're not used to it, as neither Julie nor I were. Although I have to say I've rarely been happier, and soon got to love it.

Everything was rolling along and Leigh was having a wonderful time doing the house and reading scripts. We had discovered the joys of buying at auction when we were doing up the London flat and later did the same in the cottage we'd bought at Chesterton in Oxfordshire. So when Leigh found out where the auctions were in LA, he was like a little boy with a fishing rod, full of stories of the things he'd got and the things he didn't get. And he was a brilliant buyer and found some amazing pieces: not only did he have a great eye for a bargain, but he would set himself a ceiling price and stuck to it, which is really difficult in the excitement of the moment, but incredibly important when buying at auction so as not to succumb to auction fever. Within a few months our house looked as if we'd been there twenty years. This was going to be his American period, Leigh decided. Every morning he'd wake up shouting 'God Bless America'. He bought old American colonial furniture and pictures, played American music, even got a tape of 'The Star Spangled Banner' by the Mormon Tabernacle Choir which was my early morning call. It was very funny.

By the time we were shooting the last of our eight commissioned episodes the first three had gone out and we were getting very good reviews and ratings and the studio heads liked it. Now we had to wait till the network commissioned the next batch. It never happened. The producers and the network bosses had a disagreement on the future of the series and that very sadly was that. It's not called show 'business' for nothing.

One good thing to come out of it was meeting Fran Drescher and her husband Peter Jacobson, who have since become very close friends. Fran now has a hit sitcom of her own: *The Nanny*.

She got the idea when she was staying with us in Oxfordshire and London. One day she did the tourist trail and took Carly along for company or as she says, 'schlept Carly all over town'.

'The poor thing wore her new shoes and complained about blisters. I showed no mercy. I was going to see London come hell or high water and wasn't prepared to do it alone. I told her, 'Honey just walk on the backs of your shoes.'

'Won't I break them?'

'No. You'll break them in.'

And that was the begining of *The Nanny*.

She phoned Peter with the idea — an out-of-place nanny from Queens, New York, working for an English family. Peter wrote it and it was accepted by CBS with Peter as producer and Fran starring and is now a top-rated show seen all over the world. A Hollywood dream come true for them and it couldn't happen to two nicer people.

For several weeks the cast of *Princesses* were kept on 'permament hiatus' while the network were umming and ahhing about what they were going to do with the show. But I knew it was over. One day about this time I had a call out of the blue from Patsy Kensit who I knew of from the film *Absolute Beginners*. She had something she wanted to talk to me about, she said. So we met for lunch. She was adorable. It turned out she had been approached by a production company that had got involved with Justin who, as I read it, was trying, yet again, to flog my story. They were thinking of doing a mini-series or film and had approached Patsy to play me.

She said that she was a great fan and would like to do it, but wanted to meet me first, to find out what I thought. 'I wouldn't go ahead unless I had your blessing.'

I was absolutely aghast. It made me see red. I could see that the extraordinary things that have happened to me could make a good story on film — but surely if my story is to be told, and told right, it has to be me who tells it. I don't mean act in it, but it's my story to tell and mine alone. Patsy would have been good casting but I'm here, I'm not dead — get the story from the horse's mouth, not the stable boy.

Patsy was very understanding, and told me that now she knew how I felt, she wouldn't dream of going ahead with it. What a special person. This sort of honourable and thoughtful behaviour is so rare in our business. Once Patsy dropped out, it would seem the whole package fell apart.

Carly was happy in her school and soon both Leigh and I had pilots for the following spring. I also did a two-hour pilot for a horror series, produced and directed by John Carpenter, the king of horror. It consisted of three separate stories and mine was called *Bodybags*. My co-star was Mark Hamill of *Star Wars* fame. I'd always wanted to do a really gory horror, and it was just as much fun as I thought it would be. The hardest thing is not to giggle.

Ace was just wonderful at this time. It was hard for him that we as a family were living in LA. He and Leigh have a very close and special relationship, but he was at boarding school in

England and of course his mother was there. He never once complained. He used to love coming out to see us and by the following April, his dad was back in the UK. Granada had commissioned a second series of *Kinsey*. I came back with him just for a couple of weeks, one reason being that we'd been asked to an amazing party given by Billy Connolly and his wife, Pamela Stephenson. And their parties are legendary, the sort you really would fly half-way round the world for. Once they took over a whole Highland castle for a week and invited a group of friends. We all wore traditional dress and they arranged a ceilidh and Highland games. It was quite wonderful.

Once they invited us to a birthday party they gave for Prince Andrew. We had been told dress was 'smart casual' but we all got dressed up a bit. HRH was wearing a rather smart burgundy velvet smoking jacket and his wife Sarah was in a party dress. It was all a bit glitzy, Michael Caine and Shakira were there and we all sang 'Happy Birthday' accompanied by Elton on the piano. At one point I remember we were standing chatting and behind us Jerry Hall was talking to Prince Andrew and Sarah. Jerry is six foot tall with a strong Texan drawl so we couldn't help overhearing as she said to Andrew, 'So. Where're y'all living now?' And Prince Andrew replies, 'Buckingham Palace. Mummy doesn't seem to mind, so we're staying there for a while till our house is finished.' Not very often you overhear a snippet of conversation like that at a party.

I first met Billy Connolly nearly twenty years ago, through a brilliant writer friend of Michael's called Peter McDougal who wrote the award-winning TV dramas *Just Another Saturday* and *Elephant's Graveyard*, both of which starred Billy. He and Billy had worked the shipyards together in Glasgow before either of them changed track. It was when Billy was doing J. P. Donleavy's play *The Beastly Beatitudes of Baltazar B* in the West End and Michael and I went to see it with Peter and his wife Glenn. Billy Connolly has something of genius about him. Either face to face or when he's performing, he is never just a man telling jokes; what he gives you is a whole new take on people and life. He's a musician, a playwright and a gifted actor. Our paths didn't cross again for about ten years, by which time he was married to Pamela, who is just as outrageous and funny and clever as she seems, and a perfect foil for Billy. Neither of them ever does things by halves.

For both Pamela and Billy comedy is a weapon. That April 1992 Pamela had decided, hysterical as it may seem, to stand as a candidate in the general election. Her party was called the Pink Blancmange Party. Why the name, or what the issue was she was campaigning on — and I'm sure there was an issue — I can't now remember and perhaps never knew. But of course to celebrate the Pink Blancmange Party there had to be a pink blancmange party, and we all had to wear pink. So before the counting of the votes at the local town hall we were all invited as Pamela and Billy's guests to a wonderful dinner in a local restaurant where we were served pink salmon, pink potatoes, pink cauliflower, pink champagne and, of course pink blancmange. A political speech was made by the parliamentary candidate, who presided over the festivities looking amazing in an outrageous pink dress. She drove a pink Volkswagen Beetle to the polling station, while all the guests were taken in a pink bus. The officials looked sternly aghast at this pink invasion. To our amusement and amazement, when the votes were counted, she had scooped over three hundred.

But Pamela is also a serious campaigner. In 1989 she became aware of a damaging chemical called Agar sprayed on apples, which America had banned, but it was legally used in Britain. Unlike most pesticides Agar penetrates the skin of the fruit, so just peeling an apple wasn't any good. When she launched Mothers Against Agar most people in Britain had never heard of it but she galvanised all her friends with kids, including me, and through persuasion and willpower got the campaign huge publicity. More importantly within six months she succeeded in getting Agar banned in Britain. Just shows what can be done if someone is committed.

When Leigh began work on *Kinsey*, Carly and I went back to LA. I had a pilot to shoot. Then on 29 April an all-white jury had found the white police officers not guilty of the terrible beating of Rodney King, a black man who everyone had seen being beaten half to death on video by the defendants. The trial was very high profile, and the verdict was, in my opinion, a travesty. But no one quite expected what happened next. It started with one man (black) throwing a stone at a policeman (white) in south central LA. Then at half past four came news of a pitched battle at the crossroads of Florence Street and Normandy Street. I was shooting the pilot out in Studio City, over the Hollywood Hills in the San Fernando valley. It was called *For Love or Money* and I was playing the head of a publishing house.

I remember watching the news in my trailer at the studio. It was horrendous. There were riots in downtown LA not that far from Hancock Park: Fighting in the streets, and looting and setting fire to property. LA is so spread out that something can happen in one area and you don't even know about it until you see the news on TV. Obviously the producers were concerned: they were trying to shoot a pilot and we had a live audience due to come in. But nobody was thinking it would be cancelled.

Leigh was in England, on location in Birmingham on *Kinsey* and had woken at 5.30 a.m. to pictures of LA burning on CNN. He rang me straight away, obviously very worried, but I managed to reassure him. The next morning, I called a few other Marlborough parents to see what they thought and called the school, who said everything was fine, though I didn't let Carly go on her bike that morning. We usually went by bike because her school was only six blocks away.

I rang the studio, just to check. Everything was still on, they said, but they'd decided to cut the live audience. We'd record it today, so that in case anything happened on the Friday they had it in the can.

Just as I was leaving for the studio, Dustin Hoffman, who lived on the other side of town, called.

'No arguments. A car's coming. I know Leigh's in England. I'm not even discussing it. You and Carly are coming to stay with us.'

When I told him that I was working he said that the car would pick us up from the studio at the end of the day.

When Leigh was offered *The Merchant of Venice*, he had been slightly worried about working on stage with such a big Hollywood star. But Dustin was a dream. He'd just won the Academy award for *Rain Man* but he wanted to do Shakespeare in Shakespeare's country. A very brave choice and he was a wonderful Shylock. Dustin's great love is the theatre — it's where he started — and so is Leigh's, and he and Leigh became really good friends. Leigh says he's the kindest man he's ever met, and the funniest. When Dustin's wife Lisa and their children came over, it was only natural that we should link up. Like us, they're a very close family. We adored Lisa straight away, anyone would, and their lovely children hit it off immediately with Carly and Ace.

Dustin does such wonderful things, things that people never hear about. When the Peter Hall Company went to New York with *Merchant*, the leads could come but smaller parts had to be recast with Americans. American Equity are a very strong union. Basil Henson, a veteran classical actor had been playing the Duke, and Dustin knew it was his dream to play Broadway. He was then in his seventies. Dustin adored him; he was the one who would go to Dustin and say, 'No, you can't do it like that.' And Dustin would listen.

So Dustin went to the office of Equity in New York and pleaded with them to let Basil come in.

'I need him, he helps me with my lines.'

So then they said he could come in as his coach. But Basil said no. 'If I come to Broadway, I come to Broadway.' So back Dustin went. And he did it. You feel you want to give him a medal for that. He could have just said, 'Sorry Basil, can't get you in', but that isn't Dustin's way. When he was in New York Dustin made sure Basil was well taken care of. He died a year later.

Leigh said it was like working with Father Christmas. He's just so generous. In spirit as well as everything else. Because he didn't think the dressing rooms were up to scratch he personally paid for them to be decorated and carpeted and had fresh flowers and fruit delivered every week to members of the cast.

While they were doing *Merchant* there was a story on one of the morning shows about a woman who needed some very expensive operation for her child and didn't have the medical insurance to cover it. So without anyone knowing, Dustin paid for her. And in America medicine doesn't come cheap. He does this sort of thing all the time but keeps quiet about it.

Dustin's mainstay is his family. He's been with Lisa for nearly twenty years. How they met is a story in itself. Everyone thinks Dustin is a New Yorker but he's a Los Angelino born and bred. He came back one time for a family party and was sitting playing the piano — he's a gifted musician — when a little ten-year-old girl came in and sat on his lap and they played a little duet together. And that was Lisa. Dustin is wonderful with kids and after he left, Lisa went to her grandmother and said, 'When I grow up I'm going to marry that man.' And everyone said, 'Yeah. How sweet.' Ten years or so later she did.

And she is the best. Nothing to do with show-business, just a wonderful mother and wife. She says she's got five children of her own, four plus Dustin, and two step-children from Dustin's previous marriage.

At lunchtime on 28 April, all hell broke loose. I was in make-up and everywhere you went in the studios that day we had all the newsreels on. Then came the announcement from City Hall. A state of emergency was called and everybody was told to go home. So suddenly the whole of LA left their offices and within minutes it's gridlock. A solid traffic jam. Not that I knew that then. I rang the school and they told me they'd been told to send the kids home. Carly had gone home with a friend and her father, who we knew quite well. He offered to bring Carly over to me at the studio. Normally it would be a fifteen minute drive over the hills.

It took him over two hours. It was the longest two hours I had ever lived through.

I had called Dustin and a car was on its way. He didn't send the limo because he said it would be too conspicuous; by then people were being pulled out of posh cars by the rioters. He sent a four-wheel drive instead. Dustin and Lisa lived in Brentwood, a smart suburb to the north-west, a long way from the troubles. Normally you would take the freeway, then down a canyon, but very cleverly his driver had a better idea.

Across the top of the range of hills that separate LA from the San Fernando valley runs a little twisty road called Mulholland Drive. Lots of big stars still live along Mulholland, like Jack Nicholson and Warren Beatty. The houses are usually ultra-modern but Mulholland is still one of the most desirable addresses. The idea is that you are above the smog and you do get the most amazing views. So that's the way we went, along this twisty road like a corniche. And when we hit the top the amazing views were there, though not the ones the film stars pay for. The city below was covered in a pall of smoke and flames. LA really was burning.

What had started in South Central was moving north towards Beverley Hills. But Beverley Hills being its own city, and very rich, it was completely encircled with armoured vehicles. All the private security firms in the city were booked within an hour of the first disturbance. Everyone was so frightened. And no wonder. Over the five days of the riots, fifty people were killed, 17,000 people were arrested and 5,000 ended up in court. One billion dollars' worth of damage to property was done. Although the flashpoint had been the Rodney King verdict, the riots were completely multi-racial. The first ever. And a lot of the hatred from the black community was directed toward the Koreans who were the latest immigrants to the city and who were running the stores, working hard and doing very well.

Amazingly Mulholland Drive was clear but when we hit the freeway for the last mile and a half to Brentwood, it was nose to tail and took us an hour and a half to reach Dustin and Lisa's house. We stayed there for four days, until we flew back to London the following Saturday. I felt very safe and I figured that if it got really bad, they'd have plans. I knew Dustin would hire an army if necessary to protect his family. There was a moment where it could have gone either way. The National Guard was called in and eventually calmed the situation down.

The riots were the beginning of the end for us. Just knowing that if you were in the wrong street at the wrong time you could get your head blown away is very scary. Back in England we saw Chrissie Hynde, lead singer of one of my favourite bands, The Pretenders, who is a friend of Linda and Paul's. An American by birth, she's a real anglophile; she moved to the UK years ago. 'Sell your house,' she said. 'It's only the beginning.'

We spent that summer at our cottage in Oxfordshire, and although we went back to LA and Carly spent another term at Marlborough, we had more or less decided to move back to England. But it took one more disaster to finally convince us — the earthquake. English GCSEs need two years of study and if we wanted Carly to join the English education system, we had to go now, so I arranged for her to start at Bryanston, a boarding school in Dorset, in January.

Shortly after we returned to England I got a message from Los Angeles. There was to be a gala tribute to Tommy Tune. Tommy was guest of honour, and he was asked who he would like to have on the show. He said, 'I know it's impossible, she's in England, but I'd love Twiggs to be here.' So as a surprise Leigh and I flew over. I was the last guest, and as I came forward, I reached out my hand from the stage to the table where he was sitting.

'Come on Tommy,' I said and asked him to join me on stage, which he did, and we sang our duet from *My One and Only*, 'Boy Wanted' and 'Soon'.

When we'd finished I went back to the table where Leigh was sitting, and I saw there were tears on his cheeks. Joel Grey, who had performed earlier and was another old friend of Tommy's, was at the same table. Leigh later told me that as the music began Joel leant over to him and said, 'Watch this.' Joel knew that although Leigh and I had been together seven years, he had never seen me perform on stage before. He says it was one of the most moving and magical experiences of his life.

21

The negativity I had felt when I had lived in LA with Michael had long gone, so it was with mixed feelings that we finally packed our bags. We had lots of good friends and we would miss them. Although I knew we would see each other again, as you do in this business, it would be hard to recapture that close sense of community we had shared in Los Angeles, particularly with our English friends like Bruce Robinson and his wife Sophie. Bruce is now best known as the writer and director of the cult film *Withnail and I*, and *How to Get Ahead in Advertising*. He also wrote the screenplay for the Oscar-winning, *The Killing Fields*. Leigh and Bruce go back to the time when they were young actors, both discovered by Zeffirelli. After *The Merchant of Venice* finished in New York Leigh did a pilot for a one-hour series in LA called *The Phantom* in which he played the title role. It was all shot at night in Los Angeles and I'm just thankful it didn't get picked up: five years of night shooting is a recipe for madness. I wasn't able to be in LA with him but Bruce and Sophie were then living there and they very sweetly had Leigh to stay with them. The film company Bruce was working for at the time on his film *Jennifer 8* had rented them an amazing Spanish mansion which belonged to Gore Vidal. It was beautiful, twenties, with a garden filled with orange and lemon trees. They have a gorgeous little girl called Lily and a son Willoughby and they were like a second family to Leigh while he was there.

Dinner with the Robinsons is always a delight: Bruce is such a talent, a brilliant wit with an outrageous sense of humour, while Sophie is a very clever English rose who illustrates children's books and her drawings are divine. They have now moved back to Britain, and live on a farm on the Welsh/English borders and we miss seeing them as much as we used to in LA.

Another couple that we were close to in England and LA were Trevor Eve and Sharon Maughan. Leigh had known both of them since RADA days. Their children, Alice and Jack (George wasn't born then) got on really well with Carly and Ace, although they were younger. So we were always doing family things together, like getting together for barbecues round the pool. That's one of the great things about the west coast. Plan a barbecue in England and it pours with rain, but ninety-nine times out of a hundred in LA it's hot and sunny. On Sundays we'd sometimes meet up and go to Venice beach, built in 1905 to recreate a Mediterranean resort on the Pacific. It's not like anywhere else in Los Angeles, much more European, a place for pedestrians, all colonnades and rather romantically run down, because when they discovered oil there in the 1920s, Venice stopped being smart.

We would hire rollerblades or bicycles. I tried rollerblading once or twice, but I tended to bicycle. The food in LA is sensational and we'd ride along the coast path to a restaurant that did a great brunch. If you got bored with the beach, running alongside the path there were masses of little shops selling everything from clothes to tarot cards and incense, really hip and fun, with street entertainers, some awful but some quite wonderful, mime artists, portrait painters, fortune tellers, jugglers, musicians and singers. I remember one Rastafarian who used to go along on rollerblades in exotic dress with an electric guitar with some kind of energy pack strapped to his back playing and singing. They were fun times. It was just like being on holiday. Now, like so many of our ex-pat friends Sharon and Trevor and their lovely kids have forsaken tinseltown and are back in England so we can still enjoy some good times together. As time goes on the longevity of friendships seems to grow more and more important.

Holidays were always a big part of my childhood. We were the first family in our street to go on holiday every year; working-class families could rarely afford proper holidays before the fifties. But then came holiday camps; pure *Hi-Di-Hi*. A week every summer, and always somewhere different: Bognor, the Isle of Wight, Hayling Island. Always on the south coast and Pontins rather than Butlins because Butlins was too big; bad for Mum's nerves.

We always left at six in the morning to avoid the traffic and even going at 30 m.p.h. we'd get there far too early. I remember one year sitting in a café in Hayling Island, probably not long after breakfast, having to wait till lunchtime before we could get in to the camp, but so excited knowing that we'd soon be in our chalet. Even the word chalet sounded romantic to me. As a holiday it was brilliant: always plenty of other children to play with and in the evenings Mum and Dad could have their entertainment, knowing I was tucked up in bed, quite happy and safe with patrols going around checking up on the juniors. There were swings and slides and swimming pools and always competitions: knobbly knees for the dads, legs for the mums, and beautiful babies. For me there was the fancy dress. This was always the high spot for Mum, who took such pride in making my costume. Once I went in a tennis outfit which she made me: a little white skirt and frilly knickers and a borrowed racket. I must have been about four. There was a famous tennis player known as Little Mo though it didn't mean anything to me. I went as Half a Mo. All Mum's idea. For all her contrariness she could be very funny and kind. Even now, all these years later, I can still remember her standing in the kitchen in Neasden, while she knelt on the floor beside me, her mouth full of pins as she turned up the hem of the dress she'd just finished sewing, trying to get her fidgety daughter, so excited by the new frock, to keep still. Then, when it was finished, the light in her eyes as she would say to me, 'Right, Les, give us a twirl.' And I spun round and round, the skirt ballooning out like a whirlwind.

Now my idea of the perfect holiday is very different: books, beaches, eating and sleeping.

When I first met Leigh he had a beautiful old village house in Andratx on Mallorca. He was determined to have a view of the sea, so he'd opened up the flat roof and at night when it was hot we would take blow-up mattresses and lie there and look at the stars, the kids asking amazing questions, and we'd have wonderful conversations and laugh until one by one we all fell asleep. Happy, happy days.

Holidays with Leigh are always special. I see things differently when I'm with him. Peter Asher and his wife Wendy are two of our dearest friends and when they bought a house in Tuscany and invited us to stay, it gave Leigh a great opportunity to do the *Brother Sun, Sister Moon* trip down memory lane with a very willing me in tow, Assisi, Montelceno, Banya Vinyoni, Gubbio, Leigh charging this way and that saying, 'Here's the church where we shot that scene; here's the café where Peter Firth, Kenneth Cranham and I got drunk. Here's the hot springs we bathed in.' The Ashers now live in Los Angeles, where Peter, who back in the sixties was half of the singing duo Peter and Gordon, is a big-time record producer and manager and now a big wheel at Sony Records. In early 1996 he rang us to say he was going to be over in Europe looking for new talent, new bands. An English band he was really interested in, he told us, was called Kula Shaker.

'You do know who that is, don't you?' laughed Leigh. 'That's Crispian's band.'

The now chart-topping Kula Shaker is none other than Ace's half-brother Crispian Mills, who I first met that fateful Sunday on the Thames at Henley when he was eleven. Crispian wasn't an overnight success: he has played guitar since he was twelve and for several years did his apprenticeship on the road, playing gigs in pubs and clubs for a few pounds a night. But in 1996 Kula Shaker hit the big time with a Number One album, *K*, that stayed at the top for several months.

Crispian had always said he was going to be a rock star. But many little boys say that, though he's always been talented musically. When Crispian got his first guitar, which was pink, he was so in love with it, he used to sleep with it. Naturally we're all incredibly proud of him, especially Leigh, who taught him his first few chords.

Whatever they say, when you marry someone you do take on their family. And the wonderful thing is that Leigh is as lucky in his family as I am in mine. Leigh has always been very close to his nephew Saul, an exceptional human being. He's a six feet tall, handsome and a successful DJ in London's West End clubs, yet Saul doesn't drink, doesn't smoke, is totally anti drugs and devoted to his family — therefore the most incredible role model for our children. He's the best grandson to Leigh's mother. When Leigh's sister Gloria's marriage to Saul's father broke down, Saul was only tiny. They left Bermuda where his dad, who was an MP, comes from, and resettled in England. As a result Leigh became very important in Saul's life and Saul in his. They are almost as close as father and son and so Saul is a very important part of our family.

In early 1995 Saul brought his new girlfriend Cali round to the flat to see us. She is nearly six foot tall and so beautiful that your heart misses a beat. When I first saw this amazing creature, long fair hair, fabulous blue eyes, without a trace of make-up, I did what I had never done before. I asked her if she had ever thought of becoming a model. The answer was no. She was then at St Martin's College of Art and Design, where all those years ago I had dreams of studying fashion, and where she was doing a course in textile design. And Cali was adamant that that was what she wanted to do. But I said if ever she changed her mind to give me a call. With the money models earn these days, even a couple of years could set her up to do what she wanted with the rest of her life. And it could be quite fun.

About six months later another student at St Martin's asked Cali to model her end-of-year collection for the course show. It was Stella McCartney. Neither of them knew that there was any connection between them other than both being students at the same college. Like most young people they don't go around talking about their parents, let alone their parents' friends.

Stella's clothes were fabulous. I know because I was there. Linda had called and asked us if we would like to go along. When I saw it was Cali up there on the catwalk I was nearly speechless. It was the first time she'd done it and she was a complete natural, totally at ease appearing alongside Kate Moss and Naomi Campbell.

That night, after the show Paul and Linda gave a bash for Stella and it was there that I first met Kate Moss. And Linda took a photograph of the two of us, which she later sent to me as a memento. Quite historic. The two superwaifs who get all the blame for anorexia.

'They're actually the same articles the papers were running thirty years ago,' I told her, 're-hashed with your name instead of mine.'

She was there with her mum and is very natural, charming and funny, and very refreshing.

Paul has lived in that house in St John's Wood since early Beatles days and on a wall in one of the living rooms is still a hand-painted mural, that John Lennon and he did in the sixties. It must have been at the height of psychedelia. When they had it redecorated Paul just got them to paint around it. Everyone knows John was a talented artist, but perhaps they don't realise that Paul is too.

A couple of days after the show Cali telephoned and said she'd so enjoyed doing Stella's show, she thought she might give modelling a go after all. So I called a couple of photographer friends and Models One, the agency I am with, and said I thought they should see her. Modelling is such a tough world, so competitive, unless you have one of the top agencies representing you it's virtually impossible. She needed them to confirm my intuition, that she had something really special. When they saw her they signed her immediately and rang to thank me and to ask me if I had any others up my sleeve. Now Cali Rand is one of the hottest new models around. As for Stella McCartney, in the spring of 1997 the fashion world was stunned when, at only twenty-five, she took over from Karl Lagerfeld at House of Chloe in Paris.

Before Carly started at her new school, we decided to celebrate her fifteenth birthday in style, courtesy of Miss World, which was held that December 1993 in Sun City, the casino and golf resort built by Sol Kerschner in South Africa. I had been asked to be one of the judges along with Christie Brinkley, Frederick Forsyth and Vanessa Williams. Sun City was extraordinary, entirely man-made, with a beach and a 'sea' complete with wave machine all laced with Las Vegas glitz and glamour. A thrill for us and Christie and her daughter was a dawn ride in a hot air ballon that took us right to the heart of a safari park. Because the balloon makes no noise, it doesn't disturb the animals and we could come quite low. We saw elephant, giraffe, zebra, and warthogs with their babies, all in their natural habitat. Wonderful. The sweetest memory from this trip was when they told me a three-year-old hippo had just arrived at the park, and I was asked if they could they name her Twiggy after me. Throughout the whole photo session with the press, she just ate. Very endearing but incredibly fat.

Then it was on to Mauritius, a completely unspoilt island in the Indian Ocean, four hours from Johannesburg. Le Tousseroc is the most beautiful hotel I have ever been lucky enough to stay at. In Sun City Carly's room had been across the corridor from us and this time she wanted to be next door. The man who showed us to our room said that this might be a bit of a problem:

'You are in the Royal Suite and the nearest single room is down the corridor.'

Leigh said we should go and see it anyway. The door opened and we were speechless. The sitting room was about forty foot square, with French windows out onto a private patio and then the beach. There were two bathrooms as big as most people's sitting rooms, one outside open to the sky, one inside with a huge Jacuzzi bath big enough for us all, and a vast bedroom. Not to mention a dining area that seated twenty-four. All marble floors and high ceilings.

'Forget the single room,' said Leigh. 'We'll find somewhere for her in here.' And he asked them to bring a day bed. The first night Carly slept in the living room outside our bedroom. But in the morning she said she'd been a bit nervous of the shadows. So we moved the bed closer to our door. The next morning it was the same story.

'Just move your bed where you want it,' said Leigh and left her to it. We came back to find she'd pushed her bed into our bedroom right up against our big double, where it stayed for the rest of the ten-day holiday. So much for a second honeymoon. But it was fun — our only sadness that Ace couldn't be there because he was studying for his GCSE exams.

The island was incredibly beautiful, possibly the most beautiful place I've ever been to. A hundred yards from the beach was another island belonging to the hotel, on which Carly had her fifteenth birthday. Lunch was just Leigh, Carly and me, one cook and one waiter, salad and barbecued fish. When it was time for the birthday cake, the waiter picked up a guitar and serenaded her. Absolutely magical. The day's celebrations ended with a wonderful dinner back at the hotel with our friends Frederick Forsyth who, apart from being one of the world's most successful writers is a brilliant raconteur, and his charming wife Sandy.

Life back in England began to take shape. There were old friends to catch up with and a whole roster of new friends to make. We met Richard Curtis, who later wrote *Four Weddings and a Funeral*, in London. Carly and Ace had discovered *Blackadder*, which he co-wrote, and introduced it to us. Then of course came *Mr Bean*, and we are all avid fans. After the opening in London of the musical of *Sunset Boulevard*, there was a huge party at the Savoy Hotel. As we were introduced Richard joked, 'I've always wanted to ask you to marry me.'

'Well,' I said, 'you'd better ask my husband.'

We spent the evening laughing and talking to him and his gorgeous, clever lady Emma Freud and have been friends ever since. Every year coming up to Christmas they have a party in the converted Baptist chapel they live in and serve mulled wine and mince pies and everyone sings carols and Christmas songs. It is joyous. It's through Richard and Emma that we met Ben Elton and Lenny Henry and Dawn French. There are some people who just make your life richer for knowing them. I hold such happy memories of hysterical nights round our dining table with these talented people.

In the spring of 1996 I was approached to record a new album. It happened through Tony Walton. Not only is Tony a brilliant award-winning designer — including an Oscar for *All That Jazz*, the life story of Bob Fosse, and endless Tonys for his work on Broadway — he's a walking theatrical encyclopaedia. If we want to know anything about the theatre, a play, a writer, a songwriter, a director, Tony will have the answer. He had been having dinner with Bruce Kimball, a record producer friend from California. Bruce was telling Tony about the series of period albums he was doing.

'I want the next one to be songs from British musicals. But I'll need to find an English singer who's done Broadway.'

'What about Twiggs?'

'Do you think she'll do it?'

'Ask her.'

We call the Waltons' rambling Manhattan apartment our New York home, because they are almost family and always make us so welcome — we even have our own key. It's on Broadway and 79th, in a splendid old building called the Apthorpe.

The album is called *London Pride*, the title taken from one of the two Noel Coward tracks we had chosen. And the first night we were in

New York to record, Tony told us the story behind the title song: that London Pride is the common name for the wild flower you used to see pushing through the cracks and crannies on old bomb sites in London. Coward used it as a metaphor for the grit and determination of the Londoners to survive the Blitz. Knowing what was behind it, the song took on a whole new meaning.

The next morning Leigh and I went to the flat of my very talented arranger/conductor Todd Ellison to set my keys and Bruce was there with a young lady who he introduced as his assistant. She smiled. We went through a few songs, then just before I'm about to do 'London Pride', Leigh interrupted.

'Before you start, I've got to tell them the story.' So he did. And when Leigh tells a story like that he really knows how to pull the heartstrings. Wonderful plucky Cockneys against the fucking Nazis. And then I went into the song. When I finished there was complete silence. I was quite choked up and Leigh and the others had a tear in their eyes. It is a very moving song, especially put into context.

'God, that really affected me,' I said. 'Although I wasn't alive in the war, my parents and sisters were and I've heard all their stories. We even had a bomb come into the garden. It must have been absolutely awful.'

'Yes, my parents too,' said Bruce's young assistant.

'Oh, are you English?' I asked.

'No, German.'

I wanted the ground to swallow me up. But she was sweet. Not fazed at all. It was just one of those moments. And afterwards we really laughed about it.

Although I am naturally a soprano, (I can hit top C and more), I don't like using my high voice too much and prefer to sing lower, from my chest. There's a lot more to singing than just keeping in tune and I try to keep up regular singing lessons, increasing the power, controlling the breathing, filling the note and giving it a life, making it true. The voice is something one has to keep working on, not rely on a crash course when you suddenly get a project to do. And I have the best singing teacher, Ian Adam. He has really improved my voice. When I sing in my high register I don't think I sound like an old cat anymore. Apart from anything else I love my classes; I get to sing things I could never do in public, like bel canto operatic arias. My favourite is Puccini's 'O Mio Bambino Caro'. It's very good for me and stretches my voice although it's really hard. But I love the challenge.

My favourite singer of all time is one not everyone has heard of, Ruth Etting. When I do those period songs my singing style is stolen from her. I love the way she sings, her phrasing, those lovely slidey notes. Ruth Etting was the subject of a 1955 bio-pic called *Love Me or Leave Me* (her most famous song) which was rather good, although Doris Day was totally miscast. Ruth Etting was a torch singer whose career spanned the end of the twenties and early thirties and she was working in nightclubs in New York, making no money, when she met this racketeer, played by James Cagney in the movie, who pushes her to the top but drives her to drink and despair. Ruth Etting was way before her time. In those days white singers were still doing lightweight musical comedy, not breaking your heart with songs of betrayal and loss.

London Pride marked the beginning of Leigh's and my Noel Coward period. Not only were there two Coward tracks on the album, but one of my favourite songs on it is 'The Physician', which Cole Porter wrote for Gertrude Lawrence, Noel Coward's muse.

I first met Noel Coward in the summer of 1970 when I was in Jamaica, staying with Tommy Steele and his wife Annie. We'd met Tommy through Grover Dale who did my choreography on the Diet Rite ad. Grover had worked with Tommy on Broadway in *Half a Sixpence* and they had stayed friends. It wasn't a good introduction to the Caribbean. The whole two weeks we only got three days of sun. I'd never been anywhere tropical and I was terrified of all the big flying things and huge grasshoppers. They still frighten me now.

Noel Coward was a neighbour of Tommy and Annie's so one day we went over to visit. Young as I was, I knew I was meeting this legend and I'd heard he had a wicked tongue. He was very tanned and had his trademark dressing gown on, not his big posh one, but a thin silky one. It was very hot. He had such a great turn of phrase. When he noticed that Emma, Tommy and Annie's daughter had a crumb on her lip he turned to Annie and said, 'Dear Lady. I think your child has something alien on her upper lip.'

Around that time the *Sunday Times* did one of these silly celebrity ring-arounds asking who they thought was sexy. Mick Jagger nominated Noel Coward and Noel Coward nominated me. But as I didn't comment it stopped with me.

About a year after this Robert Stephens rang me in London, as he recounts in his autobiography.

'Noely is here and he's at the Savoy but he's not very well,' he said. 'I've been taking a surprise present every afternoon this week and tomorrow I want to take you. He told me how much he loved meeting you.'

So the next day we went to the Savoy where he had this very grand suite. The great man was sitting in his sitting room, in the familiar dressing gown, and he seemed fine, very up and chatty. Then there was a knock on the door and this woman walked in. I nearly died. It was Merle Oberon. It's funny how people get stuck in the era when they were at their most glamorous. She was wearing a big black polka dot chiffon dress, with a big black bow around her waist, like a Givenchy model. All for afternoon tea. She was quite small and voluptuous with high, high heels. But she looked gorgeous, rather wonderful and exotic, which all made sense in the light of her Indian background which then of course not many knew about. I was completely star-struck and speechless. When she left she didn't say goodbye to me. But as she reached the door she blew her old friend another last kiss, smiled at me and with great charm joked, 'Goodbye Noely, and tell that ugly child over there goodbye too.'

Eventually Noel was taken to St Thomas's Hospital and Bob Stephens rang me again to suggest I go and visit him. I don't like hospitals and I thought it would be very distressing but it wasn't, because he was so funny. He wanted a whisky and they wouldn't let him have one, though he was still smoking non-stop. As one went down he'd light up another. The nurses talked to him as if he was a child.

'Now Mr Coward, how would we like a nice glass of sherry?' one ventured.

'I would absolutely hate a glass of sherry.'

I should think he was a nightmare patient. Before I left he asked me to do a tap dance routine for him from *The Boyfriend* which I happily did. That was the last time I saw him. He died a few months later, but I feel so lucky and privileged to have known him.

While I was in New York cutting *London Pride*, Leigh was in London at the Barbican, the RSC's London base, doing *The Relapse* a rip-roaring Restoration comedy directed by the immensley talented Ian Judge. It was the first time he'd worked for the RSC and he was loving it and dreading it ending. When he first left RADA Leigh had been offered a job at the RSC — one line parts or 'spear carrying', as first rung acting jobs in our great classical theatres are known, but at the time he'd opted for playing lead parts in Coventry rep. Twenty-five years later he was at the RSC playing a lead role and loving it. On the last day of *The Relapse*, Leigh left for the theatre sad to be leaving the RSC and not knowing what he would be doing next. That afternoon Tony Walton rang me.

'Has Leigh got a green card?'

'Yes. Why?'

'Brilliant. Because at short notice I'm directing two Coward plays, a double bill at the Bay Street Theatre. And Leigh would be just perfect.'

No one can work on the American stage without a green card. I looked out the two plays, *Song at Twilight* and *Come into the Garden Maud*, from our Coward collection and telephoned Leigh immediately with the good news and got them to him to read between shows.

The Bay Street Theatre in Sag Harbor, Long Island, is run by Tony's daughter Emma, whose mother is Julie Andrews, together with Emma's husband Steve and Sybil Burton, who was married to Richard Burton, and is still wonderfully Welsh. They started it in the early 1990s: they were all working in the theatre on and off, and one day thought 'Why don't we open our own?' They managed to get it off the ground with hard work and very little money, although with Tony Walton and Julie Andrews being Emma's dad and mum they did have amazing connections. Julie did a concert for free. It must have been just like the old days: 'let's go on the road and be a family together'. The theatre is converted from an old warehouse, right on the dock. It's non-profit-making and only seats about 200 people but they attract all sorts of high-profile actors and directors and playwrights because the shows are short runs and it's such a lovely place to be for the summer. The downside is that because it's non-profit-making nobody gets much money. Which means they often have to cope with last minute changes of cast and director; the case this time. Tony's debut as director was by default. A high-powered Broadway director was originally going to direct the Coward double bill, but something else came up. So Emma said, 'Come on Dad, you've got to help us' — after all he lived there — and he had been thinking of directing for a while. That only left the casting.

Of course Leigh said yes. Then two days later Tony rang again. Would I consider being one of the women? He tried to convince me but I knew I was totally wrong. Another time maybe.

The Coward double bill was a really beautiful production and got absolutely rave reviews. My favourite was 'Leigh Lawson has flashes of acting genius'. Neither play had been done in the States since the seventies when Hume Cronin and Jessica Tandy did them off Broadway. Although the Bay Street Theatre is small it has made Sag Harbor the cultural heart of fashionable Long Island. Everybody goes. And not just rich socialites. During the run Mike Nichols, Karel Reisz, Sidney Lumet, Robbie Benson, Blake Edwards and Julie Andrews came to see the play. It was like Broadway. And Leigh was brilliant, playing two completely different parts; one American, one English; the two plays are connected by being set in the same hotel room in Switzerland. His co-stars were Bobby Calavari, Bebe Neuewirth of *Cheers* and Broadway fame and Dee Hoty, also from Broadway, both musical comedy actresses and for both of them their first straight play. They were all magnificent and also got rave reviews.

It was a fabulous way to spend the summer. Our favourite place in all the world, among some of our favourite people, staying at Tony and Jen's magical house where we were married. Our mutual friend Julie Christie came to stay. And as soon as school was over, Ace and Carly came out to join us. The plan was then we would go on to Bermuda, not that far from Long Island, where Leigh's sister Gloria has now gone back to live. Gloria had found us a house to rent, Saul and Cali were going too, and Leigh wanted to spend time with his other sister Carol, whose daughter Kim had recently been taken from us tragically by cancer at the age of thirty. It was going to be a lovely healing family holiday. But just before the first night at Bay Street, Leigh got a call from his agent. The Royal Shakespeare Company wanted him back to play Oberon in *A Midsummer Night's Dream*, a part he very much wanted to play, with the RSC's artistic director the wonderful and talented Adrian Noble directing. He jotted the dates down on the back of an envelope: London, Stratford, five other towns in the UK, and a five-and-a-half week tour in the Far East.

'Surely you can't do Japan, Hong Kong, Australia and New Zealand in five and a half weeks,' I said. 'Well, it'll be a killer, darling, a week in each place.' But there was just one small problem: rehearsals started on the first day of our holiday . . . In the acting world there's an old saying, if you want a job, book and pay for a holiday. So he came to Bermuda for one night, then flew back to the UK. It was with mixed feelings on both sides that we all waved him goodbye.

A few nights later came the real shock. On the first day of rehearsals back in London, he opened the tour schedule and one of the other actors remembers his face turning white. The tour wasn't five and a half weeks. It was five and a half months. He'd jotted the dates down wrong. Too late then to change his mind. In a way it was a good thing we didn't know at the beginning. It would have been a terrible decision to make. And although we were missing him dreadfully, it was such a wonderful experience and the most thrillingly inventive production of a Shakespeare play that I have ever seen. Over the months I must have seen it twenty times and I never tired of it. But five and a half months is just too long apart. Never again.

While we were in Bermuda my LA agents Marian Rosenberg and Matthew Lesher called to say that I too had been offered a job, a film in North Carolina. It started the week I got back from holiday and meant missing Leigh's first night. But that's the way it goes in our business, and at least I would be back in time for his last night on the main stage of the Barbican Theatre, the RSC's London base, and also back in England for our wedding anniversary and my birthday.

Something Borrowed, Something Blue was a TV film for CBS, the people I'd done *Princesses* for. Almost from the beginning things started to go wrong. We shot it in September in Wilmington, North Carolina. First came Hurricane Fran. The Caribbean was still reeling from Hurricane Bertha earlier in the summer. And as we watched Hurricane Fran's course as it drifted in from the Atlantic, bypassing the Bahamas, we realised poor little Wilmington, a beautiful old plantation town, was where it was heading. Shooting was cancelled and under terrifying charcoal skies Connie Selecca, my co-star, and I drove eight hours across Carolina and Georgia to Atlanta to escape the hurricane. We had a great time. It turned out Connie and I had met fifteen years before in Hawaii where I was doing a Helen Redy special for American TV. Her then husband was also on the show, so he and Connie and Michael and me had had dinner one night. Small world.

Four days' shooting were lost because of the hurricane, and worse, it turned out that our beach location along the coast had been devastated. More delay. In the meantime Wilmington stank. The hurricane had caused havoc with the local sewerage plant. And didn't we know it. When we finally got to the posh South Carolina resort that stood in for the original one, we were just about to start shooting there when the heavens opened up. It turned out to be a blessing in disguise. The next day another crisis. The technicians' union called everybody out. North and South Carolina are non-union states and this was an attempt to hold CBS to ransom. Needless to say it brought back dreadful memories of *Betty*. There is one other non-union state, Utah. And in extraordinary secrecy, all the key players with scenes left to do flew to Salt Lake City to complete the film with a non-union crew. We all had to pretend that we were going home, and the LA-based actors flew home first so that their ultimate destination wouldn't get out. It was like being in a spy story. We were warned not to talk to anyone at all. Nobody knew who the union moles were. I just sat in my hotel room for a day under a pseudonym. Everyone else was led to believe that the film had been abandoned.

I flew to Salt Lake City and *Something Borrowed, Something Blue* got finished, thanks solely to the sheer grit and chutzpah of its wonderful producer J.C. Shardo, who had nurtured the project from the beginning and clung to it with the tenacity of a mother to her child. But what should have been three and a half weeks had turned into five. And I missed being with Leigh for his last night on the main stage at the Barbican and our anniversary and my birthday. However I made up for it when I got back. Over the next two months I was able to spend every weekend with him up at Stratford. And I loved it. He was staying in one of the RSC apartments and for Leigh it was just like being a student again. I'd never been one, which is probably why I enjoyed it so much. I must have seen the *Dream* more times than any other play ever. After Stratford and the English tour, I was able to go with him to Japan and Hong Kong and I had been hoping to join him later in Australia. But, as always happens, another offer came up. My London agent Paul Lyon-Maris at ICM called me with an offer I could not refuse.

I had never been given the opportunity to do straight theatre in England; it had been a dream that had always eluded me. In 1988, towards the end of August, I got a call from Peter Hall. This was before Leigh did *The Merchant of Venice* with him. But I had met Peter when Leigh was doing *Yonadab* at the National Theatre in 1985. He wanted me for Tennessee Williams' play *Orpheus Descending*, with Vanessa Redgrave. ('Peter Hall, Vanessa Redgrave: Oh My God.')

I told him that the timing wasn't great. The rehearsals were beginning the week Leigh was planning our marriage. Not that I officially knew. ('Don't ask questions.') But I couldn't tell Peter that, because first, it was only my guess and second, it was supposed to be secret. So I explained that we were off to the States to do publicity for *Madame Sousatzka* as indeed we were. Peter Hall is charm personified and I found it so hard to say no. He's a brilliantly inspired director and I felt it a huge honour for me even to be asked.

The next year he offered me the role of the wife in Ibsen's *The Wild Duck*. It was a smaller part and I would have been very happy doing it. But we had just got the green light from the BBC for *Betty* the second time around. As it turned out with the fiasco of *Betty*, I could have done it, but I couldn't have known that then. I suppose it was fate and hope it'll be third time lucky with him — if he hasn't given up on me. I'd adore to work with him.

When I first met Noel Coward all those years ago in his house on Jamaica, I had been just about to start shooting *The Boyfriend* and he had said that what he'd really like to see me in was one of his plays. And as soon as I got back to England I went out and bought all that I could find and devoured them. I had decided not to do the Coward in Sag Harbor because it wasn't right for me. Now, only six months later, the phone rang and I was being offered a Coward part perfect for me and a part Noel had wanted me to play, Elvira in *Blithe Spirit* at the Chichester Festival Theatre. This time, right time, right place.

Epilogue

So there it is — or some of it. It's not possible to mention everyone who has helped this story along. And drawing to a close on my second autobiography while I'm still in my forties, I can only look forward with optimism, excitement and I suppose some caution at what is to come: Elvira in *Blithe Spirit*, at last a chance to do a play by the master as he wished, a new album of Noel Coward songs due early in 1998; plans for a new musical production, this time in England, directed by my friend the brilliant Ian Judge; talk of a line of Twiggy products — clothes, perfume, accessories . . .

Maybe it's not such a silly name then after all, recognisable, remembered, the only one. Not surprising perhaps with a name like Twiggy I should be tempted to branch out on occasion.

Blessed with a wonderful family, adorable children, my loving husband, true happiness at last: it's been a Cinderella story of sorts. Tap shoes instead of a glass slipper, that's true, and a long time to wait for my Prince Charming. But whether in a gilded carriage or a pumpkin, the journey when I look back has been quite extraordinary.

The Road Not Taken

Two roads diverged in a yellow wood,
And sorry I could not travel both

And be one traveller, long I stood
And looked down one as far as I could
To where it bent in the undergrowth;

Then took the other, as just as fair,
And having perhaps the better claim,
Because it was grassy and wanted wear;
Though as for that, the passing there
Had worn them really about the same,

And both that morning equally lay
In leaves no step had trodden black.
Oh, I kept the first for another day!
Yet knowing how way leads on to way,
I doubted if I should ever come back.

I shall be telling this with a sigh
Somewhere ages and ages hence:
Two roads diverged in a wood, and I —
I took the one less travelled by,
And that has made all the difference.

Robert Frost

Other titles in the Charnwood Library Series:

LEGACIES
Janet Dailey

The sequel to THE PROUD AND THE FREE. It is twenty years since the feud within his family began, but Lije Stuart, son of the Cherokee chief The Blade, had never forgotten the killing of his grandfather. Now, a promising legal career beckons, and also the love of his childhood sweetheart, Diane Parmalee, the daughter of a US Army officer. Yet as it reawakens, their love is beset by the beginning of civil war.

'L' IS FOR LAWLESS
Sue Grafton

World War II fighter pilot Johnny Lee had died and his grandson was trying to claim military funeral benefits, but none of the authorities have any record of Fighter J. Lee. Was the old man once a US spy? When PI Kinsey Millhone is asked to straighten things out, she finds herself pursued by a psychopath bearing a forty-year-old grudge . . .

BLOOD LINES
Ruth Rendell

This is a collection of long and short stories by Ruth Rendell that will linger in the mind.

THE SUN IN GLORY
Harriet Hudson

When industrialist William Potts sets himself to build a flying machine, his adopted daughter, Rosie, works through the years as his mechanic. In 1906 Pegasus is almost ready, and onto the scene comes Jake Smith, a man who has as deep a love of the air as Rosie herself. But Jake sparks off a deadly rivalry, and the triumph of flight twists into tragedy.

A WOMAN SCORNED
M. R. O'Donnell

Five years after the tragedy that ruined her fifteenth birthday, Judith Carty returns to Castle Moore and resumes her flirtation with its heir, Rick Bellingham. The tragic events of the past forge a special bond between the young couple, but there are those who have a vested interest in the failure of the romance.

PLAINER STILL
Catherine Cookson

Following the success of her previous collection of essays and poems, LET ME MAKE MYSELF PLAIN, Catherine Cookson has compiled a further selection of thoughts, recollections, and observations on life — and death — together with another collection of the poems she prefers to describe as 'prose on short lines'.

THE LOST WORLD
Michael Crichton

The successor to JURASSIC PARK.
It is now six years since the secret disaster of Jurassic Park, when that extraordinary dream of science and imagination came to a crashing end — the dinosaurs destroyed, and the park dismantled. There are rumours that something has survived . . .

MORNING, NOON & NIGHT
Sidney Sheldon

When Harry Stanford, one of the wealthiest men in the world, mysteriously drowns, it sets off a chain of events that reverberates around the globe. At the family gathering following the funeral, a beautiful young woman appears, claiming to be Harry's daughter. Is she genuine, or is she an impostor?

FACING THE MUSIC
Jayne Torvill and Christopher Dean

The world's most successful and popular skating couple tell their own story, from their working-class childhoods in Nottingham to world stardom. Finally, they describe how they created their own show, FACE THE MUSIC, with a superb corps of international ice dancers.